A History of God
Elohim, Yahweh, and Allah

Dr. Joseph Lumpkin

Dr. Joseph Lumpkin

A History of God: Elohim, Yahweh, and Allah

By Dr. Joseph Lumpkin

Fifth Estate Publishers,

First Printing 2017
Cover art by Heidi Milliken

Printed on acid-free paper

Library of Congress Control No: 2016963812
ISBN: 9781936533893

Fifth Estate
2017
http://www.fifthestatepub.com

Dr. Joseph Lumpkin

Dedicated to those who have courageously laid aside religion in
search of God.

Table of Contents

Dr. Joseph Lumpkin

In the Beginning...

In this book we will look at the history and "evolution" of the three deities making up the bulk of the world's religions and the evolution of the religions formed from the worship of these three deities.

We will examine the history and development of Elohim, Yahweh, and Allah. In doing so, we will also look at the teachings of Jesus and Mohammed, and their influence on the Christian and Islamic faiths respectively. By an objective examination of the Gods of the Jewish, Christian, and Muslim faiths we shall see how man's views of these deities changed over time, and with those changes we will examine how the faiths evolved.

It is impossible to directly examine God, so we are forced to view God and the resulting religions through the lens of their followers, along with the doctrine, faith, and actions connected to their worship.

No God or religion exists in a vacuum. Ideas and beliefs build on previous ideas and beliefs, combining to form new insights and forms of worship. Customs change when exposed to other cultures. So it is that religions and their gods grow and evolve as one religion or culture meets another. Ideas of who and what God is change and morph in time with the expanding views. God's focus and strength change according to what a tribe or nation needs at the time.

To begin our study we must go back to a time before there were Jews, Christians, or Muslims. In the primitive mind of man, there was God. Whether God was conceived or recognized is a matter up for discussion.

Before the Jewish people were named or assembled there were religions. It was from the religions in the area of Palestine that the Jewish God sprang.

The concept of a god seems to appear around the same time humans began to express themselves through arts and crafts. Their expanded ability to express themselves reveals to us their ideas of god.

Through the ages, humans have believed in a god, or gods, but what drove mankind to create or express the idea of god?

7

Whether it was by way of sun, moon, or idols of wood or stone, humans all over the world invented or expressed their own ideas of god. Humans were attempting to answer eternal questions of how and why the world worked as it did. They felt helpless and sought a way to explain and influence the elements and the events in life. They could then appeal to their gods in hopes of hedging the outcome of a life out of their control. This is not to say God does not exist, but rather our idea of what God is may be a temporary construct changing over time. Starting with an external idea carved in stone or represented by the elements, and ending in an internal mystical experience, God continues to change as mankind continues to seek God.

As society evolved and the needs of mankind changed, so did their deities. As some men rose to power and the stations of leaders and priests were established, their gods reflected the desires, hopes and fears of the leaders and priests. Powerful men used their gods to threaten and control the common people. Idols eventually began to desire human sacrifice, then the sacrifice of children. At least that is how the people interpreted the silence of their gods as they worked harder and harder in an ever-escalating attempt to appease them. In time, these gods evolved from protectors to murderers. It was the price of protection. Even the gods of the Jews, Yahweh and El, were gods of war and destruction. Their evolution into a single, compassionate deity took centuries and reflected changes within the Jewish world.

This evolution of God and the doctrine that followed are what we shall examine.

In the Judeo-Christian world, and in the Muslim world, it is a surety that God has always been. Man simply awoke to the truth. This is the history of that awakening and the subsequent evolution of God and the development of the Jewish, Christian and Muslim religions.

Hebrews 13:7-9
King James Version (KJV)
7 Remember them which have the rule over you, who have spoken unto you the word of God: whose faith follow, considering the end of their conversation.
8 Jesus Christ the same yesterday, and to day, and forever.
9 Be not carried about with divers and strange doctrines. For it is a good thing that the heart be established with grace; not with meats, which have not profited them that has been occupied therein.

Hebrews 13:7-9
The Message (MSG)
7-9 Appreciate your pastoral leaders who gave you the Word of God. Take a good look at the way they live, and let their faithfulness instruct you, as well as their truthfulness. There should be a consistency that runs through us all. For Jesus doesn't change – yesterday, today, tomorrow, he's always totally himself. Don't be lured away from him by the latest speculations about him. The grace of Christ is the only good ground for life. Products named after Christ don't seem to do much for those who buy them.

God, the supreme maker of all things, may not have changed. Indeed, if he is perfect how could he change? However, by reading the two interpretations of the same scripture printed above we see in an instant that the way we view God changes and the way we articulate our view of God varies immensely. This is the story of those changing views of god, which took us from monotheism to polytheism and idolatry back to what one might view as a "modified" monotheism.

"We despise all reverences and all objects of reverence which are outside the pale of our list of sacred things and yet, with strange inconsistency, we are shocked when other people despise and defile the things which are holy for us" - Mark Twain

In the recesses of time, when humankind began to search for and conceive of "god", the idea of a single, powerful, father figure was born. This "god" was a reflection of the life they led in a patriarchal society with a head of a family or tribe guiding them. Possibly, monotheism is the oldest and most enduring form of religion. This is impossible to prove, however, there is some evidence coming from ancient, untouched tribes that shows a very old and unbroken religious lineage of worshipping a single god above all others.

Primitive cultures did not worship the same god or recognize tribal gods as the same deity. They acknowledged the existence of other gods of neighboring tribes, but chose to worship their own idea of the creator or high god. Their form of worship included the sacrifice of animals and humans, with an eye toward appeasing or influencing their god. They worshipped through rites, rituals, and ceremonies led by priests and holy men whom they believed to be intuitively connected with their deity. How can one believe in other gods and still be monotheistic? It comes down to a focus of worship.

Outside the Bible, the oldest records of religion come from Ebla in Syria. The ancient city of Ebla once was situated where Tell Mardikh is today, about half way between Hamath and Aleppo. There is a mound and a small village about one kilometer off the highway where excavations began in the 1960's. In the 1970's, a series of tablets were discovered among the ruins.

These 17,000 tablets became known as "The Ebla Tablets." They were originally discovered under the direction of two professors from the University of Rome, Dr. Paolo Matthiae and Dr. Giovanni Petinato. These tablets appear to have been written during the two last generations of ancient Ebla's existance, around 2300 to 2250 B.C. Even more extraordinary was the discovery of "a creation hymn" in the tablets. Three different versions of the Eblaite "creation hymn" were found. Dr. Petinato translated one of the creation hymns as follows:

"Lord of heaven and earth: the earth was not, you created it, the light of day was not, you created it, the morning light you had not [yet] made exist."

These tablets, written long ago, are established proof of monotheism. Here is strong evidence of early monotheism that refutes the theory that monotheism was born from some consolidation or evolution of polytheism. Additionally, the fact that systems and ideas tend to begin in simplicity and end in complexity backs up this evidence. This could possibly follow the pattern of society. In fact, the idea of polytheism could have evolved along side the beginning of the specialization of gods within the human community. Polytheism could have begun when tribes with certain gods interfaced with other tribes with different gods, each taking and worshipping the additional god as a lesser deity.

People within tribes and communities developed trades such as dying cloth, stonework, weaving, and working with wood. These designated tasks within the community could have produced the idea of polytheism wherein gods had defined purposes and powers. Humans had difficulty relating to a single god that was omnipresent or omnipotent. God needed to be more human in scope and power. The all-powerful god was too removed from being human. People wanted gods to be more approachable, which, in their minds, meant more limited.

Ancient Ebla was primarily a pagan culture having gods such as Dagon, Baal, and Ishtar that were very important to the people of that time. Conversely, they conceived of one true and powerful God, with the lesser gods serving as his sons and servants. These sons and servants are the forerunners of the angels and demons of today's religions.

The theory that monotheism was the earliest form of worship is further bolstered as we look to Africa, the continent that scientists believe is the birthplace of humankind. The traceable, primitive religions of Africa all reveal an explicit monotheism. The noted authority on African religions, John S. Mbiti, wrote about the 300 traditional religions in Africa. He states, "In all these societies, without a single exception, people believed in a god, who was the Supreme Being." Their belief in a sky-god or high-god shows this belief in a singular god.

In 1912, Father Wilhelm Schmidt wrote extensively about the idea of primitive monotheism in his book, "The Origin of the Idea of God." The good father put forth one of the most intriguing questions in the study of religious history. Was the idea of a remote god who was absent in the daily life of his subjects impossible for the primitives to continually relate to? In time, did god simply fade away to be replaced by gods more human, close to earth, and easier to understand? Was this the root of polytheism?

Religions begin with simple revelations or beliefs and become more ritual, ceremony, and doctrine ridden over time. God is lost within the maze of manmade controls. This was and is the case with religion in general.

What purpose did the religions of the ancients serve? As they constructed and developed their myths, were they telling stories of an imaginary god, or were they weaving subconscious symbols into tales to express their amazement and awe of their mysterious world? Was the primitive mind capable of deep subjective thought? Was primitive man able to see himself as part of a race, a world, or the cosmos?

Prehistoric man lived in communion with earth and heaven. To the primitive mind, all things were related, whether it was messages in the starry skies or mother earth bringing forth food. However, they related these events to their god or gods and how the deities felt about

11

them and their actions at the time. Everything seemed inter-related, but in an objective, outward looking, purely external sense. Plainly, primitive man had no ability to internalize his belief. They sought god and god's favor only by the outward forms of ritual, ceremony, and sacrifice.

Hidden somewhere deep inside the ritual and ceremony lurked the symbols of spirituality, knocking on the door of the subconscious mind. Why was humankind incapable of stepping out of religion and into a spiritual, internal search for god?

The Axial Age – Explaining the Unexplainable

"In religion and politics, people's beliefs and convictions are in almost every case second-hand, and without examination, from authorities who have not themselves examined the questions at issue but have taken them at second-hand from another." *Mark Twain*

The Evolution of God could be tied directly to the enlightenment and expansion of the human mind.

In 1949, Karl Jaspers, the German psychologist and philosopher, published *"The Origin and Goal of History,"* and coined the term, **"The Axial Age"**, to describe a general period from around 800 BCE to approximately 200 BCE. During this span of time, which in relation to the age of humanity was a blink of an eye, revolutionary religious and spiritual awakenings appeared in synchronicity around the world, with major hubs in China, India, and throughout the Middle East.

Anatomically modern humans arose in Africa approximately 200,000 years ago. Modern behavior was established only 50,000 years ago. Spiritually, humans may have come into their present stage only 3000 years ago. This is a single grain of sand in the archeological hourglass.

Jaspers saw in the recent shift of religious and philosophical thought, similarities that could not be accounted for without direct transmission of ideas between regions, and there was no evidence of "cross-pollination" of ideas or concepts to be found.

Jaspers argued that during the Axial Age "the spiritual foundations of humanity were laid simultaneously and independently."

In Karen Armstrong's book, *"The Great Transformation,"* Armstrong expands on Japers' thesis, stating that the insights representing liberal religion occurred almost simultaneously and independently about 2500 years ago in four different areas of the world: China, India, Greece, and the Middle East.

Religion can be broadly understood as a system of beliefs and practices concerned with sacred things and/or symbols uniting individuals into a single moral community. These religious laws, rituals, and beliefs form a cohesive moral structure. If "religions" did specifically relate to the sacred, one could use the same definition for governments. Moreover, religions can become governments unto themselves. Therefore, a "religion" does not require a supernatural being as the object of worship, but it does have to represent a commitment to a particular moral or ethical code.

In the pre-Axial Age, religion always revolved around a deity. After the Axial Age, some religions, such as Buddhism, did not revolve around a god, but involved an inward journey toward deeper self-awareness.

Armstrong further suggests that the history of the last two and a half millennia is seen as a continuous struggle between those who acknowledge and value the newly evolved spiritual insights and those who may have a much older and more restrictive concept of the nature of religion. There is no way to know the number of mystics or progressive religious thinkers that influenced any changes in the ancient world's religions, but archeology shows us that changes were molded mostly, if not totally, by migrations to and from adjacent regions, mixing cultures and gods.

This does not answer the nagging questions of why we persist in "structured" religions, and why all major religions carry the same moral or ethical imperatives. Jesus, among others, so beautifully summed up these imperatives: "Love God and treat others as you want to be treated." The rest is commentary.

Immanuel Kant (1724–1804) was a German philosopher. Kant sought to find and identify the foundational principle of the metaphysics of morals. He attempted to analyze and articulate commonsense ideas about morality. Kant looked for the principles on which we base all of our ordinary moral judgments. He took the position that all rational people are born with an innate sense of morality. Thus, normal, sane, adult human beings will usually make the same judgment calls based on an inborn sense of right and wrong.

This is a wonderful idea, but seems rather naïve considering the amount of crime and abuse we see today. Neither does it answer certain questions such as, "If man is intrinsically good, why did we insist on human sacrifice in our past?" Today, crime runs rampant and Kant's theory does not seem to hold water. Possibly Kant's arguments only come to light when there are few negative social pressures involved. Studies have shown that the number of human sacrifices in primitive cultures rises rapidly under pressures of famine and pestilence. Under extreme circumstances, they sometimes turned to cannibalism.

There are at least two "wired in" processes going on here. The highest and oldest is self-preservation. The secondary impulse, which Kant describes, is based on following a social norm in order to enable the group, family, or tribe to survive. In other words, we are inclined to work as a team. This may explain our ability to stand by and see humans killed or sacrificed as long as the group acts in accord. We can call this a "mob mentality."

However, maybe there is something to this idea of humans drawing on some very widely shared moral viewpoint that contains some general judgments. Outside of the religious ceremony for punishing someone who has broken a moral imperative, such as – do not murder, do not steal – most societies do have the same basic moral structure.

Kant sought to discover a rational basis for one's sense of duty, and from this devise a principle by which one can distinguish between right and wrong. Right and wrong hinge on the intent. The intention or motive for the action determines whether it is right or wrong. It opposes the view that the end justifies the means and does not account for the outcome of an action. The morality of an action has no regard for its current situation. It is universal and does not take into account the outcome of an action regardless of circumstance.

Kant's starting point was his observation that we all experience an innate moral duty. Conscience triggers feelings of shame and guilt when we violate our internal moral compass. In this way, morality stands an empirical test. Since we seek to avoid the negative feelings of a disturbed conscience, we first attempt to do good. The highest form of good is good will. To have good will, one must perform one's duty for the sake of duty and for no other reason.

From this, Kant concluded that moral duty is objectively revealed through reason. Morality can be known by using reason and can be verified or falsified.
To quote Kant:
"To act morally is to perform one's duty, and one's duty is to obey the innate moral laws."
"A good will is not good because of what it affects or accomplishes… it is good through its willing – that is good in itself."

If only a small seed of Kant's ideas are correct, it could answer the question of why religions in every corner of the globe have the same basic moral laws. Moral laws, however, are separate from religion. Religion is simply a vehicle for a moral code, since both religion and its commandments developed around the need to solidify and guide a society. Primitive man did not have courts. They had priests acting as judges.

So, why did this moral compass develop in humans? Possibly, it was due to a consequence of evolutionary pressures. Humans were weak, slow, hairless creatures in a world of beasts and natural elements. The only way to survive was to ban together. If a person went against the family, tribe, or group, he or she would be ostracized and would have to face the world alone. Loners did not survive well. Over time, those with the highest social quotient for teamwork flourished in the hostile environment. The good of the many won out over the good of the individual. This could be the beginning of our internal moral code. This code is at odds with the older code of individual survival. The greater imperative is personal survival at all cost. This impulse must be consciously overridden by communal cooperation. Herein is the difference between what Kant describes and what we see in society. Some people are balanced one way and some another.

This code is wired in to our developing brains on a subconscious level. Meaning, the code could not be subjective since we had no way to "think" about it. However, it was made objective through the development of codified laws. Later, we grew and developed enough to intensely consider our laws, our conscience, and the internal battles.

Until the Axial Age, the focus of religion was external, particularly on rituals and ceremony intended to influence or control a god or gods to protect the family or tribe, bring rain, guarantee success in battle, and so on.

During the Axial Age, this changed and an internal search for god began. There may have been several influences driving this evolution. The world became smaller with migrations and the advent of transportation via horseback. Cities grew and developed. Continuous warfare mixed gods as the conquered tribes adopted the beliefs of the victors, considering their gods more powerful. The amalgam or unity of tribes and formation of armies began the demise of tribalism and the splitting of families through death and conscription into military service. The shattering and absorption of tribes and families brought about the rise of individual focus. Previously, consequences or punishment from actions of one individual or tribal member affected the entire family or tribe. With individuals separated from families and tribes, the perpetrator carried the consequences alone.

Continual hardships of war, disease, and changes in societies caused people to question the efficacy of their traditional god and religious practices prompting them to look for alternatives.

In China, India, Greece, and Israel, the spirit of humankind awakened in a flash. Wise men, shamans, sages, prophets, philosophers, and scholars independently articulated their insights. The religious traditions they created or influenced are alive in the major religions of today. Confucianism, Taoism, Hinduism, Buddhism, philosophical rationalism, and monotheism arose as though they were orchestrated and coordinated by a single hand.

The insights common to all religious enlightenment of the Axial Age include the ideas of reciprocity, compassion, love, altruism, and the individual's mandate to end the suffering of others. The ideas of compassion and reciprocity are summed up in the actions of treating other justly and as you wished to be treated. Judaism would go on to embody these values in their laws. In turn, the newly awakened Judaism translated that ideal, which has evolved into a monotheistic religion in which members seek communion with God.

In the years centering around 500 BCE, great advances in religion, philosophy, science, democracy, and many forms of art occurred independently and almost simultaneously in China, India, the Middle East, and Greece. Today, humanity still uses the spiritual foundations laid in that ancient time. In those times of social upheaval and political turmoil, spiritual and religious pioneers became the standard-bearers of a new religious, cultural, and social order. Great religious leaders rose up in various areas of the world attracting many followers, thereby changing many sociological, cultural, economic and spiritual beliefs.

In China, many individual thinkers, such as Confucius, Lao-Tse, and Mo Tzu, began to reflect on the ethical and spiritual implications of human existence. In time, their teachings became known throughout the world. Confucianism, Taoism, and Jainism are only a few religions to be founded or affected by them.

In India, the authors of the Upanishads expanded the scope of their explorations to include metaphysical thinking in the search for the ultimate truth and the meaning of life and death.

India experienced a dramatic social and intellectual transformation, and produced the teachings of the Buddha and

Mahavira. New teachings ran the whole gamut of philosophical schools of thought, including skepticism, materialism, and nihilism.

In Palestine, the prophets Elijah, Isaiah, and Jeremiah made their appearance. Although the law and moral code of the Israelites dates back before this age, and may have been influenced by the code of Hammurabi of 1750 BCE, the prophets reached beyond the law and called believers into a relationship with Yahweh.

In Mesopotamia, cultural and art developed but the concept of an omnipotent and omniscient creator God did not exist.

In Greece, developments were more philosophical than spiritual. Greece witnessed the appearance of Thales, Xenophanes, and Heraclitus who regarded all existence to be in a state of flux, exemplifying his concept by stating, "one cannot step in the same river twice." Parmenides commented on the nature of permanent "being" as opposed to the impermanent phase of "becoming". Democritus devised the first atomic theory of nature, which later gave way to the scientific nature of matter and atoms.

These philosophers influenced the minds of Socrates, Plato, and Aristotle. They examined the very nature of existence, life, and thought, itself.

Each philosopher and thinker forced his or her culture to question and reinterpret previously devised cosmologies. Until that point in time, every cosmology was a cosmology put forth by a religious myth and none were based in reason or science. Philosiphers attempted to impose reason, even on religion.

Even as philosophers were dividing science from religion, mystics were emerging from crystallized religions of old to seek the real internal world that lay beyond the senses.

Buddhism propagated the preaching of the eight-fold path. Right View and Right Intention are the wisdom factors of the Noble Eightfold Path. Right Speech, Right Action, and Right Livelihood address ethical conduct. Right Effort, Right Meditation, and Right Concentration address mental cultivation. The wisdom factors continually affect ethical conduct and mental cultivation.

This leap became the source of major and lasting cultural traditions enduring to the present time, giving way to a secondary stage or influence of spiritual transformation in which religions such as Judaism spawned the world's two major religions of Christianity and Islam.

The almost simultaneous changes in China, India, Palestine, and Greece seem too remarkable to be accidental; especially considering the lack of influence one movement could have had on another, seeing the countries are widely separated from each other. The only example of intellectual communication among these countries appears to be the conjecture that in the 6th century BCE the Greek poet Alcaeus may have known the prophecies of Isaiah.

Religions began to influence and build on each other within different countries. Some religions became opposed to killing their fellow man, while others valued all life. Ideas and beliefs of Jainism influenced a newly developing Hinduism and the new religion of Buddhism. The dualistic idea of good and evil contained within Zoroastrianism would influence the Jewish ideas of good and evil and the notion of Satan. The new face of Judaism would give way to Christianity and Islam.

The idea of an "Axial Age" has no specific timeline. It is a general idea based around a broad period of time wherein a global awakening occurred. Figures such as Jesus and Mohammed came after the Axial Age. However, Jesus and Mohammed both reaped the rewards of the spiritual awakening. This spiritual awakening within Judaism was the foundation that took the religion into a search for communion with Yahweh, El, God, or Allah. Jaspers' concept of the Axial Age is an observation and not a law of history. Yet, there were mighty spiritual changes taking place within the "Axial Age."

Possibly, Zarathustra, the founder of Zoroastrianism, lived before the Axial Age. The history of Zoroastrianism varies widely. Some sources say the founder appeared around 1200 BCE in what is now Iran. Perhaps Zoroastrianism emerged from a prior religion in a common prehistoric Indo-Iranian belief system dating back to the early second millennium BCE. According to Zoroastrian tradition, Zoroaster was a reformer who exalted the deity of Wisdom, Ahura Mazda, to the status of Supreme Being and Creator, while demoting various other deities and rejecting certain rituals.

Zoroastrianism only enters recorded history in the mid-5th century BCE. It was within this period that the religion came into its own.

In the Middle East, Judaism was undergoing a tremendous upheaval. Recent studies and archeological excavations reveal that the Jews were not only polytheistic, but may have been in the midst of changing deities, from the war god El, to the god Yahweh, who invited them into communion and protection. Although the Jews vacillated between the two differing deities with differing personalities, the change began.

In the late 18th century, Bible scholars refined their abilities to follow the wording and phrasing within the Old Testament and determine that it was the result of several writers and an editing process that took place in successive layers over centuries. Each writer's contribution brought current events and their individual spiritual or religious viewpoints, which drove the evolution of Judaism.

Scholars in Germany noted that in most of the duplicated stories, one set described God using the Hebrew word El or Elohim (usually translated "God"), while the other set used God's name of Yahweh (written as the tetragrammaton of Y-H-W-H with the Hebrew letters of yodh, he, waw, he.) Evidently, there were at least two different authors. The main authors used the label "E" for Elohim and the other called "J" (German for Y), for Yahweh. YHWH is also seen as YHVH. This because W and V is reversed when pronouncing the name or letters in German. Thus, YHWH becomes YHVH and yields the name, Jehovah.

Later, closer and more precise analysis of grammar, vocabulary, and writing style within the Old Testament revealed evidence of at least four authors. There was a writer obsessed with laws and genealogy called "P" for the Priestly author. His hand is seen most clearly in Leviticus. The other is called "D" for the Deuteronomist, since the book of Deuteronomy is grammatically and politically different from the earlier books. Writer "J" focused on humanity and "E" pontificates about religious and moral concerns. The multiple-author view is now called the "Documentary theory."

Later, an editor, called the Redactor, combined the four different books. Sometimes, the Redactor put different authors' stories of the same events in succession, for example, the creation stories. Some he interwove, such as the two stories of Noah's Flood and of Joseph's mistreatment by his brothers. Evidence of varying stories of the flood has been uncovered, but the story in the Bible seems to weave many of them into a single narrative. The Redactor also added transitional phrases such as, "and it came to pass," "and it was so," and "in the fullness of time" between sections to tie them together.

Armstrong indicates, at this point, the shift from legalism to compassionate equality is evidence of Axial Age spirituality. This can be seen in Leviticus, chapter 19.

Leviticus 19:33-34
*33 When an alien lives with you in your land, do not mistreat him. **34** The alien living with you must be treated as one of your native-born. Love him as yourself, for you were aliens in Egypt. I am the LORD your God.*

Leviticus 19:18
"Thou shalt not avenge, nor bear any grudge against the children of thy people, but thou shalt love thy neighbour as thyself: I am the LORD."

Although it is held as one of the main principles of the entire Bible and the statement sounds universally fair, the term "neighbor" meant roughly "kinsman," and could be interpreted as applicable only to fellow Jews.

Tobit 4:14-15
"Take heed to thyself, my child, in all thy works; and be discreet in all thy behavior. And what thou thyself hatest, do to no man."

Armstrong points out that the Axial insight moment did not last long after the return of the Jews from captivity. The wrathful god was back with a vengeance. This tenuous hold on spiritual evolution is somewhat childlike, and is seen in our everyday lives. When the Jews were in captivity or under military or political oppression, it was easier for them to see how all men should be treated with equal compassion. Once they were free and had a superior hand, it became easier for them to be the despot. Following this, their god again reflected his warlike and oppressive attitude.

The sixth century BCE, in particular, was a period of radical changes in basic religious concepts and the sudden emergence of new ideas. A radical change in humanity's spiritual development occurred and became a major source of most of our present-day faith traditions.

Any acceptable theory of causation cannot satisfactorily explain the rapid transformation. Eventually, most of the new doctrines became organized as religious systems, concerned with world-views and world-values. Although we may trace many of the old traditions, rituals, beliefs, and ceremonies back to pre-Axial Age religions, they were incorporated into new religions and were remade and redefined afresh.

Princeton University psychologist, Julian Jaynes, postulated one theory of the rapid and global change in his book, *The Origin of Consciousness in the Breakdown of the Bicameral Mind*, published by Houghton Mifflin/Mariner Books (1976, 2000)

At the heart of this book is a revolutionary idea that human consciousness did not begin in our "animal" stage of evolution, but was a learned process. Jaynes presents a theory of the bicameral mind which speculates that ancient peoples could not "think" as we do today and were, therefore "unconscious," a result of the domination of the right hemisphere. Only catastrophe and cataclysm forced humankind to "learn" consciousness, and birthed our modern state of consciousness out of an earlier mentality only 3,000 years ago. We are still developing along these lines. Before 1,000 BCE, human history and culture issued forth from the brain's left hemisphere. The implications of this new paradigm extend into virtually every aspect of human psychology, history, culture, and religion.

In general, the left and right hemispheres of your brain process information in different ways. We know that the cerebral cortex is the part of the brain that houses rational functions. It is divided into two hemispheres connected by a thick band of nerve fibers (the corpus callosum), which sends messages back and forth between the hemispheres. In addition, brain research confirms that, in nearly every human activity, the brain involves both hemispheres. We know that the left side of the brain is the seat of language and processes thought in a logical and sequential order. The right side operates more visually and processes thought intuitively, holistically, and randomly. The right side of the brain produces intuition and "gut feelings."

Nobel Prize Winner (1981), Roger Sperry, conducted what are sometimes called the "split-brain" experiments. A patient suffering from uncontrolled seizures had an area of his brain surgically removed in an attempt to control his illness. The area was the corpus callosum, the wiring between the left and right hemispheres, suspected of having lesions.

Following his surgery, he conducted a series of tests wherein he isolated each "half" of the patient from the other. The left and right eyesight and hands had a divider coming up to the face and chest. He then presented different visual and tactile information to the patient's left or right side, without the other side knowing. The results were astounding.

With their communications link severed, each side of the patient's brain functioned independently. Although this did not prevent normal daily functions, he encountered some unexpected findings when each side was examined independently of the other.

With the left side of the body isolated, the right hand and eye could name an object, but the patient could not explain the use of the object. When shown to the left hand and eye, the patient could explain and demonstrate the object's use, but could not name it. Further studies indicated that various functions of thought are physically separate and localized to a specific area on either the left or right side of the human brain. This functional map is consistent for an estimated 70 to 95 percent of us.

However, the disconnection between the left and right sides of the brain did not cause the patient to revert to a "pre-Axial-Age" condition of being emotionally, intuitively, or spontaneously driven, nor was the patient rendered incapable of thinking about future events as related to present decisions. Whether the patient functioned from a dominant left or right side of the brain, no "spiritual de-evolution" occurred. This observation alone could engender skepticism regarding the Bicameral Mind theory as being the driving force behind our spiritual leap into internalization of God and our ability to see ourselves in others and others within ourselves. Moreover, the theory does not speculate about the interconnectivity between the hemispheres specifically, but rather it speaks of an odd unilateralism within the brain. Humans, if healthy, are bi-lateral creatures with a balanced left and right side. Bicameral Mind theory asks us to assume that one side of the brain is so dominant that the other side of the brain is overwhelmed or silenced.

Sperry determined the function of each side of the brain and labeled the modes of each.

"The main theme to emerge... is that there appear to be two modes of thinking, verbal and nonverbal, represented rather separately in left and right hemispheres respectively and that our education system, as well as science in general, tends to neglect the nonverbal form of intellect. What it comes down to is that modern society discriminates against the right hemisphere."
-Roger Sperry (1973)

The basic breakdown of left and right brain functions are as follows:

LEFT	RIGHT
Logical	Emotional
Detail oriented	Big Picture oriented
Facts	Imagination
Science	Religion
Order	Spatial Perception
Form	Images
Functionality	Symbols
Reality	Fantasy
Rational	Philosophy and Faith

Ideally, both sides of the brain work together in people with optimum mental ability. This coordinating ability may be the key to superior intellectual abilities. In most people, however, the left-brain takes control, choosing logic, reasoning, and details over imagination, holistic thinking, and artistic talent, due to the present demands of society. This was not the case a few thousand years ago.

Now, this is where the concept of a dominant right-brain human may get confusing. If the right brain is in charge of our intuitive and philosophical side, why did its dominance not allow us to plunge into our mystical, altruistic, compassionate, spiritual inward journey? The answer seems to be that the right brain cannot clearly conceive of future events, cause and effect, or our relationship to the cosmos. Although the right brain thrives on the big picture, it does not see the full picture in a logical way. In other words, it seems to take both the left and right sides of our brain working together to keep a balanced and correct perspective of where we are and where we are going in an internal search.

In human history preceding the Axial Age, man believed he needed to make sacrifices, of both human and animal, to the gods. In order to appease and influence the gods, man carried out particular rituals and ceremonies, placing their priests and religious leaders in high esteem. Today, modern society has not only eclipsed, but also suppressed these right brain activities.

Our personality, and to a certain degree, our abilities are a result of the degree to which these left and right brains interact, or, in some cases, do not interact. "Left brain" types are analytical and orderly, while "right brain" types are artistic, unpredictable, and creative.

Experiments show that most children are classified as "highly creative" (right brain) before entering school. Because our educational system places a higher value on "left brain" skills such as mathematics, logic, and language than it does on drawing or using our imagination, only ten percent of these same children will classify as highly creative by age 7. By the time we are adults, high creativity remains in only 2 percent of the population.

These experiments discount the idea of pure evolution in brain size as a springboard into the Axial Age. Although there is a general correlation between brain size and intellectual ability, the form and function of the brain is as important. Homo erectus, our distant ancestor, had a brain size of about 1200 cc. Modern Homo Sapiens have an average brain of about 1400 cc. However, the Neanderthal people who failed to evolve into humans had a brain size of 1500 cc, which is larger than modern man has today. There are "genius" brains measuring as small as 1000 cc. and as large as 2000 cc and is further evidence that brain size alone does not yield intelligence.

At this point, the size of the human brain at birth may be maxed out due to the natural size of a typical women's pelvic opening. In addition, larger brain size requires a highly stable temperature and a larger supply of high protein and energy. We use one quarter of our caloric intake for brain energy consumption. Yet, if our development thus far is due to changes in the "interconnectivity" of the brain and the balancing of the left and right sides, there is hope that we can finally move forward and leave the ritual and ceremony of religion behind and embrace the compassionate and humanitarian side of our spiritual journey.

At the present, we are sitting on a razor's edge attempting to decide on which side to fall. We still see the horrors of what vengeful religions and vengeful gods can do. The Christian church mounted the bloody crusades well into the 1600's, although it reached fever pitch around 1290 when the Catholic Church ordered the murder of an entire region containing the Cathar Christians in what is now France. The pre-Axial-Age frenzy is being carried out today in the forms of fundamentalism within Islam, the Zionist movement of the Jews, and the judgmental and hateful aspects of the Christian church.

Even today we see three forms of human awareness, the bicameral or god-run man; the modern or problem-solving man; and contemporary forms of pre-bicamerality man where religious frenzy, with externalized and stern concepts of god rule the day.

Thusfar we have spoken of two different and separate ideas. We have raised the issue of the inability of ancient man to look within and find the connection between himself, his fellow man, and his god. Ancient man did not have the ability to think beyond the immediate. We have also spoken of the imbalance in either strength or communication of the left side of the brain.

According to Jaynes, the right hemisphere of the brain dominated ancient man. However, after the Axial Age, there arose true mystics - men and women who departed this conventional external world and began an inward journey.

"O, what a world of unseen visions and heard silences, this insubstantial country of the mind! What ineffable essences, these touchless rememberings, and unshowable reveries! And the privacy of it all! A secret theater of speechless monologue and prevenient counsel, an invisible mansion of all moods, musings, and mysteries, an infinite resort of disappointments and discoveries. A whole kingdom where each of us reigns reclusively alone, questioning what we will, commanding what we can. A hidden hermitage where we may study out the troubled book of what we have done and yet may do. An introcosm that is more myself than anything I can find in a mirror. This consciousness that is myself of selves, that is everything, and yet is nothing at all - what is it? And where did it come from? And why?"
Julian Jaynes

This is a beautifully articulated description of the mystical experience, but it does not make the theory correct. Certain questions beg to be answered.

If the left side of the brain was quiescent and the left side controlled logic, reason, planning, form, function, and science, how then did ancient man build the pyramids?

The Great Pyramid of Giza is the most substantial ancient structure in the world. According to prevailing archaeological theory, three kings of the fourth dynasty built the three pyramids on the Giza plateau between 2575 and 2465 BC. The Great Pyramid was originally 481 feet, five inches tall and measured 755 feet along its sides, covering an area of 13 acres, or 53,000 square meters. It is large enough to contain the European cathedrals of Florence, Milan, St. Peters, Westminster Abbey, and St. Paul's. Approximately 2.5 million limestone blocks weighing on average 2.6 tons each comprise the pyramid's construction. The total mass is more than 6.3 million tons, which is a greater amount of building material found in all the churches and cathedrals built in England since the time of Christ. If Julian Jaynes' theory is correct, how could such a feat be accomplished by men driven almost exclusively by the right side of his brain? Possibly, we need to re-visit this theory.

What drove mankind to awaken spiritually between the years of 800 BCE and 200 BCE? Alternatively, is the question itself erroneous? When two contradictory statements appear, check the premise.

Recent experiments have shown real-time patterns and differences between the wakeful and sleeping brain. One of the most interesting and marked differences is the response to non-sensory input. While visually monitoring the brain with magnetic imaging, scientists generated a magnetic pulse and directed it into the sleeping brain. The brain responded by "lighting up" the area effected by the pulse. The response looked liked the brain simply echoed the pulse by a rapid "blip" of activity, which quickly died. When the same magnetic pulse was introduced into the wakeful brain, the brain resonated like a bell being struck. The echo seen in the wakeful brain did not stop with the simple response. Instead, the response activated adjoining areas, passed from one area of the brain to another, around, and through the brain as each area processed the occurrence. It is the interconnectivity of the brain that brings about consciousness. Could it be that Jaynes was actually on to something, but simply went too far in his assumptions? Maybe it was not simply a matter of balancing hemispheric dominance that caused the great shift of the Axial Age, but instead a subtle evolutionary change in the connections between the areas of the brain. This is not to insinuate that ancient man was not as conscious or wakeful as modern man is today, or any more or less intelligent. Simply, through the connections within and between areas of the brain, we may find the sense of who or what we are, and where we reside in god and in the universe. It is possible that we are over-analyzing the entire concept and what was happening spiritually was exactly what happens in all other areas of human progress. Great men have great ideas that are built upon present concepts, which push humanity forward into the next stage.

Dr. Joseph Lumpkin

We may never know the reason the Axial Age graced us. The brain and nervous system are made of soft tissue, which disintegrates. They do not withstand the ravages of time. Thus, any theory concerning the brain can only be inferred and never proven, at least not with our current science. Whether the Axial Age was brought about by the social changes driving individualism, migration, or the modes of travel on horseback occurring in certain regions, or whether it was by a change in brain connections or chemistry, we do not know. We do know, however, there was a pattern; and within a certain epoch of time, man became a spiritual creature, leaving his primitive gods behind.

How and why did this happen globally and simultaneously?

Theories of a Connected Mind

Is there a "Universal Mind" connecting us all?

In Japan, scientists were observing a type of monkey called the Macaca Fuscata. The tribe of monkeys was observed in the wild for a period of over 30 years. In 1952, on the island of Koshima, scientists began providing monkeys with sweet potatoes, which the scientists simply dropped in the sand. Then left the monkeys alone. The monkeys liked the taste of the raw sweet potatoes, but they did not like the grit or taste of the sand. An 18-month-old female monkey the scientists had named Imo found she could clean her potatoes by washing them in a nearby stream. Seeing the trick worked, the mother emulated her daughter. The playmates of the 18-month-old also learned this new way. Most of the younger monkeys picked up on the trick and some of their mothers learned the ritual. The action became a cultural innovation and was gradually picked up by various monkeys. Between 1952 and 1958 all the young monkeys learned to wash the sand from their sweet potatoes in the streams. The adults who imitated their children learned and kept up the routine, but other adults kept eating the sandy sweet potatoes.

Then, something odd took place. A collective change within the tribe occurred, as if a critical mass had been reached. In the autumn of 1958, after a certain number of Koshima monkeys had learned to wash sweet potatoes, the activity seemed to pass through the entire tribe. Almost everyone in the tribe was mimicking the action. One could explain this by saying that it was a matter of each monkey being exposed to the ritual multiple times until it was learned. However, at the same time, scientists observed that the habit of washing sweet potatoes appeared in monkey colonies in other areas that were separated from the first tribe by the sea. Colonies of monkeys on other islands and the mainland troop of monkeys at Takasakiyama began washing their sweet potatoes. This became known as the "Hundredth Monkey Phenomenon."

Later, scientists revisited the notes left by the original researchers. The follow-up group claimed that the first researchers over-stated the phenomenon. They also claimed that it was possible for a monkey to swim from colony to colony, spreading the knowledge as it went. This is possible, of course. Over time, monkeys could have traveled from place to place, but the scientists reported the phenomenon was occurring too quickly in several different locations for this to be the case, unless they over-stated that also. If the first scientists reported both pieces of data inaccurately, they may have inadvertently spawned an urban myth. The question seems to boil down to this; "Is it possible that our minds are connected or that our mind or emotions may have some minor influence over distances?"

*The following are excerpts from The New Yorker Magazine
Article "In the Air: Who says big ideas are rare?"
By Malcolm Gladwell
May 12, 2008*

In 1874, Alexander Graham Bell spent the summer with his parents in Brantford, Ontario. He was twenty-seven years old, and employed as a speech therapist in Boston. However, his real interest was solving the puzzle of what he called the "harmonic telegraph." In Boston, he had tinkered obsessively with tuning forks and electromagnetic coils, often staying up all night when he was in the grip of an idea. When he went to Brantford, he brought with him an actual human ear, taken from a cadaver and preserved, to which he attached a pen, so that he could record the vibration of the ear's bones when he spoke into it.

One day, Bell went for a walk on a bluff overlooking the Grand River, near his parents' house. In a recent biography of Bell, "Reluctant Genius," Charlotte Gray writes:

"A large tree had blown down here, creating a natural and completely private belvedere, which [he] had dubbed his "dreaming place." Slouched on a wicker chair, his hands in his pockets, he stared unseeing at the swiftly flowing river below him. Far from the bustle of Boston and the pressure of competition from other eager inventors, he mulled over everything he had discovered about sound. "

"In that moment, Bell knew the answer to the puzzle of the harmonic telegraph. Electric currents could convey sound along a wire if they undulated in accordance with the sound waves. Back in Boston, he hired a research assistant, Thomas Watson. He turned his attic into a laboratory, and redoubled his efforts. Then, on March 10, 1876, he set up one end of his crude prototype in his bedroom, and had Watson take the other end to the room next door. Bell, always prone to clumsiness, spilled acid on his clothes. "Mr. Watson, come here," he cried out. Watson came running—but only because he had heard Bell on the receiver, plain as day. The telephone was born..."

"In June of 1876, a few months after he shouted out, "Mr. Watson, come here," Alexander Graham Bell took his device to the World's Fair in Philadelphia. There, before an audience that included the emperor of Brazil, he gave his most famous public performance.

Bell was not the only one to give a presentation on the telephone at the Philadelphia Exhibition, however. Someone else spoke first. His name was Elisha Gray. Gray never had an epiphany overlooking the Grand River. Few have claimed that Gray was a genius. He does not seem to have been obsessive, or to have routinely stayed up all night while in the grip of an idea — although we do not really know, because, unlike Bell, he has never been the subject of a full-length biography. Gray was simply a very adept inventor. He was the author of a number of discoveries relating to the telegraph industry, including a self-adjusting relay that solved the problem of circuits sticking open or shut, and a telegraph printer — a precursor of what was later called the Teletype machine. He worked closely with Western Union. He had a very capable partner named Enos Barton, with whom he formed a company that later became the Western Electric Company and its offshoot, Graybar (of Graybar Building fame). Moreover, Gray was working on the telephone at the same time that Bell was. In fact, the two filed notice with the Patent Office in Washington, D.C., on the same day — February 14, 1876. Bell went on to make telephones with the company that later became A.T.&T. Gray went on to make telephones in partnership with Western Union and Thomas Edison, and — until Gray's team was forced to settle a lawsuit with Bell's company — the general consensus was that Gray and Edison's telephone was better than Bell's telephone.

In order to get one of the greatest inventions of the modern age, we thought we needed the solitary genius. However, if Alexander Graham Bell had fallen into the Grand River and drowned that day back in Brantford, the world would still have the telephone, the only difference being that the telephone company would have been nicknamed Ma Gray, not Ma Bell.

This phenomenon of simultaneous discovery — what science historians call "multiples" — turns out to be extremely common. One of the first comprehensive lists of multiples was put together by William Ogburn and Dorothy Thomas in 1922. They found a hundred and forty-eight major scientific discoveries that fit the multiple patterns.

For Ogburn and Thomas, the sheer number of multiples could

31

mean only one thing: scientific discoveries, in some sense, must be inevitable. They must be in the air, products of the intellectual climate of a specific time and place. It should not surprise us then, that calculus was invented by two people at the same moment in history. Calculus was in the air.

Yet, we are reluctant to believe that great discoveries are "in the air." We want to believe that great discoveries are in our heads — and to each party in the multiple, the presence of the other party is invariably a cause for suspicion.

However, five people came up with the steamboat, and nine people came up with the telescope, and, if Gray had fallen into the Grand River along with Bell, some Joe Smith somewhere likely would have invented the telephone instead, and Ma Smith would have run the show.
    End Citation

Good ideas are out there for anyone with the wit and the will to find them, which is how a group of people can sit down to dinner, put their minds to it, and end up with eight single-spaced pages of ideas.

This observation about scientific geniuses is clearly not true of artistic geniuses, however. You cannot pool the talents of a dozen Salieris and get Mozart's Requiem. You cannot put together a committee of extremely talented art students and get Matisse's "La Danse." A work of artistic genius is singular, and all the arguments over calculus, the accusations back and forth between the Bell and the Gray camps, and our persistent inability to come to terms with the existence of multiples are the result of our misplaced desire to impose the paradigm of artistic invention on a world where it does not belong. Shakespeare owned Hamlet because he created him, as none other before or since could. Alexander Graham Bell owned the telephone only because his patent application landed on the examiner's desk a few hours before Gray's did. The first kind of creation was sui generis; the second could be re-created in a warehouse outside Seattle.

This is a confusing distinction, because we use the same words to describe both kinds of inventors, and the brilliant scientist is every bit as dazzling in person as the brilliant playwright.

Like great ideas in science, great religious and spiritual ideas occur in multiples around the world. If we could discover the mechanism for multiple scientific ideas and notions, we would have discovered the mechanism for multiples of spiritual ideas and the reason for the Axial Age.

As it turns out, there are two experiments that have measured linked influences over great distances, Quantum Entanglement and Human Consciousness Field. Yes, this does sound like pseudo-science and new-age babble, but at least, let's examine the evidence as laid down by university scientists.

The Strange World of Quantum Entanglement
By Paul Comstock
March 30th, 2007

Brian Clegg, the author of numerous books and articles on the history of science, received a physics degree from Cambridge University. His most recent book is *The God Effect: Quantum Entanglement, Science's Strangest Phenomenon.*

Dr. Clegg explains Quantum Entanglement like this:

"Entanglement is a strange feature of quantum physics, the science of the very small. It's possible to link together two quantum particles — photons of light or atoms, for example — in a special way that makes them effectively two parts of the same entity. You can then separate them as far as you like, and a change in one is instantly reflected in the other. This odd, faster than light link, is a fundamental aspect of quantum science. Erwin Schrödinger, who came up with the name "entanglement" called it "the characteristic trait of quantum mechanics." Entanglement is fascinating in its own right, but what makes it really special are dramatic practical applications that have become apparent in the last few years."

John Bell, who devised a lot of the theories for testing the existence of entanglement, covered it in a paper called "Bertlmann's Socks and the Nature of Reality." Reinhold Bertlmann, one of Bell's colleagues, always wore socks of different colors. Bell pointed out that, if you saw one of Bertlmann's feet coming around the corner of a building and it had a pink sock on, you would instantly know the other sock was not pink, even though you had never seen it. The color difference was programmed in when Bertlmann put his socks on. However, the quantum world is very different. If you take some property of a particle, the equivalent of color, say the spin of an electron, it does not have the value pre-programmed. It has a range of probabilities as to what the answer might be, but until you actually measure it, there is no fixed value.

This is what happens with a pair of entangled electrons. Until the moment you measure the spin of one electron, neither of them had a spin with a fixed value. However, the instant you take the measurement on one, the other immediately fixes its spin (say, to the opposite value). These "quantum socks" were every possible color until you looked at one. Only then did it become pink, and the other instantly took on another color.

It took a long time to prove that entanglement truly exists. It wasn't until the 1980's that it was clearly demonstrated. But, it has been shown, without doubt, that entanglement exists, and is used in very practical ways.

The first thing most people think of, including a report produced for the Department of Defense shortly after entanglement theory was validated, is the ability to communicate faster than light. The link of entanglement works instantaneously at any distance. Therefore, it would be amazing if it could be used to send a signal. In fact, this is not possible. Although there is a real connection between two entangled particles, we do not know what information it is going to send. If I measure the spin of an entangled electron, yes, it communicates the value somehow to its twin — but I cannot use it. I had no idea what the spin was going to be. This is just as well, because faster than light messages travel backwards in time. If I could send a message instantly it would be received in the past, and that really would disrupt cause and effect. However, there are still real and amazing applications of entanglement. It can be used to produce unbreakable encryption. If you send each half of a set of entangled pairs to either end of a communications link, then the randomly generated, but linked properties can be used as a key to encrypt information. If anyone intercepts the information, it will break the entanglement, and the communication can be stopped before the eavesdropper picks up any data.

Entanglement is a wholly physical process. It is a very special particle that gives everything its mass, and has been called the God Particle, because it is so fundamental. However, that is just a label. Nobel Prize winning physicist, Brian Josephson, suggested that entanglement could explain telepathy (much to the irritation of paranormal debunker James Randi), but Josephson said, "If telepathy exists, then here's a physical mechanism that could explain it." — he wasn't indulging in mystical navel-gazing.

Entanglement (and quantum theory in general) reminds us that

the real world is much stranger than we imagine. That is because the way things operate in the world of the very small is totally different to large-scale objects like desks and pens. We cannot rely on experience and common sense to guide us on how things are going to work at this level, so that can make some of the effects of quantum physics seem mystical. In the end, this is something similar to science fiction writer Arthur C. Clarke's observation that "any sufficiently advanced technology is indistinguishable from magic."
(End of Article)

Quantum Entanglement, telepathy, instant and coordinated influences at great distances, all sound like science fiction, yet it is science that has opened the door to such possibilities. If entanglement exists, then the pairs of entangled particles could influence not only the brain, but also almost any system that is sensitive enough to be influenced by minute atomic changes.

Changes in perceptions and ideas, and even the energy creating quantum changes may travel through a field. For hundreds of years, the idea of a general and ubiquitous medium that surrounds all living things existed, and various energies could be propagated through this medium. Rupert Sheldrake calls this field the Morphic Field.

Morphic Fields and Morphic Resonance
By Rupert Sheldrake
Fields of the Mind - Morphic fields underlie our mental activity and our perceptions, and lead to a new theory of vision, as discussed in the book, *"The Sense of Being Stared At."* The existence of these fields is experimentally testable through the sense of being stared at itself. The morphic fields of social groups connect members of the group together even when they are many miles apart, providing channels of communication through which organisms can stay in touch at a distance. They provide an explanation for telepathy. There is now good evidence that many species of animals are telepathic, and telepathy seems to be a normal means of animal communication, as discussed in my book *"Dogs That Know When Their Owners Are Coming Home."*

(End of Article)

Telepathy is normal, not paranormal, natural, not supernatural, and is common between people; especially people who know each other well. In the modern world, the commonest kind of human telepathy occurs in connection with telephone calls. More than 80% of the population says they have thought of someone for no apparent reason, who then called; or that they have known who was calling before picking up the phone in a way that seems telepathic. Controlled experiments on telephone telepathy have given repeatable positive results that are highly significant statistically.

If there is a morphic field, it should influence people and events throughout the world. It should be measurable or detectable. As of yet, its existence cannot be proven, but there have been experiments that seem to indicate collective influences between people and events.

From the Global Consciousness Project - 2009:

For the past seven years, random number generators have been running all over the world, electronically flipping 200 coins each second, with the intention of measuring a global consciousness. The Global Consciousness Project (GCP), originating from Princeton, have named these random event generators Electrogaiagrams (EGGs) and are using them to test whether a human consciousness extends a field around the earth which can change the results of random events. They claim that when an important event occurs, such as the 9/11 terrorist attack or the Indian Ocean tsunami, the random event generators start to display patterns that should not exist in truly random sequences.

Creative inspiration, identical ideas, and solutions occurring globally must work under the same rules and with the same mechanism as spiritual and religious ideas. Religious and ethical thinkers in the different countries posed questions almost simultaneously. Basic religious ideas by which people have been living since the dawn of the age of man were laid down at the same time. New ideas were conceived and articulated during the same time frame. How did this happen? The theory of quantum entanglement gives us the doorway to explain how particles are connected through vast distances. Preliminary data shows how collective human minds may influence random outcomes. Minds may affect minds and groups may affect groups. To date there has been no valid explanation as to why multiple inventions and ideas occur or why there was a worldwide change in spirituality. Quantum Entanglement may offer a clue.

The evolution of religion happened in a relativity short period of time. The Axial Age did not happen over night, but was a single grain of sand in the hourglass of mankind's existence. Was the idea of mysticism and spiritual awareness floating in the air? What was the path that brought us to this place? How did religion evolve? Why does it matter that we changed?

The answer to the last question may be the most intuitively obvious. Consciousness may be the way that the universe reflects and understands itself, and deeper consciousness brings about deeper understanding. God may be beckoning us homeward in stages of greater wisdom. The ideas floating in the air could be the universal consciousness propelling us upward.

To understand the trajectory and path of our spiritual evolution we must go back to a time when man began.

An Overview of Evolution in Religion

Julian Jaspers, the man who postulated the Bicameral Mind, divides history into four major ages: the Neolithic age, the age of the earliest civilizations, the age of the emergence of great empires, and the modern age. Before the Neolithic was the Paleolithic period.

During their first and longest phase of social evolution, called the Paleolithic phase, (denoting the early phase of the Stone Age, lasting about 2.5 million years, when primitive stone implements were used), people lived by gathering fruit and nuts, hunting, and trapping animals. These "hunter-gatherer" people had primitive theories explaining nature. Life, death, food, and fire were of main importance. They likely had a limited language, which reflected limited ideas.

The first major advance in human experience was the beginning of an agrarian society. The farming villages began, and included a little animal husbandry. Since the period was still pre-history, we have no written records, and only archeological evidence. Very little is known about the social conditions that made the transition possible. The discovery of agriculture and the domestication of animals were possibly the most far-reaching changes in human history. They both apparently occurred eight to ten thousand years ago, at the beginning of the Neolithic era. Religion expanded only slightly to include concerns regarding weather and crops.

Apart from a notion that humans have always been war-like beings, and religion has always centered on praying for victory in war, whether it is tribal or national, and apart from slowly changing daily concerns, basic religious concepts remained the same for thousands of years. There was only limited religious development at this time, and on some level, one may argue that even until today, for many, there have been few changes still. Everyone continues to claim that god is on his or her side and will make them victorious in battle, no matter which side they happen to be on.

The second major advance was the building of urban civilizations. Keeping in mind that many societies combined the priestly and ruling classes, many tribes and villages were ruled by warrior/kings or priest/kings. As people began to concentrate into territories, and the coordination of efforts began to be orchestrated by the rulers, a remarkable degree of building innovation, as well as technological and aesthetic innovation took place. Specialization of skills occurred and people began to come together as communities. This allowed them to break free from the constant strain of having to work, build, and farm independently. With increased personal time and resources, people, especially the upper classes of priests and rulers, began searching for comprehensive religious and ethical concepts. Needless to say, many of these concepts were superstitious and self-serving.

Beginning in the fourth millennium BCE, and for the next three thousand years, what we call "civilization" matured in the Middle East around Egypt and the Fertile Crescent area.

Religion permeated the early civilizations. Each region or community had its patron or favorite god. All community efforts that were not related to work, building, and battles were focused on religion. Priest/kings developed theocratic government where priests and kings stood in proxy for or as conduits to the gods. Temples were built to worship tribal deities in religions ruled by a priest-king. The long-held belief that monarchies and absolute rule are the most efficient is probably true, however, those type governments are not always the most equitable. In theocracy, there was a remarkable leap in human inventiveness, creativity, and construction.

It has been said that the hearts of men are evil continually. As the priests conceived of greater and more precious sacrifice to garner favor from their god, the people were required first to sacrifice from their harvest, then their animals, and finally members of their family. The zenith of human sacrifice was reached in the worship of the deity, Moloch.

There were several societies practicing human sacrifice in the time-period at the beginning of the Axial Age.

Canaanites – 3500 – 1100 B.C. - "Canaanite" is an ancient term for what we now know as Israel, Lebanon, and parts of Syria and Jordan. Children were sacrificed to the god Moloch.

Carthaginians – 300 – 140 B.C. - The Carthaginians of North Africa were disgusted by the thought of sacrificing their own children, but in order to please their god they bought children slaves of other regions to sacrifice.

Celts – 800 – 1 B.C. - Celtic sites throughout Europe show bodies with evidence of having been sacrificed. They worshiped their gods of nature by burning people alive in structures made of woven branches known as "Wicker Men."

Etruscans – 800 – 100 B.C. Etruscans belonged to an ancient civilization in Italy between Florence and Rome. Their written records no longer exist, but their artwork shows evidence of human sacrifice.

Gauls – 700 – 500 B.C. - In roughly 50 BC, Julius Caesar wrote, in his Commentarii de Bello Gallico, that [The Gauls] believe that unless a man's life is paid for by another man's, the majesty of the immortal gods cannot be appeased.

One may also add the ancient Jews to the list. Having adopted and followed the rituals of Moloch, they burned their children alive in sacrifice to the pagan idol. In good times, the rituals usually followed certain lunar or solar events, however, in times of crisis like war, famine, or drought, sacrifices would go on, and increase in number until the gods were appeased. In such times, the children of wealthy families would be included in the sacrifices.

In 605 BC, Babylon rose again and King Nebuchadnezzar deported the Jews to various parts of Arabia. The Jews around Canaan were exposed to Moloch. Many deities of ancient Mesopotamia are recorded in the Old Testament owing to the fact that idolatry was commonplace throughout the ancient Middle East. The gods included the fishtailed Dagon of the Philistines, the he-goat Asima of the Emathites and the fly, Beelzebub, worshipped in the kingdom of Accaron. The most bloodthirsty deity was Moloch.

Several Biblical accounts record the followers' belief that by appeasing Moloch with the lives of burnt children and animals, he would renew the vitality of their king, who, in turn, could reap a plentiful harvest. The king represented the land he ruled, as it was in the much later myth of King Arthur.

The sacrifice was a noisy and morbid affair. On days of sacrifice, drums and cymbals were played at maximum volume to drown out the screams of children being burned alive.

A Greek transcription of the Hebrew Moloch, whose name means king, indicated that he was one of the main pagan deities of ancient Mesopotamia. As many Israelites burned their children alive in tribute to this idol, modern thinking holds that the name in fact derives from the Punic root MLK, meaning offering, or sacrifice, and suggests that Moloch refers not to the name of a god, but to a particular form of ritual sacrifice.

Many commentators have asserted that Milcom is simply an interchangeable variant of Moloch. This may not be true. Milcom was of Ammonite origin and did not require child sacrifice. All references to Moloch associate this god with child sacrifice, while Milcom is never associated with this practice. Deuteronomy 12:29-31 and 18:9-14 also suggest that child sacrifices were presumably to Moloch and were of Canaanite origin. Although the two can be considered as independent deities, this may simply be semantics since tribes integrated the god of neighboring tribes, changing rituals to suit local customs. Deuteronomy 12:31 bring this to a point.

Thou shalt not do so unto the Lord thy God: for every abomination to the Lord, which he hateth, have they done unto their gods; for even their sons and their daughters they have burnt in the fire to their gods.

Correction is not needed unless the deed had been done and needed correcting.

Moloch became one of the enemies of the establishment of the first stages in monotheism for the Jews. The religious practice of Moloch was forbidden in Leviticus 18:21: *"You shall not give any of your children to devote them by fire to Moloch, and so profane the name of your God."* What was the motivation to change one's religious ritual or beliefs? Some think the Ten Commandments, and the laws that issued from them, come from a Hittite form of law dating from the 12th century BCE. Others think that the basis was the "Code of Hammurabi," a Babylonian form of law dating from 1700 BCE. For the Jews, the Decalogue may have come into form and force in the 7th century BCE. The interesting dichotomy is, that in spite of laws known to restrict killing for no reason, the sacrifice continued. Why did sacrifice decrease and disappear? It would take a cynic to suggest that the decrease was related to the fact that civilizations that sacrifice their children grow slower than those who do not, and are eventually overly influenced or overrun by their neighbors. Call me a cynic.

The Jews were straying and had given themselves over to Moloch worship. Laws, doctrine, and edicts are seldom pronounced unless error has occurred. Doctrine and laws serve to correct and mitigate error and "sin."

Moloch appears in the Hebrew of 1 Kings 11:7:
"Then did Solomon build a high place for Chemosh, the abomination of Moab,

in the hill that is before Jerusalem, and Moloch, the abomination of the Sons of Ammon."

Amos 5:26:
"But you shall carry Sikkut your king,
and Kiyyun, your images, the star-symbol of your god
which you made for yourself."

The Septuagint renders "your king" as *Moloch*, which is the actual meaning of the name.

Acts 7.43 continues this rendering:
"You have lifted up the shrine of Moloch (some say Molech)
and the star of your god Repham, the idols you made to worship."

The first clues of Moloch worship appeared after the excavation of mass grave in Carthage in 1921, which produced hundreds of child and animal sacrifices, co-mingled with stones inscribed MLK (Moloch).

Maybe it was in reaction to the continued bloodletting or maybe it was a simple response to the process of civilization, but the horrors of human sacrifice began to die away. Many religions continued with animal sacrifice for many years. The Jews ended animal sacrifice, for the most part, with the destruction of the Temple in 70 AD, although various groups may have continued until the second century AD.

The faith in the principle rule of priests/kings gradually declined. As trade expanded and conquest brought amalgams of nations and societies, the people began to migrate and travel more. Wider exposure brought the realization that the basic concepts of deities were repeated throughout the then-known world. The idea arose that the peoples of the various nations worshipped the same deities, although names and rituals may differ here and there. Religious tolerance was the order of the day as travelers participated in local ceremonies, recognizing the parallelism of the religions of foreign lands.

Societies evolved and grew making it necessary to formulate and codify a more enlightened morality. Realization of individual responsibility and a person's ownership of his or her own destiny deepened. It became illegal in certain moral systems to punish a father for the sins of a son or vice versa.

Once again, religions began to evolve toward monotheism, even though the change in religious thought was inhibited by traditional beliefs.

The time-period around the beginning of the first millennium BCE was a period of economic, social, and cultural evolution. People became capable of producing an agricultural surplus, which, in turn, produced an additional income. The new wealth helped to create a society with a broader perspective. Worship of pagan gods began to dissolve into the tendency to worship a single universal God. Also, as people became more aware of social injustices, new values and new perspectives were formed. People became conscious of themselves and their place in the world of mankind. Their view of their position in the world changed fundamentally.

Almost simultaneously, around the world, prophets and philosophers began to conceive and articulate new doctrines of spiritual growth, the value and sacredness of life, the connection between all living things, the purpose and meaning of life, and the paths to attain freedom from sin or self. The first twinkling light of rational thought and science began to be seen. This was the beginning of the Axial Age.

Although great thinkers all over the world entertained the questions of god, reality, morality, justice, and human suffering, they did not respond identically to the questions. Inner peace was the main concern in the East. The harmony of order and freedom was particularly important in the West. Even within each culture, the spiritual responses were varied, but wisdom rained down on the earth like a welcomed shower in a spiritual desert.

Many great philosophers and religious leaders emerged with their "new ideas." Confucius, Siddhartha Gautama (The Buddha), Lao Tzu, Socrates, Plato, and others emerged with ideas and notions that changed the world. These are just a few of the lights that came into the darkened world during the Axial Age.

Confucius (551 B.C.E – 479 B.C.E.)

Confucius or "Kong Fuzi" was a famous Chinese thinker and philosopher. Born in 551, Confucius looked back to the Western Chou as a "Golden Age" of China. His influence became obvious during the reign of Wu-Ti, when Confucianism was integrated into the government. Consequently, everyone wanted to be in the government.

Lao-Tzu (604-531 B.C.E.)

Lao-Tzu was actually several individuals' history blended into one. The main personage was the librarian for the emperor. Many questions surround Lao-Tzu. Assuming he existed, he, or they, lived in the time-period around 604-531 BC. Lao-Tzu wrote the Tao Te Ching, a philosophical book that drew inspiration from nature. He believed in the simple life: meditation and Tai Chi. His philosophies revolved around The Tao: literally, "the way," described as a balance, a power, and an energy that flows through all living things.

Siddhartha Gautama (The Buddha) (563-483 B.C.E.)
Siddhartha Gautama was born into the noble class, and had a sheltered childhood. One day, he journeyed into the city where the poor lived. He was disturbed to find people who were suffering deeply. He saw the sick, the aging, and the dead, and was disturbed at the inequity between rich and poor, sick and healthy, living and dying. He set out to explore and understand the condition of the world and to end suffering in his life. After meditating for some time, he achieved satori, or sudden enlightenment, while sitting under a pipal tree.

The Buddha then announced the realization of the Four Noble Truths:
• Suffering (Dukha) exists wherever there is life.
• Desire is the cause of suffering.
• To be free from pain, you must relinquish desire.
• This release leads to enlightenment.

Buddhism also instructed people to follow the eightfold path:
    Right view - Right intention - Right speech - Right action -
    Right livelihood - Right effort - Right mindfulness -
    Right concentration.

Mahavira (599-527 B.C.E.)
Mahavira founded Jainism in 550 BC. Jainism's most valued trait was Ahimsa, or unconditional peace. Ahimsa is based on the idea that all living things have a soul. (A snake once bit Mahavira, but he forgave it.) Due to Ahimsa, all Jains were strict vegetarians. Jains believe that Mahavira was the 24th saint, and that people can achieve enlightenment by following the model set by the saints. His beliefs were absorbed into Hinduism and Buddhism.

Zoraster (circa 500 – 600 B.C.E.)
Zoraster was a Persian prophet who founded Zoroastrianism.

Although sources differ greatly on the time of his life, many believe he lived in early 600's and the mid-500's B.C. His religion focused on the battle between good and evil wherein, a Monotheistic belief in god is balanced with an evil enemy. This dualism informed Judaism, Christianity, and Islam.

Socrates (469-399 B.C.E.)
In his use of critical reasoning, by his unwavering commitment to truth, and through the vivid example of his own life, fifth-century Athenian Socrates set the standard for all subsequent Western philosophy.

Plato (429–347 B.C.E.)
Plato is, by any reckoning, one of the most dazzling writers in the Western literary tradition and one of the most penetrating, wide-ranging, and influential authors in the history of philosophy.

These great spiritual leaders did not change the world overnight. Like seeds blown by the wind, the ideas made their way into every corner of the world and sprouted in various forms, bringing forth the sweet flowers of compassion, reverence of life, human dignity, the family of man, and the idea of a loving and merciful god. Still, there are those who insist on killing both animals and humans in the name of their god. They missed the message of the Axial Age. Sadly, there are still religions today with sects and members stuck in the darkness of the time before the awakening.

The Stages and Faces of God

Stories of gods and their adventures could have been a way of expressing the mystical relationship between ancient man and the mysterious world in which he lived. If this is true, and the stories told around fires of the past were not meant to define worship, but to convey an inner feeling, our approach to religion may be incorrect in its very basis. To express awe for the creator and his or her creation did not have to become a religion, but it always did. In crystallizing into a religion, the awe and reverence was reduced to a set of rules, rituals and rites, which, because of rigidity, killed the awe. This was, and is, the pattern of religion. For now, let us look at how religions form.

No religion resonates in the human psyche without well-told mythic stories. One would hope the stories would be true, or accepted as true, in order to affect the psyche of the believer. However, whether true or not, the story must carry with it a sense of the overwhelming and supernatural power of the god and his ability to punish or deliver his people. One man's myth is another man's religion.

In time, stories became religion. The great god in the sky ceased being a story conveying a mystical or emotional message, and became a religion controlled by a distant and uninvolved god. As this happened, the people could not relate to such a god, even though they had constructed the religious structure over time themselves. God became inaccessible and had to be replaced by other gods.

These gods may have been more accessible, but because they were closer to human and had a division of power, talent, or dominion, they were, by necessity, inferior to the original father-god. Because of this, there needed to be more of them. Each time the template for the original God was somehow divided, by sex, geography, or power, another lesser god came into existence.

Religions holding to monotheism fought against the division of god. Judaism and later Islam built their foundations on this one unalterable statement; "God is one."

Indeed, this is why many Muslims and Jews view the idea of the trinity within the Christian faith as blasphemous. Jesus is the Christian expression of the love and accessibility of the one true God toward humanity, but the apparent division of oneness expressed by the trinity is, in itself, an affront to those who hold to the idea that God is One. However, even Jews and Muslims have made this mistake in their past.

From the time of the ancient Jews, man has struggled with the inability to understand and balance the manifold attributes of God. In an attempt to make god more integral with their society, their idea of god tended to change in order to fit better and more understandably within the society at the time. If the society is focused on family and procreation, then god must be also. If the people were focused on war, their god would be a mighty man of war. As a society, we create the image of god according to what we are familiar with and what we need. In the case of modern Christianity, even though Jesus was likely a very dark man with thick, coarse, black hair, most pictures render him as a man with a lighter complexion, with straight, flowing, brown hair. In the west, we have done a wonderful job of creating God in our own image.

Religions do not usually spring into existence and remain stable or stagnant. Religions evolve and morph, changing with the social pressures, absorbing various beliefs, customs, and practices from converts and those around whom the practitioners live. So it was with Judaism.

Scholars have long wondered why the God of the Old Testament had two names, El, usually translated as God, and Yahweh (Jehovah), usually translated as Lord. Moreover, the two deities seem to have different personalities.

The Canaanites, Eli, Il, or El was the supreme god, and the creator of all. El, or 'il-'ib was a general name for a deity, which may have been a god of the ancestors. As such, he was depicted as a grey or white haired, wise old man who guided his people. In the beginning, he was probably a desert god who, according to the older myths, had two wives and built a sanctuary with them and his new children in the desert. The idea of El having two wives shows up again in the Old Testament in a metaphorical story of El marrying Judah and Israel.

The close connection in the religions of the Canaanites and the Hebrews are notable. There are indications that the Hebrew people are a break off of the Canaanites. During the Egyptian rule of Canaan, it re-organized the territory. As a result, many peasants were left homeless and had to live in their caravans. Egyptians began calling them "caravan people." The ancient Egyptian word for caravan people was similar to the word Hebrew. This is one of several theories but seems to be probable. Remember that the titles of Jews or Israelites came from the name of the men Judah and Israel. Genesis 32:28 explains that God changed Jacob's name to Israel, which is why some also called the Hebrews Jacobites.

Three pantheon lists found at Ugarit begin with the names of gods, El, Dagnu, also known as Dagon, and Ba'l'sapan, who was also called Hadad. Hadad was a storm god, whose other name was Ba'al.

Since El is a general name for god there would be names encountered such as Tôru El, or the Bull God. ("Bull El" or "the bull god"). Other names for El are bātnyu binwāti "Creator of creatures," 'abū banī 'ili "father of the gods," and 'abū 'adami "father of man." He is also called 'ēl 'ôlam "God Eternal."

In one of the early myths, El lies with his two wives, who give birth to Shachar ("Dawn") and Shalim ("Dusk"). Again, his wives become pregnant and give birth to "the gracious gods," "cleavers of the sea," "children of the sea." The names of his wives were Athirat, also known as Asherah, and Rahmay ("Merciful"). Asherah was El's chief wife. Later, El would morph into a god of war, as the Jews would need such a deity in their conquests. Still, the compassionate face of the wise father god remained in the minds of the people and would be resurrected later in the New Testament.

In the days when Israel was fighting for land and survival they needed a god of war. We have a record of the Israelite battles both in the Old Testament and in the chiseled stone of the ancient steles.

The Merneptah Stele was discovered in 1896 and is dated to (circa) 1208 BC. The last 3 of the 28 lines of the text deal with a separate campaign in Canaan. It mentions a victory over Israel by the lines: "The Canaan has been plundered into every sort of woe: Ashkelon has been overcome; Gezer has been captured; Yano'am is made non-existent. Israel is laid waste and his seed is not;"

Mesha Stele was discovered in 1868-70 and was created around 840 BC by King Mesha of Moab. Mesha tells how Kemosh (Chemosh), the God of Moab, had been angry with his people and had allowed them to be subjugated to Israel, but at length Kemosh returned and assisted Mesha to throw off the yoke of Israel and restore the lands of Moab.

Tel Dan Stele was discovered in 1993-94 and was created in 870-750 BC. It consists of several fragments making up part of a triumphal inscription in Aramaic, left most probably by Hazael of Aram-

Damascus, an important regional figure in the late 9th-century BCE. Hazael boasts of his victories over the king of Israel and his ally the king of the "House of David".

Beyond the steles there are reliefs and records from other ancient sources.

The Lachish relief shows the siege of Lachish.
The siege of Lachish is the name given to the Assyrian siege and conquest of the town of Lachish in 701 BC. The siege is documented in several sources including the Hebrew Bible, Assyrian documents and in the Lachish relief, a well-preserved series of reliefs which once decorated the Assyrian king Sennacherib's palace at Nineveh. The siege ended with the conquest of the town. The town's inhabitants led into captivity and the leaders of Lachish were tortured to death. The town was abandoned, but resettled after the return from Babylonia.

Sennacherib's campaign in Judah was a military conflict in 701 BC between Kingdom of Judah and the Neo-Assyrian Empire; the conflict is part of the greater conflict of Sennacherib's campaigns. The conflict is considered one of the greatest victories of Judah at that time, from being a vassal state of Assyria, to beating the Assyrian empire and being completely independent.

The Battle of Qarqar took place in 853 BC, and was fought by Shalmaneser III, king of Assyria, and a coalition of 11 kings including Ahab, king of Israel. In the Kurkh Monoliths, it is mentioned that the Israelite forces constituted 10,000 troops and 2,000 chariots.

Assyrian Siege of Jerusalem occurred in 721 BCE, the Assyrian army captured the Israelite capital at Samaria and carried away the citizens of the northern kingdom into captivity. The virtual destruction of Israel left the southern kingdom, Judah, to fend for itself among warring Near Eastern kingdoms. The siege took place in approximately 701 BCE by Sennacherib, king of Assyria. The siege failed and the town did not fall by the hands of Sennacherib.

The Battle of Megiddo is recorded as having taken place in 609 BC with Necho II of Egypt leading his army to Carchemish to fight with his allies the Assyrians against the Babylonians at Carchemish in northern Syria. This required passing through territory controlled by the Kingdom of Judah and Necho requested permission from its king, Josiah. Josiah refused to let the Egyptians pass and a battle took place in which Josiah was killed. The battle is recorded in the Bible, 1 Esdras, and the writings of Josephus.

In the Jewish–Babylonian war Zedekiah was chained and brought before Nebuchadnezzar, from Petrus Comestor's, according to "Bible Historiale," 1670. The Jewish–Babylonian war was a military conflict between the Kingdom of Judah and Babylonia that lasted from 601 to 586 BC. The conflict marked the end of the Kingdom of Judah and Jewish independence until the Hasmonean revolt. After Babylonia invaded Jerusalem it destroyed the First Temple, and started the Babylonian exile.

First siege of Jerusalem occurred in 597 BC and a second siege happened in 587.

In 605 BC Nebuchadnezzar, king of Babylon defeated Pharaoh Neco at the Battle of Carchemish, and subsequently invaded Judah. To avoid the destruction of Jerusalem, King Jehoiakim of Jerusalem, in his third year, changed allegiances from Egypt to Babylon. He paid tribute from the treasury in Jerusalem, some temple artifacts, and some of the royal family and nobility as hostages. In 601 BC, Nebuchadnezzar failed to invade Egypt, the failure led to rebellions among states in the Levant including Judah. Nebuchadnezzar sieged Jerusalem in 597 BC, and managed to get in and capture king Jehoiachin, and all of the Aristocracy of Jerusalem. The siege resulted with the fall of Jerusalem and destruction of the First temple. Then Nebuchadnezzar exiled 10,000 of the officers, and the craftsmen, and 7,000 soldiers.

In July 587 BC, Zedekiah rebelled against Babylonia, making an alliance with Egypt, and Nebuchadnezzar sieged Jerusalem again, starving the people. The siege resulted in the destruction of Jerusalem and the fall of the Kingdom of Judah.

The Jews were a warrior people. They had to be to survive. The surrounding tribes and nations were constantly squabbling over land and resources. It is important to understand that most of the nations and tribes had their own gods or variations of gods. There were few if any religions that had developed a systematic or written record, history, or theology. Religion was like life. It was playing out day by day for most. In their minds, if one tribe conquered another it must be because the god or gods of the conquering tribe was stronger than the god of the defeated people. Defeat was a sign that your god was unhappy with the people, had deserted them, or was weaker. The defeated people often converted to the religion of the victorious. The Jews tended not convert if conquered. They held fast to their god. In time they would be the conquerors and the vanquished may be converted. As the history and doctrine of the Jews became a written record they would convert less and less. They would see in their history they had once been conquered but their religion could survive. Yet, the Jews were in religious transition, deciding between the gods El, Baal, and Yah (Yahweh), and between monotheism and polytheism. Things were not as clear as we may have been led to believe.

According to the book, *"Canaanite Myth and Hebrew Epic; Essays in the History of the Religion of Israel,"* written by Frank Moore, published by Cambridge, Mass., Harvard University Press, 1973, and his book, *"From Epic to Canon: History and Literature in Ancient Israel"*, published by Johns Hopkins University press, c1998, Dr. Moore states in part:

"Religion, as a phenomenon of set rules and doctrine, was unknown and would be incomprehensible to the Canaanites and Israelites. Events transpired because the gods either willed it or did not oppose it. Plans and battles failed when the god opposed the plans or the planners, or if the gods were more inclined to the plan or persons of the enemies. Such beliefs saw the gods as fickle, arbitrary, and quixotic."

"In Syria-Palestine survival depended on the annual rains and rainfall varied widely from year to year. It was clear to Canaanites and Israelites that rainfall and thus crops were provided by the god whose powers included storms, rain, and fertility. This alone may be the answer to why the deity known as Ba'al remained in the Hebrew houses and temples for so long. Ba'al was the god of storms, and thus rain and crops."

"Unlike the people, who valued the rains and crops above all, for a king it was important to have a god of power and war. El was such a god."

"El was a strong ruler and the divine warrior. We see El as the figure of the divine father. The one image of El that seems to run

through all of his myths is that of the patriarch. Unlike the gods who represent the powers of nature (such as storms, rain, or procreation), El is the first social or family god. In the Akkadian, Amorite, and Canaanite religion, El frequently plays the role of "god of the father," who is fair, stern, and wise."
(End citation)

To the ancient Israelites El was the ultimate warrior and war seemed to be a gift from God in the eyes of the Israelites.
Here is a partial "quick list" of battles listed in the Old Testament:

Battles from Abraham to Israel's Conquest
- Abraham's 318 against the Armies of Shinar (Babylon) – Genesis 14
- Pharaoh Pursues the Israelites in Exodus – Exodus 14
- The Israelites Fight Back against the Amalekites – Exodus 17:8–16
- Israel Opposes the Midianites and Moabites – Numbers 31:1–11
- Israel's Rules of War – Deuteronomy 20 (Exo. 23:24, Lev. 18:21–24, 19:24, 20:2–3, Deut 18:9–14)
- Israel Marches on the City of Jericho – Joshua 6
- Israel's Struggle with the City of AI – Joshua 7–8
- Joshua Leads Israel against the Five Amorite Kings – Joshua 10 (Deut 9:5)
- King Jabin of Hazor with a Great Army Opposes Joshua and Israel – Joshua 11
- Israel's Continuing Conquests – Judges 1:1–11
- Ehud Leads Israel against the Moabites – Judges 3:12–30
- Barak Leads Naphtali and Zebulun against Sisera, the Commander of Canaan – Judges 4
- Gideon's 300 Rise Up against the Midianites – Judges 7–8:21
- Israel Wars with Its Own Tribe of Benjamin – Judges 19–20

Battles of the Kingdom
- The Philistines Capture the Ark of Covenant – 1 Samuel 4:1–11
- Samuel Leads Israel to Repent and Repel the Philistines. 1 Samuel 7
- Saul Leads Israel to Save the City of Jabesh Gilead – 1 Samuel 11
- The Battle at Michmash – 1 Samuel 13:16-14:23 (14:47–48)
- Saul Leads Israel against the Amalekites 1 Samuel 15:1–9 (15:19, 33)
- The Battle of the Valley of Elah, David verses Goliath – 1 Samuel 17
- David Saves the City of Keilah and Out Maneuvers King Saul – 1 Samuel 23 (21:1–15; 22:1–5)
- Saul's Pursuit of David in the En Gedi – 1 Samuel 24
- David's Strategic Movements -1 Samuel 26–27
- David Saves the City of Ziklag – 1 Samuel 30
- King Saul's Final Battle – 1 Samuel 31

- War Between David's Judah and Ishbosheth's Israel – 2 Samuel 2–4
- King David's Conquest Establishes Jerusalem – 2 Samuel 5
- David's Mighty Men and Special Training 1 Chr 11:10–25; 12:1–2, 8
- King David's Great Conquests – 2 Samuel 8 (2 Chr 18)
- The Ammonite Rebellion – 2 Samuel 10
- Absalom's Rebellion – 2 Samuel 18 (2 Sam 13–17)
- Sheba's Rebellion – 2 Samuel 20
- King David Avenges the Gibeonites – 2 Samuel 21 (1 Chr 29:26–30)
  Battles of the Divided Kingdoms, Judah and Israel
- Israel's King Ambushes Judah – 2 Chronicles 13
- Ethiopia's Army, Greater than One Million, Attacks Judah – 2 Chronicles 14
- King Jehoshaphat's Army of Judah Worships and Sings in the Face of Battle – 2 Chronicles 20
- King Ahab of Israel's Battles with Syria – 1 Kings 20; 22
- Israel and Judah Joined Together to Defeat the Moabites – 2 Kings 3
- The Syrian Army Come to Conquer Israel including Elisha – 2 Kings 6:8–7:20
- Edom Revolts against King Jehoram of Judah – 2 Chronicles 21
- King Amaziah of Judah Wars against Edom – 2 Chronicles 25:1–16
- King Amaziah Stirs Up Israel to Battle – 2 Chronicles 25:17–24
- King Uzziah of Judah Fights the Philistines – 2 Chronicles 26:1–15
- Judah is Weakened by Battles – 2 Chronicles 28
- The Assyrian Invasion – 2 Kings 18–19 (2 Chr 32:20–21)
- King Josiah Goes Out to War against Pharaoh Necho – 2 Chronicles 35:20–27 (2 Kgs 23:29–30)
- The Babylonian Captivity of Judah – 2 Kings 25

Looking at El, the war God of the Pentateuch and Old Teatament we see a great difference between this god and the loving, merciful God of the Gospels. Notice, I pointed to the God of the Gospels and not the New Testament, since in the beginning of these books Jesus had not been born and had not died, forming the new covenant of the New Testament. This keeps both faces of God in the same Old Testament covenant. Thus, the change cannot be blamed on the sacrifice of Christ. Up until the sacrifice, Christians can still view everything through the eyes and laws of the Old Testament.

Even though we are taught that Judaism was always a monotheistic religion, this was not always the case. The evolution of Judaism into its current form gives us insight into the first steps away from monotheism and the balance between male and female energies and attributes contained within one God. Oddly, or maybe not so strangely, this path was followed by many belief systems, so we will use Judaism as a general example of what stages religions may go through.

For those who may doubt that the ancient Jews were polytheists, I offer the following:

Exodus 20:2-17 NKJV
"I am the Lord your God, who brought you out of the land of Egypt, out of the house of bondage. You shall have no other gods before Me."

The passage is an acknowledgement that there were other gods. In our western society, which is so different from the polytheistic societies of the time, we have learned to equate this passage as a warning against having any item or desire, such as money or success, come before God, but this interpretation is a modern one and does not fit the time or society of the text.

Another example of the implication of the acknowledgement of multiple gods is Exodus 15:

Exodus 15
Amplified Bible (AMP)
1) Then Moses and the Israelites sang this song to the Lord, saying, I will sing to the Lord, for He has triumphed gloriously; the horse and his rider or its chariot has He thrown into the sea.

2) The Lord is my Strength and my Song, and He has become my Salvation; this is my God, and I will praise Him, my father's God, and I will exalt Him.

3) The Lord is a Man of War; the Lord is His name.

4) Pharaoh's chariots and his host has He cast into the sea; his chosen captains also are sunk in the Red Sea.

5) The floods cover them; they sank in the depths [clad in mail] like a stone.

6) Your right hand, O Lord, is glorious in power; Your right hand, O Lord, shatters the enemy.

7) In the greatness of Your majesty, You overthrow those rising against You. You send forth Your fury; it consumes them like stubble.

8) With the blast of Your nostrils the waters piled up, the floods stood fixed in a heap, the deeps congealed in the heart of the sea.

9) The enemy said, I will pursue, I will overtake, I will divide the spoil; my desire shall be satisfied upon them; I will draw my sword, my hand shall destroy them.

10) You [Lord] blew with Your wind, the sea covered them; [clad in mail] they sank as lead in the mighty waters.
11) Who is like You, O Lord, among the gods? Who is like You, glorious in holiness, awesome in splendor, doing wonders?

The question, *"Who is like You, O Lord, among the gods?"* assumes there are other gods and Yahweh is mightier.

Judaism was formed in part by the pressures of the mingling of peoples and customs around Canaan, also called the Ugarit region. The ancient Canaanite city-state of Ugarit is of utmost importance to those who study the Old Testament. Writings found there have greatly aided in our understanding of the meaning of various Biblical passages, as well as in deciphering difficult Hebrew words. Ugarit was at its height around the 12th century BCE. This was the period corresponding with the entry of Israel into Canaan.

The evolution of the people we now call Jews was formed under the pressures of the polytheistic Canaanites culture. In the time of the formation of the religion of El, the city of Ugarit was a major hub of that society.

It was from tablets found in archeological excavations of this area that we find the names of deities such as El, the God in the Jewish and Christian scriptures, and then, Ba'al, the god of storms, who was his sworn enemy. Later, we shall see that Ba'al came to be represented by a bull as well.

According to the Journal of Semitic Studies, the general recognition of the "Great God, El" was recorded as far back as the first half of the second millennium B.C. E. That is around 1800 B.C.E.

During this time-period, gods were local to certain areas. Cities would have a patron deity, and individuals may have a household deity they worshiped also. The Hebrews venerated El beginning in the period before Moses, while; the Canaanites and Phoenicians were mingling and mixing religious traditions. El was a god of war and considered the father of other deities such as Ba'al.

In homogeneous cultures there tended to be fewer gods. The people were on the same page, so to speak.

"There has been much misunderstanding of the nature of Canaanite-Phoenician culture. It must be emphasized this was a relatively homogeneous civilization from the Middle Bronze Age down to the beginning of the Achaemenian period, after which it was swallowed up in large part by much more extensive cultures. Chronologically speaking, it is certain that "Phoenician" is simply the Iron-Age equivalent of Bronze Age "Canaanite".... Phoenician culture did not completely expire until the triumph of Christianity in the fourth century C.E.."

"From the geographical standpoint, there was a homogeneous civilization, which extended in the Bronze Age from Mount Casius, north of Ugarit, to the Negeb of Palestine, and in the Iron Age from north of Arvad (at least) to the extreme south of Palestine. This civilization shared a common material culture (including architecture, pottery, etc.) through the entire period, and we now know that language, literature, art, and religion were substantially the same in the Bronze Age. From the twelfth century on, we find increasing divergence in higher culture, but material culture remained practically the same in all parts of the area. The differences (except in the case of Israelite religion) were no greater than they were in different parts of the Mesopotamian area of culture, which was geographically much more extensive. The situation in Canaan is in a number of ways comparable to that in Egypt, but the civilization of Egypt was more homogeneous as compared to Canaanite culture."

"Since Israel emerged from the same Northwest-Semitic background as the Phoenicians and other Canaanite groups, which continued to exist down into the Iron Age, one would expect to find extremely close relationships in both material and higher culture. It is true that Israelite ties with Egypt were very strong, both historically and geographically, but it is doubtful whether Canaanite and Phoenician bonds with Egypt were any less close. Quite aside from the close ties of reciprocal trade, remember that Palestine, Phoenicia, and Egypt were, as a rule, part of the same political organization, in which Egypt generally played the controlling part. So far as we know, the only exceptions, during the period, which interests us particularly, were during the 18th century B.C., again at the end of the 13th, and from the middle of the 12th to the late tenth. After the early ninth century B.C., Egyptian political influence in Asia decreased greatly, but was compensated by the steady development of reciprocal trade relations." *(W. F. Albright, Some Canaanite-Phoenician Sources of Hebrew Wisdom in "Wisdom in Israel and in the Ancient Near East," edited by M. Noth and D. Winton Thomas, published by Brill, 1969)*

The Sumerians, around 3,000 BC, living around the modern-day

Syria and Iraq were the first civilization to leave carvings and reliefs depicting a prototype angel. To their complex religion and the pantheon of gods, they added messengers of the gods. These messengers of the gods ran errands and delivered communications between gods and humans.

As Samaria declined and Babylon and Assyria rose in power, the idea of "angels" spread into the two rising powers. Carvings of angels around this time bear this out. By 2,500 BC, angles, or messenger gods, had started to appear in the Egyptian culture as well.

Around 1900 B.C.E., Semitic tribes, who also had multiple gods, conquered Samaria. The Semitic tribes added the Samarian messengers or angles to their own pantheon of gods. Then, they made this more complex by ranking the forces of the angels, creating a blend, which found its way into Zoroastrianism, monotheistic Judaism and beyond.

What need does an omnipresent and all-powerful god have for ethereal messengers, servants, and soldiers? If god can be anywhere and do anything at any time, why does he need any other creature to do his bidding? The answer is found in the difficulty of simply doing away with the gods of old. The idea of polytheism within Judaism was kept alive in the concept of angels. Could angels be a polytheistic escape clause for a religion that was becoming monotheistic? Could we be viewing the evolution of a religion over a period of three millennia?

When we look at the history of gods and their servants, we see remnants from a time when man could only conceive of a god similar to himself. The all-powerful and all knowing god had been replaced with gods of war, and gods of weather, and gods of procreation, etc. There were male gods and female gods. Were we attempting to balance the male and female parts of our society through God?

In a society built upon war and survival, the world and our view of God must have taken on a harsh tone. It is easy to assume that a male-driven theology would have only male attributes, and certainly, this monocular approach had its effect, but that is only part of the story. There is also the love prose of Solomon, and the passionate and flowing poetry of King David.

Around 1500 BC, the next major worship to appear was that of Mithras, Mithras was a light-bringer god, whose cult flourished between 1500 BC and the time of Christ. The religion based itself in what was then known as the Persian angels and the god, Mithras. Mithras was often depicted as more of an Angel in the broad horizontal bands of sculpted and painted decorations on the walls and ceilings of buildings, called friezes, which were created around this time.

The Phoenician era saw a shift in Canaanite religion. The larger pantheon was pushed to the side in favor of previously, less important, singular deities who became or, in the case of Baalat, already was, the patron city-gods, affirmed by ruling priest-kings. Baal or Ba'al is the root of Baatat.

Early scholars and demonologists, unaware of Hadad, or that "Ba`al" in the Bible referred to any number of local spirits, came to regard the term as referring to only one personage. Until archaeological digs at Ras Shamra and Ebla uncovered texts explaining the Syrian pantheon, the Ba'al Zebûb (or Beelzebub) was frequently confused with various Semitic gods. Ba'al and Beelzebub, in some Christian writings, might refer to Satan, himself. The Biblical and historical evidence shows that the Moabites worshiped Ba'al. Pre-Islamic and Muslim sources reveal that the Meccans took over the idol, Hubal, from the Moabites.

It is likely that Ba'al was the idol of the golden calf that the Israelites worshiped while Moses was upon the Mountain receiving the Ten Commandments. The vision of the people and the idol drove Moses to break the original tablets. What is more difficult to follow is that the symbol of El was, at one time, the bull or calf, and could have been associated with an old and idolatrous way of worshipping El or Ba'al.

Several deities bore the title "Baal" (Lord) and more than one goddess bore the title "Baalat" (Lady). Biblical references to Baals associated with various places include Baal Hazor, Baal Hermon, Baal Heon, Baal Peor, Baal Perazim, Baal Shalisha, Baal Tamar, Baal Zephon and others. However, as early as the period of the Book of Judges, we find references to a more generalized sense of the term — Baal Berith — Lord of the Covenant. Thus, the conception of Baal was clearly in universal as well as place-specific terms. (Similarly, the Israelites conceived their God as the God of the whole earth, the God of Issac, the God of Jacob, the God of the Hebrews, and the God of one specific mountain: Sinai.)

The deity opposed by the biblical prophets as "Baal" was usually a version of Baal-Hadad, the major deity of the Hittites, Syrians, and Assyrians. Baal-worship extended from the Canaanites to the Phoenicians. Both Baal and his consort Astarte were Phoenician fertility symbols. The "Baal" worshiped by Queen Jezebel is referred to as

Baal-Melqart. Both Hadad and Melqart are found in lists of Phoenician deities, but it is difficult to know whether Jezebel's form of Baal-worship differed much from the worship of Baal-Hadad. The King of Aram was named after this deity.

1 King 20
ASB
1 Now Ben-hadad king of Aram gathered all his army, and there were thirty-two kings with him, and horses and chariots. And he went up and besieged Samaria and fought against it. 2 Then he sent messengers to the city to Ahab king of Israel and said to him, "Thus says Ben-hadad, 3 'Your silver and your gold are mine; your most beautiful wives and children are also mine.'" 4 The king of Israel replied, "It is according to your word, my lord, O king; I am yours, and all that I have." 5 Then the messengers returned and said, "Thus says Ben-hadad, 'Surely, I sent to you saying, "You shall give me your silver and your gold and your wives and your children," 6 but about this time tomorrow I will send my servants to you, and they will search your house and the houses of your servants; and whatever is desirable in your eyes, they will take in their hand and carry away.'"

Baal Hammon, generally identified by modern scholars either with the northwest Semitic god El or Dagon, was the supreme god of the Carthaginians.

One of the most important points to understand is in the early periods, the minds of the people "cross-connected" the gods El, Yahweh, and Baal. In one mythology, El is the father of gods and sits in court judging and directing other gods, one of whom is his son, Baal. These early cross-connections and mutual identifications become confusing. To simplify the contorted flow of this period in our religious history, remember that Baal, El, and Yahweh were all gods and all were worshipped together at one time or another. We see that in time, El and Yahweh became identified as the same god, due in part to one mythology that has the father, El, and the son, Baal, at odds and in conflict.

Part of the confusion comes from the fact that the names and biblical renderings of the names overlap. For example, the name "Baal" means lord. However, in the English bible the name Yahweh is usually rendered as "Lord". The name El is translated as God, but the people of the time considered all of these deities to be a god. These various issues have led to a tangled and confusing history.

Since the name "Baal" means lord, the name has been attached to many deities. One famous name is Baal Zebub (Beelzebub). Scholars continue to be unsure of the meaning of the name. Many believe that zebub may substitute for an original "zbl" which seems to mean "prince," and is a title frequently attributed to Baal in mythological texts. However, some believe the word means "flies" and is connected to an Ugaritic text in which Baal affects the expulsion of the flies, which were thought to be the cause of a person's sickness.

Other versions of the deity Baal are Beelzebub and Beelzeboul. The names are clumsy transliterations and the name is more accurately "Baal Zebûb." He was a deity worshiped in the Philistine city of Ekron (2 Kings 1:2). Scholars have also suggested that the term was originally Baal Zebu, which means "Lord Prince." However, the Jews seized on the fact that zebûb was a Hebrew noun meaning 'fly', so they berated the deity by calling him Baal Zebub or "Lord of Flies," pointing to the fact that flies were always found on dung.

Baals were often worshiped in "high places where a priest or prophet of the local "baal" would offer animal, vegetable, or wine offerings. The Book of Kings describes the prophets of Baal engaged in shaman-like ecstatic dances. The prophets of Baal are also described as engaging in self-mutilation. In mythology, Baal died. During the mourning of Anat, between Baal's death and resurrection, she cut herself:

She cuts cheek and chin.
She lacerates Her forearms.
She plows like a garden Her chest,
Like a vale, She lacerates Her back.
"Baal is dead!"

Temples of Baal existed in or near larger towns. Worship involved ritual sex between a king or priest and a female priestly counterpart, symbolizing the union of heaven and earth, which brings on the blessing of rain and crops. Later this ritual would spread into the use of Temple Prostitutes, who would be used by the followers in exchange for donations and ritual practice. It was this practice that so provoked prophetic objections to Baal-worship.

The first religion involving ritual sacred prostitution associated with the goddess Ishtar began in Babylon. Possibly, the Canaanite worship of Astarte, the consort of Baal was linked to the worship of

Istar / Ishtar.

Israelites allegedly participated in such rituals also. This is illustrated by the story of Judah when he fathered twin boys through his daughter-in-law Tamar, who had disguised herself as a sacred prostitute in the town of Timnah (Gen. 38:15-38). The practice was widespread, and is hard to say at what point the Israelite tribes began to think of the practice as something condemned by God.

Child sacrifice is another issue. The prophet Jeremiah indicates that infant sacrifice was offered to Baal as well as to other gods (Jer. 19:5). However, it seems to be more prevalent with other deities such as Moloch.

Up to this point, the gods of El and Baal were closely connected. El was a god of war and Baal was a thundering storm god. Both were powerful and were related in some of the early stories. They were part of the same mythos, pantheon, and family of gods.

The people of the region worshiped a god called, "El." The wife of El was Ashtoreth, whose title was, "The Queen of Heaven." Ugaritic polytheism consists of a divine council or assembly. The divine family, made up of the chief god, his wife, and their offspring, populates this assembly. The chief god, El, and his wife, Ashtoreth, are said to have produced seventy divine children, some of whose names may be familiar, as they include Baal, Astarte, Anat, Resheph, the sun-goddess Shapshu, and the moon-god Yerak. Some sources also list the name, Yah, or Yahweh. These children came to be called, "the stars of El." Below the divine counsel are the helpers of the divine household. Kothar wa-Hasis was the head of these helpers. Some scholars believe that the servants or helpers of the divine household came to be known as the entities the Bible calls "angels." The word for angel means messenger, and these helpers were in fact, messenger-gods. Ashtoreth would become Asherah in the Israelite's worship.

In the book of Jeremiah, we see one of these gods called out by name. Asherah, The Queen of Heaven, is the title given to the wife of God. Exavations have uncovered a vast number of small staues and other objects venerating her. The number and significance of the objects of veneration to her confirms the suggestion that the people held this goddess in high regard. So many pillar figurines have been excavated in Judah that they are now regarded as "a characteristic expression of piety" for those who worship El and his consort.

Dr. Joseph Lumpkin

In the earliest stages of this religion, Yahweh appears to be simply one of these seventy children, each of whom was the patron deity of the seventy nations. We see this idea of city-state having patron gods brought into the ancient Greek religions as well. The idea also appears in the Dead Sea Scrolls reading and the Septuagint translation of Deuteronomy 32:8.

Deuteronomy 32:8-9
Douay-Rheims 1899 American Edition (DRA)
8) When the Most High divided the nations: when he separated the sons of Adam, he appointed the bounds of people according to the number of the children of Israel
9) And his people Jacob became the portion of the Lord, Israel was the line of his inheritance.

Some sources, including the Masoretic Text; Dead Sea Scrolls (see also Septuagint) renders "children of Israel" as "sons of God."

As the patriarch, El, had divided the land, each member of the divine family received a nation of his own: Israel is the portion of Yahweh. The statement, "according to the number of the children of Israel" is thought to include the seventy children.

Psalm 82 also presents the god, El, presiding over a divine assembly at which Yahweh stands up and makes his accusation against the other gods.

Psalm 82
Amplified Bible (AMP)
A Psalm of Asaph.
1) GOD stands in the assembly [of the representatives] of God; in the midst of the magistrates or judges He gives judgment [as] among the gods.
2) How long will you [magistrates or judges] judge unjustly and show partiality to the wicked? Selah [pause, and calmly think of that]!
3) Do justice to the weak (poor) and fatherless; maintain the rights of the afflicted and needy.
4) Deliver the poor and needy; rescue them out of the hand of the wicked.
5) [The magistrates and judges] know not, neither will they understand; they walk on in the darkness [of complacent satisfaction]; all the foundations of

the earth [the fundamental principles upon which rests the administration of justice] are shaking.

6) I said, You are gods [since you judge on My behalf, as My representatives]; indeed, all of you are children of the Most High.

7) But you shall die as men and fall as one of the princes.

8) Arise, O God, judge the earth! For to You belong all the nations.

Why did Baal split away to become the archenemy of El? The answer may be as simple as assimilation versus annihilation. As it is with kingdoms, so it is with religions. If there is a close enough fit and the opponent is weaker, there can be assimilation, but if the opponent is stronger or there is strong opposition between the factions, there can be little assimilation. Destruction is the only recourse. El was the head or father of the gods. In the mythos of the people, El divided the lands into sections and gave each of his sons a separate region to rule. This made Yahweh the patron god of Israel. There would be an obvious fit and a way to integrate the belief in the father god and the son, who protects Israel. However, the tension between Baal and El was different in the eyes of those serving Yahweh. Baal was not their patron deity. Baal and El were often at odds in the stories and lore of that mythology. Baal could not be assimilated easily. There was no way to bring in an opposing force when Yahweh, a parallel force, was already becoming associated with El. The natural response was to oppose the spread of Baalish beliefs and combine the gods of Yahweh and El, thus identifying them as one, that one being the high God, God the father, the Lord, God all mighty. However, the worship of Baal had ritual sex and both male and female sacred prostitutes. The people did not wish to leave their god or their sex.

Modern scholars suggest that the Lord of the Hebrews, Yahweh, the Canaanite deity, Baal, were possibly not so distinct.

Psalm 82:1 states: "*God presides in the great assembly; he gives judgment among the gods.*"

Many commentators believe this verse harkens back to a time when the Hebrew religion was not yet monotheistic. Some suggest that Yahweh and Baal were originally considered sons of El. Since they were "brothers" and both "Sons of El", the worship of Yahweh and Baal could have been nearly indistinguishable.

The later prophets and temple priests condemned worshiping

Yahweh in the "high places," declaring that only Jerusalem's altar was authorized. Yet earlier prophets, and even Elijah himself, offered sacrifices at these very high places. Similarly, the establishment of sacred pillars was condemned as related to the worship of Baal and Ashera. Both Baal and Ashera (or Asherah) were considered fertility gods, and the sacred pillars were phallic symbols of stone.

The goddess, Ashera, came to be identified as the wife of god. The Jews lost or did not establish the idea of the all-powerful and complete god having a male and female side or force. To account for the feminine force with humankind, they substituted a pagan goddess. To understand the muting of the original feminine force within Judaism and later within Christianity, one must delve back into a history that, until recently, was hidden, if not occluded. We will cover the wife of god later.

The worship of El was firmly established within the Old Testament. The patriarch Jacob erected a stone pillar in honor of El at Bethel (Gen. 28:18-19); Moses set up twelve pillars at Mount Sinai where he offered sacrifices. (Exodus 24) and Joshua established a sacred pillar at Shechem (Josh. 24:26). Even the name, Beth-El, tells the story that this was the house of El. With El as the main and more powerful god, and the prohibition of the worship of Yahweh and Baal in the high places, the worship of Baal and Yahweh resemble each other closely in the early days of Israel's history. However, we shall see that El and Yahweh began to merge into a single deity, and the worship of Baal would be more distinct later. This is clearly reflected through the teachings of both prophet and priest.

Whether Yahweh was the son of El in the beginning of the mythos or not, at some time in the 8th century BCE, the names and deities begin to merge and be identified as one. Where El was a patriarchal and punitive God, Yahweh tended to interact with mankind. We see this merging in the story of Abraham, as he rejects his father's god and is called into communion with the "one true God." In Genesis 14, Abraham interacts with Melchizedek, a priest of El Elyon, and Abraham verbally equates Yahweh with El Elyon. Remember, as a rule, in our Bible "El" is translated as "God" (Elyon means the highest or the most high), and "Yahweh" is translated as "Lord."

Genesis 14
Amplified Bible (AMP)

17) After his [Abram's] return from the defeat and slaying of Chedorlaomer and the kings who were with him, the king of Sodom went out to meet him at the Valley of Shaveh, that is, the King's Valley.

18) Melchizedek, king of Salem [later called Jerusalem] brought out bread and wine [for their nourishment]; he was the priest of **God Most High**,

19) And he blessed him and said, Blessed (favored with blessings, made blissful, joyful) be Abram by **God Most High**, *Possessor and Maker of heaven and earth,*

20) And blessed, praised, and glorified be God Most High, Who has given your foes into your hand! And [Abram] gave him a tenth of all [he had taken].

21) And the king of Sodom said to Abram, "Give me the persons and keep the goods for yourself."

22) But Abram said to the king of Sodom, "I have lifted up my hand and sworn to **the Lord, God Most High**, *the Possessor, and Maker of heaven and earth,*

23) That I would not take a thread or a shoelace or anything that is yours, lest you should say, I have made Abram rich."

Because the two identities were merging into one, the deity now known as Yahweh-El (Lord God) was the husband of the goddess, Asherah, also known as the "Queen of Heaven."

According to the Old Testament book of Genesis in the Hebrew text, there was a balance of male and female forces within God from the beginning. Neither male nor female, both male and female, God showed the male energy of forming and shaping, as well as the female energy of nurturing and brooding. Although one may have a difficult time in distinguishing God the Spirit from the Spirit of God, the word for "spirit" is "ruach" and is a female word.

Genesis 1
Amplified Bible

1) In the beginning God (prepared, formed, fashioned, and) created the heavens and the earth.

2) The earth was without form and an empty waste, and darkness was upon the face of the very great deep. The Spirit of God was moving (hovering, brooding) over the face of the waters.

The Holy Spirit is the designated representation of the feminine principle. This idea is supported by the Hebrew word for "spirit."

Jerome, the author of the Latin Vulgate, knew this when he rendered the passage into Latin. He is quoted as saying:
"In the Gospel of the Hebrews that the Nazarenes read it says, 'Just now my mother, the Holy Spirit, took me.' Now, this should offend no one, because "spirit" in Hebrew is feminine, while in our language [Latin], it is masculine, and in Greek, it is neuter. In divinity, however, there is no gender."

In Jerome's Commentary on Isaiah 11, the explanation contains a pointed observation. There was a tradition among a sect of Early Christians, which believed that the Holy Spirit was our Lord's spiritual mother. Jerome comments that the Hebrew word for "spirit" (ruach or ruak) is feminine, meaning, that for the 1st Century Christians in the Aramaic world, the Holy Spirit was a feminine figure. This was likely because in the beginning, the converts to this new cult of Judaism, called Christianity, were mostly Jews. The gender was lost in the translation from the Hebrew into the Greek, rendering it neuter, and then it was changed to a masculine gender when it was translated from the Greek into the Latin.

The Bible, in the book of Genesis, describes a male/female God with the male creating and the female brooding. Except, man could not hold onto that unfamiliar concept, and the primitive Jews chose to take up the Canaanite deities of the God, El, and his wife, Asherah. But, she was simply a fertility goddess. Although scholars argue that she was not a god because she had no headdress, the fact that she was the wife of God makes her a goddess.

Although the balance of male and female energies was presented in Genesis from the outset, primitive man was not ready to accept or understand the spiritual truth of balance. Instead, they made themselves a goddess to balance out the nature of their god, and embraced her fully and completely.

The most dramatic indication of this is the many figurines from the biblical period (the Iron Age) that have been discovered in Israel. These are figurines of females; male figurines are practically nonexistent. They are not "Canaanite" figurines: images of upright female figures with divine symbols that were very common in the late Bronze Age (Canaanite occupation), but disappeared in Israelite times. Even the earliest Israelite figurines, which date from the time of the Judges (the Early Iron Age), are markedly different from those of Canaan. These Israelite figurines are plaques that represent women lying on beds. The style shows considerable continuity with Late

Bronze Age styles. However, the Israelite difference is obvious. The females in the Israelite figurines have no divine headdress or any other symbols of divinity. Even in this early period, the time of the settlement of Canaan, Israel was modifying earlier traditions to eliminate rival deities.

The plaque figurines disappeared from Judah by the time of the monarchy. A new type of figurine became quite prominent in the eighth century; a solid figure in the round, with a "pillar" base, breasts, and molded head, sometimes with no arms, sometimes with arms holding breasts, and sometimes with arms raised. These figurines are found in areas, which appear cultic in some respect; neither have a sacrificial or incense altar; and both show evidence that food preparation, eating, and drinking took place there. This activity was clearly not part of the official sacrificial cult, but may have been a tolerated, nonconformist worship. These pillar figurines are also found in domestic settings, interestingly, from the last years of settlement.

These pillars hold no divine insignia, wear no crowns, and carry no symbols of their power. The pillars arise; moreover, long after the Canaanite plaques have disappeared. They are not Canaanite goddess figurines. There is also no reason to suspect that these figurines represent the development of an Israelite goddess. They may not be personalized goddesses at all. Instead, they are a visual metaphor, which show in seeable and touchable form that which is most desired. In other words, they are a kind of tangible prayer for fertility and nourishment.

Could it be possible that the figurine is a kind of tree with breasts? Such a tree of nourishment is known from an Egyptian painting. Here the tree is identified with Isis; elsewhere such a tree is an attribute of Hathor. There is an inscribed cult stand discovered in Ta'anach, dated from the late tenth century B.C.E. that has a naked goddess flanked by two lions and, on another register, a tree flanked by two lions.

It is significant that there are no trappings of divinity on these figurines. Moreover, the same people who had these figurines in their houses did not name their children with a name that called for Asherah's blessings or protections. Just as the asherah associated with the stele and altars at the local shrines was not seen by the people to be in conflict with the worship of YHWH, so too it would seem that these figurines were not idolatrous in their eyes. There is no evidence at all to suppose that the people imagined the figurines to represent God's consort. They have no pubic triangle, nothing to suggest attachment, and they appear alone, not as part of a male-female couple. The figurines and the altar asherah to which they may be analogous, may represent a divine power, not fully articulated, or personified, and not "worshiped" as some sort of a goddess that could rival YHWH.

The dating of these figurines is significant, for they come into being in the eighth century, precisely the period in which the official royal cult has removed the asherah from Samaria. The asherah with its tree associations had brought the divine and natural worlds closer together. These tree-based breast-figurines may do the same. The breasts, and possibly the tree trunk, address a desire for and anxiety about fertility. Through these figurines, the people could be reminded that the divine blessings of fertility are in their midst, that the divine is indeed a beneficent bestower of abundance. A religion that states that fertility depends entirely upon people's behavior creates enormous strain: it places a great responsibility on the people to behave well and, at the same time, requires them to understand the difficult abstract idea that fertility is indeed automatically attendant upon such good behavior. The asherah-tree at the altars and the tree-based figurines at cult sites and in houses are a way of ensuring and demonstrating the fact that there really is a power of fertility that can be seen and touched, which guarantees the rewards of right relationship with God. In Israel, where YHWH is the one who grants "the blessings of breast and womb," the force for fertility, represented by the figurines, may not have been seen as a separate deity. Quite possibly, it was not consciously personalized at all. In this way, the people were able to add a reminder of divinity to their homes, and a visualization of abundance (the lactating tree) while they continued to maintain devotion to the one invisible transcendent God.

Frymer-Kensky, Tikva, In the Wake of the Goddesses: Women, Culture, and the Biblical Transformation of Pagan Myth, The Free Press, MacMillan 1992

In the Hebrew Bible, there is a very strong association of Asherah with trees. For example, she is found under trees (1K14:23; 2K 17:10)), is made of wood by human beings (1K 14:15, 2K16:3-4) and is erected by human beings (2K17:1). The Asherah often occurs in conjunction with shrines on high places, which may also be to other gods such as Baal, and is frequently mentioned in association with the host of heaven.   Richard Pettey (1990:153-4) has catalogued each reference and produced tables showing all combinations of Asherah with images, pillars, high places and altars. Using these, he argued that Asherah, always associated with the worship of a deity whether YHWH or Baal, is a cultic object used along with the altars, high places, and pillars in the service of such deities, which included Yahweh [this is also the position of widely quoted biblical exegete, Saul Olyan. 1988]. It is rather surprising, considering the numerous references to trees in connection with Asherah, that Pettey does not include them in his formula. To the question, was Asherah a goddess of the Israelites? He answers both no and yes. "Certainly no," he says, "the biblical authors were unanimous in their abhorrence of Asherah worship, but, yes, she was, without doubt, popularly accepted as the goddess of Israel. One thing is certain: the Asherah with attendant asherim has many forms, but is never far from trees or the wood of trees...." *(Pettey 1990: 210)*

The Mishnah's definition of an Asherah is: "any tree worshipped by a heathen, or any tree, which is worshipped..." The great rabbi Akibah said, "wherever thou findest a high mountain or a lofty hill and a green tree know that an idol is there." (Danby: 1933:441). "Trees described by the rabbis as being an asherah, or part of an asherah, include grapevines, pomegranates, walnuts, myrtles and willows." (Danby: 1933: 90,176).   From this, we see that these early lawmakers denied Asherah as part of the Hebrew religion, but recognized her as a divinity worshipped by the "heathen," and treated her as a living tree or living part of a tree. (Mishnah – collection of Jewish oral traditions.)

John Day's third category has Asherah as both a sacred object and a goddess. This reading he believes is now most accepted and most consistent with the evidence (1983: 398). Ruth Hestrin, of the Israel Museum in Jerusalem, goes further, and built this into an extremely satisfactory solution to the conundrum. (Hestrin 1991:50-59) She maintains that the goddess Asherah is represented in the Bible by three of her manifestations - as an image representing the goddess herself, as a green tree, and as the asherim, tree trunks. She points out that this interpretation fits well with that of the rabbi's statement in the Mishnah. (Interestingly, the question, "Is She One or Many?" is one of the most pressing questions now being addressed by the present-day goddess movement (see Long: Feminist Theology, May 1997), and although it cannot be pursued here, it seems as if a study of biblical Asherah may provide some clues to answers.)

We see traces in the Bible of Asherah worship when King Solomon brought the practice to Jerusalem. Solomon "loved YHVH," but "also burned incense in high places." This refers to the practice of burning incense to Asherah whose statues were always placed in high areas, on hilltops, etc. Solomon married the daughter of Pharaoh, a Sidonian Princess, and a Hittite Princess, and daughters of the ruling elite of Moab, Ammonites, and Edomites. Many of these women came from the old pagan religions that worshipped Asharah, also known by some as Ishtar. To appease his wives, Solomon allowed the idols to be placed in the Holy of Holies next to the Ark of the Covenant.

The worship of Asharah ended in the Kingdom of Israel, at least, when the Assyrians sacked it in 721 BCE. There was a remnant of the Israelites who still remained behind in Samaria and tried to continue the Asherah worship along with the worship of YHVH.

Excepts from an article by Christopher B. Siren – May 25th, 1998 based on John C. Gibson's Canaanite Mythology and S. H. Hooke's Middle Eastern Mythology

Little is known of the history of the God, El, and his family. Most information came from an excavation of the city of Ugarit in 1928 and the digs there in the late 1930's. The Canaanite myth stories recovered from the city of Ugarit, in what is now Ras Sharma, Syria dates back to at least 1400 B.C.E., in its written form, while the deity lists and statues from other cities, particularly Gubla date back as far as the third millennium B.C.E. Gubla, during that time, maintained a thriving trade with Egypt and was described as the capital during the third millennium B.C.E. Despite this title, like Siduna (Sidon), and Zaaru (Tyre), the Egyptians colonized the city and lorded over the whole region. Between 2300 and 1900 B.C.E., many of the coastal Canaanite cities were abandoned, sacked by the Amorites, with the inland cities of Allepo and Mari lost to them completely. The second millennium B.C.E. saw a resurgence of Canaanite activity and trade, particularly noticeable in Gubla and Ugarit. By the 14th century B.C.E., their trade extended from Egypt, to Mesopotamia, and Crete. All of this was under the patronage and dominance of the 18th dynasty of Egypt. Zaaru managed to maintain an independent kingdom, but the rest of the Caananite cities soon fell into unrest, while Egypt lost power and interest. In 1230 B.C.E., the Israelites began their invasion and, during this time, the Achaean "Sea Peoples" raided much of the Eastern

Mediterranean, working their way from Anatolia to Egypt. This led to the abandonment of Ugarit in 1200 B.C.E., and in 1180 B.C.E., a group of them established the country of Philistia, i.e. Palestine, along Canaan's southern coast.

The practice of the day was that whenever a people were conquered, they would take up the religion of the victors, believing the gods of those who conquered them must be more powerful than their god. This was not the case when Israel was sacked. Instead, the Israelites held fast to their belief that they alone were the chosen people of God. The question then became, "Why is our God angry with us that he would allow us to be destroyed?" For the answer, they turned back to the Ten Commandments and the Law. This was the turning point when the Jewish people became monotheistic. A ground swell arose against the worship of the consort of God, and she was banished from the nation, leaving a void of the Sacred Feminine in the psyche of the people. After all, the total of all female attributes and energy was tied up in the fertility and mother goddess, the queen of heaven, who was no longer welcome.

Jeremiah 7
Amplified Bible (AMP)
    15) And I will cast you out of My sight, as I have cast out all your brethren, even the whole posterity of Ephraim.
    16) Therefore do not pray for this people [of Judah] or lift up a cry or entreaty for them or make intercession to Me, for I will not listen to or hear you.
    17) Do you not see what they are doing in the cities of Judah and in the streets of Jerusalem?
    18) The children gather wood, the fathers kindle the fire, and the women knead the dough, to make cakes for the queen of heaven; and they pour out drink offerings to other gods, that they may provoke Me to anger!

Jeremiah 44
Amplified Bible (AMP)
    15) Then all the men who knew that their wives were burning incense to other gods, and all the women who stood by a great assembly, even all the people who dwelt in Pathros in the land of Egypt, answered Jeremiah:
    16) "As for the word that you have spoken to us in the name of the Lord, we will not listen to or obey you.
    17) But we will certainly perform every word of the vows we have made: to burn incense to the queen of heaven and to pour out drink offerings to her as we

71

have done, we and our fathers, our kings and our princes - in the cities of Judah and in the streets of Jerusalem; for then we had plenty of food and were well off and prosperous and saw no evil.

18) But since we stopped burning incense to the queen of heaven and pouring out drink offerings to her, we have lacked everything and have been consumed by the sword and by famine."

19) [And the wives said] "When we burned incense to the queen of heaven and poured out drink offerings to her, did we make cakes [in the shape of a star] to represent and honor her and pour out drink offerings to her without [the knowledge and approval of] our husbands?"

20) Then Jeremiah said to all the people to the men and to the women and to all the people who had given him that answer.

21) "The incense that you burned in the cities of Judah and in the streets of Jerusalem, you and your fathers, your kings and your princes, and the people of the land, did not the Lord [earnestly] remember [your idolatrous wickedness] and did it not come into His mind?

22) The Lord could no longer endure the evil of your doings and the abominations, which you have committed; because of them therefore has your land become a desolation and an [astonishing] waste and a curse, without inhabitants, as it is this day.

23) Because you have burned incense [to idols] and because you have sinned against the Lord and have not obeyed the voice of the Lord or walked in His law and in His statutes and in His testimonies, therefore this evil has fallen upon you, as it is this day."

It is difficult to know why the void of the feminine was not filled with the principles the people once understood, just as it is difficult to know why the people could not fully conceive of such an abstract form of God as a spirit containing both male and female energies. Perhaps Genesis, being written around the 5th or 6th centuries B.C.E., articulated an understanding of what the Hebrews worked out after hundreds of years of polytheism. Many parts of the Old Testament were written after the decision to adopt monotheism, but before the transition was completed.

With biblical condemnations of her cult and the eradication of symbols and inscriptions in the Jerusalem temple, eventually the wife of god disappeared from view. The idea of a divine family, with a god and his wife, was established again in the teachings of the Church of Jesus Christ of Latter Day Saints.

As the religion of Yahweh developed, God El was cast in the role of the Divine King ruling over all the other deities. This religious outlook appears, for example, in Psalm 29:2, where the "sons of God," or divine sons or children, are called upon to worship Yahweh, the Divine King.

Psalm 29
Amplified Bible (AMP)
A Psalm of David.

1) ASCRIBE to the Lord, O sons of the mighty, ascribe to the Lord glory and strength.

2) Give to the Lord the glory due to His name; worship the Lord in the beauty of holiness or in holy array.

3) The voice of the Lord is upon the waters; the God of glory thunders; the Lord is upon many (great) waters.

4) The voice of the Lord is powerful; the voice of the Lord is full of majesty.

5) The voice of the Lord breaks the cedars; yes, the Lord breaks in pieces the cedars of Lebanon.

6) He makes them also to skip like a calf; Lebanon and Sirion (Mount Hermon) like a young, wild ox.

7) The voice of the Lord splits and flashes forth forked lightning.

8) The voice of the Lord makes the wilderness tremble; the Lord shakes the Wilderness of Kadesh.

9) The voice of the Lord makes the hinds bring forth their young, and His voice strips bare the forests, while in His temple everyone is saying, Glory!

10) The Lord sat as King over the deluge; the Lord [still] sits as King [and] forever!

11) The Lord will give [unyielding and impenetrable] strength to His people; the Lord will bless His people with peace.

The temple revealed various expressions of polytheism, such as images of lesser gods in the forms of cherubim and seraphim and thus demonstrated that this place was Yahweh's palace, and was populated by those under his power. The other gods became mere expressions of Yahweh's power, and the divine messengers were understood as little more than minor divine beings expressive of Yahweh's divine nature. The idea of angels and demons began to emerge as lesser beings that were controlled by the One True God. This head god became the godhead of today.

Since Baal simply means 'Lord', Yahweh could be called "Lord". Also, there is no reason why the term could not be applied to Yahweh as well as other gods. The Israelites did not always consider Baal and

Yahweh worship incompatible.

Several prominent Israelites bore "ba'al" names. The judge, Gideon, was also called Jeruba'al, meaning, "Ba'al strives." A descendant of Jacob's firstborn son was named Ba'al (I Chron. 5:5). An uncle of King Saul was also named Ba'al (I Chron. 9:35-39). One of Saul's sons was Eshba'al, Saul's grandson was Meriba'al, and Be'eliada was a son of David. 1 Chronicles 12:5 mentions the name Bealiah, meaning either Ba'al-Yahweh, or "Yahweh is Ba'al", that is to say, "Yahweh is Lord."

After Gideon's death, according to Judges 8:33, the Israelites started to worship a Ba'al Berith ("Lord of the Covenant"). Was this the god the Jews came to call "Lord", which is Yahweh? Shechem supported Abimelech's attempt to become king by giving him 70 shekels from the temple of Ba'al Berith (Judges 9:4). This "Lord of the Covenant" appears similar to the one described in Joshua 24:25 as involving a covenant with Yahweh.

Judges 9:46 goes on to say that these supporters of Abimelech entered "the House of El Berith," which was apparently the same temple earlier referred to as belonging to Ba'al. Thus, all three names of Ba'al mean, "lord." El, usually rendered as "God" in our Bible, and Yahweh, normally rendered as "Lord" (with a capital "L"), all refer to a Covenant Deity at Shechem. If the terms and names merged or somehow were interchangeable in this period, the three names could refer to one deity.

The fact that altars devoted to Yahweh, even in the Temple of Jerusalem itself, were characterized by horned altars that also indicates a carryover from more primitive days with El and Baal (both of whom were sometimes portrayed as bulls), and were not worshipped on common hilltop altars with Yahweh.

It is also possible that some hymns, which originally described Baal, may later have been ascribed to the worship of Yahweh. Psalm 29 is thought to be an adaptation of a Canaanite hymn originally devoted to Baal.

The voice of the Lord is over the waters;
The God of glory thunders,
The Lord thunders over the mighty waters...
The voice of the Lord strikes with flashes of lightning.
The voice of the Lord shakes the desert;
The Lord shakes the Desert of Kadesh.
The voice of the Lord twists the oaks and strips the forests bare.

And in his temple all cry, "Glory!"

Psalm 18 also describes the Hebrew God in terms that could easily apply to storm god Baal, the "Rider of Clouds."

The earth trembled and quaked
and the foundations of the mountains shook;
They trembled because he was angry.
Smoke rose from his nostrils;
consuming fire came from his mouth
burning coals blazed out of it.
He parted the heavens and came down;
dark clouds were under his feet.
He mounted the cherubim and flew;
he soared on the wings of the wind.
He made darkness his covering
his canopy around him — the dark rain clouds of the sky.
Out of the brightness of his presence clouds advanced
with hailstones and bolts of lightning.
YHWH thundered from heaven
the voice of the Most High resounded.

It is quite plausible that in the minds of many Israelites, the Lord Baal and the Lord Yahweh were two names for the same deity, an awesome God who thundered from on high and yet lovingly blessed them with rain to bring fertility and prosperity.

The prophet Jeremiah reminded his followers that various evil practices were something that God never commanded, nor would allow (Jer. 7:31; 19:5; 32;35). Since scripture and doctrine, like laws, are written to correct an error, we can assume that the Jews believed these practices were what God wanted and the prophet was setting them straight. However, not before some offered up their children. In fact, the victorious judge, Jephthah, is recorded as offering his own daughter as a burnt sacrifice, not to Ba'al or some pagan deity, but to Yahweh himself (Judges 11). Jeremiah later condemned this practice. Worship such as this was condemned as the wrongful practice in the worship of God.

As the rites and rituals of Yahweh became established, the prophets condemned the false worship of Yahweh, that is, the worship emulating the manner of the worship of Baal, further separating

75

Dr. Joseph Lumpkin

worshipers of Ba'al from the worship of Yahweh.

Lines of style and persona were drawn between Yahweh and Baal. Prophets etched it more and more clearly. The Book of Kings records the words of Elijah to those assembled on Mount Carmel: *"How long will you waver between two opinions? If the Lord is God, follow him; but if Baal is God, follow him" (1 Kings 18:21).*

This is the story of the battle of miracles between the prophets of Ba'al and the prophet of God. Elijah gives the prophets of Ba'al a chance to call down the power of their god to bring fire down to the alter to consume a sacrifice. After dancing, chanting, and cutting themselves for hours, they fail. Elijah's God sends fire from heaven; consuming the sacrifice, even after Elijah demand water to be poured on it. The people respond by killing the prophets of Ba'al.

The prophet Hosea put the issue more subtly when he declared: *I will seduce Israel and bring her into the wilderness, and I will speak tenderly and to her heart.... And it shall be in that day, says the Lord (Yahweh), that you will call Me 'Ishi' (Husband), and you shall no more call Me 'Baali' (your Lord). For I will take away the names of the baalim (other lords) out of her mouth, and they shall no more be mentioned or seriously remembered by their name (Hosea 2:14-17).* When a Hebrew word has a suffix of "im" it is a plural word. Ba'alim would refer to more than one Ba'al or lord.

Israelite Opposition to Baal

In the beginning, the Israelites shared many religious beliefs with the Canaanites, but as the people established regional differences, and the gods of El and Yahweh began to meld, monotheism began to develop. As the worship of Yahweh and Ba'al became further separated, and Yahweh and El were being identified as the same deity, Ba'al became the rival to El and the adversary of god and the Israelite people.

Remember, that in Canaanite mythology, El and Ba'al are at odds. This amplified as lines were drawn between the worship styles of the various gods and the proper way to worship El-Yahwee. Ba'al finally devolves into the satanic archetype in the Bible during the time of Moses.

Numbers 25
The Message Bible
The Orgy at Shittim

76

1-3 *While Israel was camped at Shittim (Acacia Grove), the men began to have sex with the Moabite women. It started when the women invited the men to their sex-and-religion worship. They ate together and then worshiped their gods. Israel ended up joining in the worship of the Baal of Peor. GOD was furious, his anger blazing out against Israel.*

4 *GOD said to Moses, "Take all the leaders of Israel and kill them by hanging, leaving them publicly exposed in order to turn GOD's anger away from Israel."*

5 *Moses issued orders to the judges of Israel: "Each of you must execute the men under your jurisdiction who joined in the worship of Baal Peor."*

6-9 *Just then, while everyone was weeping in penitence at the entrance of the Tent of Meeting, an Israelite man, flaunting his behavior in front of Moses and the whole assembly, paraded a Midianite woman into his family tent. Phinehas son of Eleazar, the son of Aaron the priest, saw what he was doing, grabbed his spear, and followed them into the tent. With one thrust he drove the spear through the two of them, the man of Israel and the woman, right through their private parts. That stopped the plague from continuing among the People of Israel. But 24,000 had already died.*

10-13 *GOD spoke to Moses: "Phinehas son of Eleazar, son of Aaron the priest, has stopped my anger against the People of Israel. Because he was as zealous for my honor as I myself am, I didn't kill all the People of Israel in my zeal. So tell him that I am making a Covenant-of-Peace with him. He and his descendants are joined in a covenant of eternal priesthood, because he was zealous for his God and made atonement for the People of Israel."*

14-15 *The name of the man of Israel who was killed with the Midianite woman was Zimri son of Salu, the head of the Simeonite family. And the name of the Midianite woman who was killed was Cozbi daughter of Zur, a tribal chief of a Midianite family.*

16-18 *GOD spoke to Moses: "From here on make the Midianites your enemies. Fight them tooth and nail. They turned out to be your enemies when they seduced you in the business of Peor and that woman Cozbi, daughter of a Midianite leader, the woman who was killed at the time of the plague in the matter of Peor."*

The sin was so great that even Phinehas, the son of Aaron, was sent to run through an Israelite man and his forbidden Midiante woman with his spear, which ha did in one stroke. The Midianites, as well as the Moabites, now became mortal enemies of Israel.

Over and over, the lure of the sex and fertility cults took the Israelites back to Ba'al and Asherah worship. Over and over God punished, corrected, and saved the Israelites. (Below you will see the name "Othniel". He was the first judge of Israel.)

Judges 3
The Message Bible
¹⁻⁴*These are the nations that GOD left there, using them to test the Israelites who had no experience in the Canaanite wars. He did it to train the descendants of Israel, the ones who had no battle experience, in the art of war. He left the five Philistine tyrants, all the Canaanites, the Sidonians, and the Hivites living on Mount Lebanon from Mount Baal Hermon to Hamath's Pass. They were there to test Israel and see whether they would obey GOD's commands that were given to their parents through Moses.*
⁵⁻⁶ *But the People of Israel made themselves at home among the Canaanites, Hittites, Amorites, Perizzites, Hivites, and Jebusites. They married their daughters and gave their own daughters to their sons in marriage. And they worshiped their gods.*

Othniel
⁷⁻⁸ *The People of Israel did evil in GOD's sight. They forgot their GOD and worshiped the Baal gods and Asherah goddesses. GOD's hot anger blazed against Israel. He sold them off to Cushan-Rishathaim king of Aram Naharaim. The People of Israel were in servitude to Cushan-Rishathaim for eight years.*
⁹⁻¹⁰ *The People of Israel cried out to GOD and GOD raised up a savior who rescued them: Caleb's nephew Othniel, son of his younger brother Kenaz. The Spirit of GOD came on him and he rallied Israel. He went out to war and GOD gave him Cushan-Rishathaim king of Aram Naharaim. Othniel made short work of him.*
¹¹ *The land was quiet for forty years. Then Othniel son of Kenaz died.*

Ehud
¹²⁻¹⁴ *But the People of Israel went back to doing evil in GOD's sight. So GOD made Eglon king of Moab a power against Israel because they did evil in GOD's sight. He recruited the Ammonites and Amalekites and went out and struck Israel. They took the City of Palms. The People of Israel were in servitude to Eglon fourteen years.*
¹⁵⁻¹⁹ *The People of Israel cried out to GOD and GOD raised up for them a savior, Ehud son of Gera, a Benjaminite. He was left-handed. The People of Israel sent tribute by him to Eglon king of Moab. Ehud made himself a short two-edged sword and strapped it on his right thigh under his clothes. He presented the tribute to Eglon king of Moab. Eglon was grossly fat. After Ehud finished presenting the tribute, he went a little way with the men who had*

carried it. But when he got as far as the stone images near Gilgal, he went back and said, "I have a private message for you, O King." The king told his servants, "Leave." They all left.

20-24 Ehud approached him — the king was now quite alone in his cool rooftop room — and said, "I have a word of God for you." Eglon stood up from his throne. Ehud reached with his left hand and took his sword from his right thigh and plunged it into the king's big belly. Not only the blade but the hilt went in. The fat closed in over it so he couldn't pull it out. Ehud slipped out by way of the porch and shut and locked the doors of the rooftop room behind him. Then he was gone.

When the servants came, they saw with surprise that the doors to the rooftop room were locked. They said, "He's probably relieving himself in the restroom." 25 They waited. And then they worried — no one was coming out of those locked doors. Finally, they got a key and unlocked them. There was their master, fallen on the floor, dead!

It was after this event that King Ahab and his Phoenician wife, Jezebel, introduced the worship of her god, Ba'al, once again to the courts. When the prophets of Yahweh protested, she attempted to rid the court of all influences of Yahweh. Once again, enter Elijah onto the scene to conduct the famous test between Ba'al and Yahweh. Elijah and the prophets of Ba'al fought for control of the high place at Mount Carmel. The contest came down to who could produce an irrefutable sign from their god. Baal's prophets fail to produce a sign that Ba'al has accepted their sacrifice, while Yahweh consumes Elijah's sacrifice with fire from heaven. The crowd rewards the failure of Baal's prophet by massacring all 450 of them (I Kings 18).

Later, the massacre continued when King Jehu took Ahab's throne and killed everyone in Jezreel who was related to Ahab, as well as all his servants, generals, priests, and close friends. (2 Kings 10:11). Jehu finished the purging by pretending to throw a party in honor of Ba'al," stating: "Ahab served Ba'al a little, but Jehu will serve him much." After gathering together anyone who wished to worship or celebrate in Baal's temple, Jehu and 80 of his soldiers killed all those in attendance and burned the temple to the ground.

(2 Kings 10:27 - 29)
The Message Bible
And the bloody slaughter began. The officers and guards threw the corpses outside and cleared the way to enter the inner shrine of Baal. They hauled out

the sacred phallic stone from the temple of Baal and pulverized it. They smashed the Baal altars and tore down the Baal temple. It's been a public toilet ever since.

28 And that's the story of Jehu's' wasting of Baal in Israel.

29 But for all that, Jehu's didn't turn back from the sins of Jeroboam son of Neat, the sins that had dragged Israel into a life of sin — the golden calves in Bethel and Dan stayed.

However, as verse 29 indicates, Jehu did not go far enough. He failed to stop the unauthorized manner of worship on the unsanctioned altars to Yahweh/El at Dan and Bethel. The golden calf, which was a left over relic of the Canaanite worship of El as a pagan deity, remained. The god, El, evolved from an idol into the name used to identify the one true god. The idolatry of the past with its dead, lifeless statues had to be destroyed to make way for the new idea of a god that needed no representation and no restrictions. It was not. Not only did the incorrect manner of Yahweh worship continue, but also Ba'al worship remained and would later spread.

Based on the continued worship of El/Yahweh using idols of a calf, we should raise an eyebrow and ask an obvious question. Was this the same problem with the Golden Calf the people of Israel worshipped while Moses was on the mountain receiving the Ten Commandments? Was the golden calf an idol to the correct god who was being worshipped in an incorrect way? Yes. Look closely at Young's Literal Translation:

Exodus 32:1-6
Young's Literal Translation (YLT)
Exodus 32

1)And the people see that Moses is delaying to come down from the mount, and the people assemble against Aaron, and say unto him, `Rise, make for us gods who go before us, for this Moses -- the man who brought us up out of the land of Egypt -- we have not known what hath happened to him.'

2) And Aaron smith unto them, `Break off the rings of gold which [are] in the ears of your wives, your sons, and your daughters, and bring in unto me;'

3) and all the people themselves break off the rings of gold which [are] in their ears, and bring in unto Aaron,

4) and he received from their hand, and doth fashion it with a graving tool, and doth make it a molten calf, and they say, `These thy gods, O Israel, who brought thee up out of the land of Egypt.'

5) And Aaron seethe, and bidet an altar before it, and Aaron called, and smith,
`A festival to Jehovah -- to-morrow;'
6) and they rise early on the morrow, and cause burnt offerings to ascend, and
bring nigh peace-offerings; and the people sit down to eat and to drink, and rise
up to play.

"A festival to Jehovah (Yahweh) tomorrow." The golden calf was the idol made to the god Yahweh/El, taking the form of the old El worship of the Canaanite war god, whose image was a calf or a bull.

It seemed that the kings of Israel, along with the priesthood of Yahweh, which had been now firmly established, kept a policy of zero tolerance against Ba'al worship for a short while. However, the people were difficult to control, and there were always kings that were more permissive.

Let's face facts. If a religion advocated sex and parties in the name of worship, it would be difficult for many to refuse. We shall look deeper into this in a moment when we discuss the existence of Temple Prostitutes in the house of God.

It was around this period of time that the Torah began to develop. Although some writings in the Torah are much older, we know that Deuteronomy was composed or completed in the 6th century BCE.
I Chronicles, II Chronicles, Esther, and Malichi were all written between 450 and 420 B.C.E. Orthodox Jewish scholars tell us the Pentateuch or first five books of the Torah were written by Moses around 1300 BCE, but it appears the Torah was actually written by at least four authors.

By the end of the 19th century, it was generally agreed there were four main sources of writers of the Torah. These four sources came to be known as the Yahwist, or Jahwist, J (J being the German equivalent of the English letter Y); the Elohist, E; the Deuteronomist, D (the name comes from the Book of Deuteronomy, D's contribution to the Torah); and the Priestly Writer, P.

It is generally thought that the sources or contributers can be dated. The Yahwist source (J) : written c. 950 BCE in the southern Kingdom of Judah.
The Elohist source (E) : written c. 850 BCE in the northern Kingdom of Israel.

81

The Deuteronomist (D) : written c. 600 BCE in Jerusalem during a period of religious reform.
The Priestly source (P) : written c. 500 BCE by Kohanim (Jewish priests) in exile in Babylon.

This theory is contrary to the view of Orthodox Rabbis but both could be true if the original document of the Pentateuch began to be written around 1300 B.C.E but were redacted and completed in their present form around 500 B.C.E.

The Torah, being the Jewish scripture, would solidify the Jewish people under one coherent faith, but that faith would continue to settle and mature. The existence of the Torah gave the Jews a distinct and different upper hand. Most religions of the time had no written doctrine and history. The ones that had no written and stable doctrine would splinter, morph, and become diffused, weaken and die. The Jews had the Torah, which served as a touchstone and a guide to keep the Jews together as a religion and people, no matter how far they wondered from their geographic religious seat or temple. Historical records indicate that although the Jewish people were once a unified community of people living in the Fertile Crescent in an area referred to as Canaan, around 597 B.C.E. they had spread into separate groups of Jewish people living in Babylon, Judea and Egypt. This separation into recognizable and distinct communities is recognized as the beginning of the Jewish Diaspora. However, around this time the Torah was being compiled and it would save the faith from dispersion. No matter how far Jews would travel, they would keep their faith, kept their ways, their laws, keep their religion, and their customs because these were preserved in a written form, which guided them. The dispersal or scattering of Jewish people seeded Judaism into separate communities in different parts of the world.

Some books of the Torah were dated from 950 BCE and passed down from priest to priest. The fact that various books of teachings had been preserved did not mean that Judaism would not continue to face its problems with various heresies and worship of other gods. Even though a book guided the faith does not mean the book would be followed.

The Torah was not the only book the Jews relied on. Later, around 500 CE, the Talmud would become part of Jewish rabbinical life. The

Talmud has two components: the Mishnah (c. 200 CE), a written compendium of Rabbinic Judaism's Oral Torah, and the Gemara (c. 500 CE), an elucidation of the Mishnah and related Tannaitic writings The Gemara is the component of the Talmud comprising rabbinical analysis of and commentary on the Mishnah. The Mishnah is an authoritative collection of exegetical material embodying the oral tradition of Jewish law and forming the first part of the Talmud. After the Mishnah was published by Judah HaNasi (c. 200 CE), the work was studied exhaustively by generation after generation of rabbis in Babylonia and the Land of Israel. Their discussions were written down in a series of books that became the Gemara, which when combined with the Mishnah constituted the Talmud.

The entire Talmud consists of 63 tractates, and in standard print is over 6,200 pages long. It is written in Tannaitic Hebrew and Jewish Babylonian Aramaic and contains the teachings and opinions of thousands of rabbis (dating from before the Common Era through the fifth century CE) on a variety of subjects, including Halakha (law), Jewish ethics, philosophy, customs, history, lore and many other topics. The Talmud is the basis for all codes of Jewish law, and is widely quoted in rabbinic literature.

The Tulmud would not be available for a thousand years, but even the Talmud and Torah were completed and widely circulated it probably would not have changed the fact that politics influences religion and religion influences politics. In the case of Ba'al worship, the people and the king seemed to like it and held on to Ba'al while worshipping El.

Ba'al worship remained in practice, always causing the prophets of Yahweh to complain. Hosea grumbled, "The more I called Israel, the further they went from me. They sacrificed to the Ba'al and they burned incense to images. " (Hosea 11:2)

Even the occasional king relapsed. Manasseh, the son of King Hezekiah (c. 687 B.C.E.) allowed altars to Ba'al to be rebuilt. It seemed that, even then, politics won out, and kings gave into the people for the sake of pleasing the people and strengthening their following.

As the common folk continued to worship the fertility and storm gods, the evidence of that worship built up and was left behind. Some survived the passage of time. Archaeologists found evidence that the worship of Ba'al and Asherah was practiced consistently alongside that of Yahweh and at times, it was not only condoned, but also sanctioned by the temple priesthood. Most of the evidence was found outside of Jerusalem. By the time King Josiah (640–609 B.C.E.) took the throne, even the Temple of Jerusalem sported temple prostitutes. These "sacred vessels" were involved in the fertility cult associated with Ba'al and Ashera.

2 Kings 23
The Message Bible
1-3) The king acted immediately, assembling all the elders of Judah and Jerusalem. Then the king proceeded to The Temple of God, bringing everyone in his train – priests and prophets and people ranging from the famous to the unknown. Then he read out publicly everything written in the Book of the Covenant that was found in The Temple of God. The king stood by the pillar and before God solemnly committed them all to the covenant: to follow God believingly and obediently; to follow his instructions, heart and soul, on what to believe and do; to put into practice the entire covenant, all that was written in the book. The people stood in affirmation; their commitment was unanimous.
4-9) Then the king ordered Hilkiah the high priest, his associate priest, and The Temple sentries to clean house – to get rid of everything in The Temple of God that had been made for worshiping Baal and Asherah and the cosmic powers. He had them burned outside Jerusalem in the fields of Kidron and then disposed of the ashes in Bethel. He fired the pagan priests whom the kings of Judah had hired to supervise the local sex-and-religion shrines in the towns of Judah and neighborhoods of Jerusalem. In a stroke he swept the country clean of the polluting stench of the round-the-clock worship of Baal, sun and moon, stars – all the so-called cosmic powers. He took the obscene phallic Asherah pole from The Temple of God to the Valley of Kidron outside Jerusalem, burned it up, then ground up the ashes and scattered them in the cemetery. He tore out the rooms of the male sacred prostitutes that had been set up in The Temple of God; women also used these rooms for weavings for Asherah. He swept the outlying towns of Judah clean of priests and smashed the sex-and-religion shrines where they worked their trade from one end of the country to the other – all the way from Geba to Beersheba. He smashed the sex-and-religion shrine that had been set up just to the left of the city gate for the private use of Joshua, the city mayor. Even though these sex-and-religion priests did not defile the Altar in The Temple itself, they were part of the general priestly corruption and had to go.
10-11) Then Josiah demolished the Topheth, the iron furnace griddle set up in the Valley of Ben Hammon for sacrificing children in the fire. No longer could

anyone burn son or daughter to the god Molech. He hauled off the horse statues honoring the sun god that the kings of Judah had set up near the entrance to The Temple. They were in the courtyard next to the office of Nathan-Melech, the warden. He burned up the sun-chariots as so much rubbish.

12-15) The king smashed all the altars to smithereens – the altar on the roof shrine of Ahaz, the various altars the kings of Judah had made, the altars of Manasseh that littered the courtyard of The Temple – he smashed them all, pulverized the fragments, and scattered their dust in the Valley of Kidron. The king proceeded to make a clean sweep of all the sex-and-religion shrines that had proliferated east of Jerusalem on the south slope of Abomination Hill, the ones Solomon king of Israel had built to the obscene Sidonian sex goddess Ashtoreth, to Chemosh the dirty-old-god of the Moabites, and to Milcom the depraved god of the Ammonites. He tore apart the altars, chopped down the phallic Asherah-poles, and scattered old bones over the sites. Next, he took care of the altar at the shrine in Bethel that Jeroboam son of Neat had built – the same Jeroboam who had led Israel into a life of sin. He tore apart the altar, burned down the shrine leaving it in ashes, and then lit fire to the phallic Asherah-pole.

After the exile, Ba'al is not mentioned again. However, "Bel and the Dragon," a book in the apocrypha which was part of the Book of Daniel in some versions of the Bible, tells the story of the prophet Daniel as he de-bunks the trickery of the priests and their deceptive practices by which they attempted to make the people believe that Bel (which is likely Ba'al) was alive and eating the sacrifices offered. The story takes place in Babylonia where the worship was that of Bel/Marduk.

Bel.1
[1] And king Astyages was gathered to his fathers, and Cyrus of Persia received his kingdom.
[2] And Daniel conversed with the king, and was honoured above all his friends.
[3] Now the Babylons had an idol, called Bel, and there were spent upon him every day twelve great measures of fine flour, and forty sheep, and six vessels of wine.
[4] And the king worshipped it and went daily to adore it: but Daniel worshipped his own God. And the king said unto him, Why dost not thou worship Bel?
[5] Who answered and said, Because I may not worship idols made with hands,

but the living God, who hath created the heaven and the earth, and hath sovereignty over all flesh.

[6] Then said the king unto him, Thinkest thou not that Bel is a living God? seest thou not how much he eateth and drinketh every day?

[7] Then Daniel smiled, and said, O king, be not deceived: for this is but clay within, and brass without, and did never eat or drink any thing.

[8] So the king was wroth, and called for his priests, and said unto them, If ye tell me not who this is that devoureth these expenses, ye shall die.

[9] But if ye can certify me that Bel devoureth them, then Daniel shall die: for he hath spoken blasphemy against Bel. And Daniel said unto the king, Let it be according to thy word.

[10] Now the priests of Bel were threescore and ten, beside their wives and children. And the king went with Daniel into the temple of Bel.

[11] So Bel's priests said, Lo, we go out: but thou, O king, set on the meat, and make ready the wine, and shut the door fast and seal it with thine own signet;

[12] And to morrow when thou comest in, if thou findest not that Bel hath eaten up all, we will suffer death: or else Daniel, that speaketh falsely against us.

[13] And they little regarded it: for under the table they had made a privy entrance, whereby they entered in continually, and consumed those things.

[14] So when they were gone forth, the king set meats before Bel. Now Daniel had commanded his servants to bring ashes, and those they strewed throughout all the temple in the presence of the king alone: then went they out, and shut the door, and sealed it with the king's signet, and so departed.

[15] Now in the night came the priests with their wives and children, as they were wont to do, and did eat and drink up all.

[16] In the morning betime the king arose, and Daniel with him.

[17] And the king said, Daniel, are the seals whole? And he said, Yea, O king, they be whole.

[18] And as soon as he had opened the dour, the king looked upon the table, and cried with a loud voice, Great art thou, O Bel, and with thee is no deceit at all.

[19] Then laughed Daniel, and held the king that he should not go in, and said, Behold now the pavement, and mark well whose footsteps are these.

[20] And the king said, I see the footsteps of men, women, and children. And then the king was angry,

[21] And took the priests with their wives and children, who shewed him the privy doors, where they came in, and consumed such things as were upon the table.

[22] Therefore the king slew them, and delivered Bel into Daniel's power, who destroyed him and his temple.

By 400 B.C.E., monotheism and the worship of Yahweh were so well established that it pushed out Israel's pagan past. However, owing to the sordid and violent opposition to the Baal cult by the Yahweh priests, kings, and followers, Ba'al was typecast as the main enemy of El/Yahweh and became a demon. Later, Ba'al was reputed to be a great demon, and has been named by many Rabbis as the "Prince over Persia."

Daniel 10   NIV
10) A hand touched me and set me trembling on my hands and knees. 11) He said, "Daniel, you who are highly esteemed, consider carefully the words I am about to speak to you, and stand up, for I have now been sent to you." And when he said this to me, I stood up trembling.
12) Then he continued, "Do not be afraid, Daniel. Since the first day that you set your mind to gain understanding and to humble yourself before your God, your words were heard, and I have come in response to them. 13) But the prince of the Persian kingdom resisted me twenty-one days. Then Michael, one of the chief princes, came to help me, because I was detained there with the king of Persia. 14) Now I have come to explain to you what will happen to your people in the future, for the vision concerns a time yet to come." 15) While he was saying this to me, I bowed with my face toward the ground and was speechless. 16) Then one who looked like a man touched my lips, and I opened my mouth and began to speak. I said to the one standing before me, "I am overcome with anguish because of the vision, my lord, and I feel very weak. 17) How can I, your servant, talk with you, my lord? My strength is gone and I can hardly breathe."
18) Again the one who looked like a man touched me and gave me strength. 19) "Do not be afraid, you who are highly esteemed," he said. "Peace! Be strong now; be strong."
When he spoke to me, I was strengthened and said, "Speak, my lord, since you have given me strength."
20) So he said, "Do you know why I have come to you? Soon I will return to fight against the prince of Persia, and when I go, the prince of Greece will come; 21) but first I will tell you what is written in the Book of Truth. (No one supports me against them except Michael, your prince.

Puritan Christians preached that Ba'al was Satan, or the demon we now know as Metastophilis, Satan's helper.

The Development of Satan

In the beginning, in the days of the birth of religion, where primitive man worshipped a supreme, all-powerful deity, whether it was a Sun god, or some idea represented by an idol, there was no duality. That is to say, there was no anti-god, no opposite force, no Satan, no Devil, no spiritual adversary. God was the only force in the universe. Although it is now common to find Christians speaking of the universe as a place divided between the good and evil forces of God and Satan respectively, this was not how primitive man, nor even the Jewish writers of the Old Testament, viewed the world. As far as the writers of the Old Testament were concerned, everything that happened was an act of God. God was the only real power in the universe. When bad things happened to people, they did not blame a devil or Satan, since he was still a "bit player" or "an extra" in the cosmic drama, and was only a creation and tool of God. When bad things happened, people assumed that they had offended God in some way. If crops failed or disease invaded the land, it was because God was unhappy and needed to be appeased. This was commonly done through rituals and sacrifice.

The peaceful meadows will be laid waste because of the fierce anger of the Lord. Like a lion he will leave his lair, and their land will become desolate because of the sword of the oppressor and because of the Lord's fierce anger. (Jeremiah 25:37-38)

When good things happened, people believed that they had pleased God in some way. Deuteronomy 28:1-68 sums this up by saying that blessings and curses are set out for obeying and disobeying God.

The LORD will send on you curses, confusion and rebuke in everything you put your hand to, until you are destroyed and come to sudden ruin because of the evil you have done in forsaking him. The LORD will plague you with diseases until he has destroyed you from the land you are entering to possess. The LORD will strike you with wasting disease, with fever and inflammation, with scorching heat and drought, with blight and mildew, which will plague you until you perish. (Deuteronomy 28:20-23)

The ancient notion of God's blessing or punishment was assumed to be in play in all aspects of human life. Something as ubiquitous as infertility was considered to be a sign of God's curse. (Genesis 30:1-2). Crop failure was traced back to God's punishment for failing in the Garden of Eden. In Genesis 3:17-19, the ground is cursed by God to produce thorns. God, and only God, was the source of both good and evil in the world. When the Jewish nation was taken into exile by the Babylonians in 586 BCE, and the temple in Jerusalem was destroyed, the prophets believed this catastrophe was the result of God's judgment against the people for becoming too lax in following the law and worshipping God.

As time went on, there were lesser gods, sons of god, or other types of entities, which could ultimately be controlled by the supreme god but who, from time to time, may do the "dirty work" of god. This was the beginning of a growing feeling that God was good and thus would not bring harm to his children. The idea of the gray haired fatherly God was bumping up against the idea of evil in the world. How to solve this problem? The religious belief of "Dualism", the absolute evil enemy of God, was born in the minds of the people.

Job 1
The Message Bible
6-7 One day when the angels came to report to God, Satan, who was the Designated Accuser, came along with them. God singled out Satan and said, "What have you been up to?"
Satan answered God, "Going here and there, checking things out on earth."
8 God said to Satan, "Have you noticed my friend Job? There's no one quite like him — honest and true to his word, totally devoted to God and hating evil."
9-10 Satan retorted, "So do you think Job does all that out of the sheer goodness of his heart? Why, no one ever had it so good! You pamper him like a pet, make sure nothing bad ever happens to him or his family or his possessions, bless everything he does — he can't lose!
11 "But what do you think would happen if you reached down and took away everything that is his? He'd curse you right to your face, that's what."
12 God replied, "We'll see. Go ahead — do what you want with all that is his. Just don't hurt him." Then Satan left the presence of God.

In the text, the word "Satan" is "accuser" and the word "angels" is actually, "Sons of God."

The founder of Persian dualism was Zarathustra, or, as the

Greeks called him, "Zoroaster"--a name which in its literal translation means "golden splendor." Zoroaster was the prophet of Mazdaism. In Persia, Mazda was a god, the Omniscient One. In an essay titled, "On the Date of Zoroaster," Prof. A. V. Williams Jackson places the life of the prophet between the latter half of the seventh and the middle of the sixth century. Dr. E. W. West points out that the calendar reform introduced in the year 505 B. C., the names of the months were supplanted by Zoroastrian names.

There were two religious parties in the days of Zoroaster: the worshippers of the daêvas or nature-gods, and the worshippers of Ahura, the Lord. Zoroaster appears in the Gathas as a priest of the highest rank who became the leader of the Ahura party. Zoroaster not only degraded the old nature-gods, the daêvas, into demons, but also regarded them as representatives of a fiendish power which he called *Angrô Mainyush*, or *Ahriman*, which means "the evil spirit," and *Druj*, meaning "falsehood."

The Scythians in the plains of Northern Asia who worshipped their highest deity under the symbol of a serpent were a fierce enemy of Persia. As it is human nature to demonize one's enemy, it was natural that their snake god, Afrasiâb, became identified with the archfiend Ahriman, or the evil one who was in opposition to Mazda.

According to Zoroaster, as the sun received divine worship, so the flame, which is lit in praise of Ahura Mazda, is a symbol only of him who is the light of the soul and the principle of all goodness.

Zoroaster taught that Ahura did not create Ahriman, but that he was possessed of independent existence. The evil spirit was not equal to the Ahura Mazda in dignity or power, but both were original beings that were creative, although one was good and the other evil. Neither could die in the conventional sense, because they were, by our standards, uncreated. They were the representatives of opposing and contradictory principles. This doctrine, in a nutshell, is the doctrine of dualism and seems to have first originated in Persia, where it found its way into Judaism, and then into Christianity and Islam. The idea of dualism is expressed in the words of the thirtieth Yasna, or saying.

"Well known are the two primeval spirits correlated but independent; one is the better and the other is the worse as to thought, as to word, as to deed, and between these two let the wise choose aright."

Since dualism expresses itself in couplets of opposites, Ahura

Mazda, the Omniscient Lord, reveals himself through "the excellent, the pure and stirring word." On the rock inscription of Elvend, which had been made by the order of king Darius, we read these lines:

> *"There is one God, omnipotent Ahura Mazda,*
> *It is He who has created the earth here;*
> *It is He who has created the heaven there;*
> *It is He who has created mortal man."*

Their worship continues:

"May Ahura be rejoiced! May Angrô be destroyed by those who do truly what is God's all-important will.

"I praise well-considered thoughts, well-spoken words, and well-done deeds. I embrace all good thoughts, good words, and good deeds; I reject all evil thoughts, evil words, and evil deeds.

"I give sacrifice and prayer unto you, O Ameshâ-Spentâ! even with the fullness of my thoughts, of my words, of my deeds, and of my heart: I give unto you even my own life.

"I recite the, 'Praise of Holiness,' the Ashem Vohu:

"'Holiness is the best of all good. Well is it for it, well is it for that holiness which is perfection of holiness!

"'I confess myself a worshipper of Mazda, a follower of Zarathustra, one who hates the daêvas (devils) and obeys the laws of Ahura.'"

Lenormant characterizes the God of Zoroaster as follows:

"Ahura Mazda has created asha, purity, or rather the cosmic order; he has created both the moral and material world constitution; he has made the universe; he has made the law; he is, in a word, creator (datar), sovereign (ahura), omniscient (mazdâo), the god of order (ashavan). He corresponds exactly to Varuna, the highest god of Vedism."

"This spiritual conception of the Supreme Being is absolutely pure in the Avesta, and the expressions that Ormuzd has the sun for his eye, the heaven for his garment, the lightning for his sons, the waters for his spouses, are unequivocally allegorical. Creator of all things, Ormuzd is himself uncreated and eternal. He had no beginning and will have no end. He has accomplished his creation work by pronouncing the Word,' the 'Ahuna-Vairyo. The Word existed before everything else,' reminding us of the eternal Word, the Divine Logos of the Gospel."

Histoire Ancienne de l'Orient, V., p. 388.

Concerning Ahriman, Lenormant says:

"The creation came forth from the hands of Ormuzd, pure and perfect like himself. It was Ahriman who perverted it by his infamous influence, and labored continually to destroy and overthrow it, for he is the destroyer (paurou marka) as well as the spirit of evil. The struggle between these two principles, of good and of evil, constitutes the world's history. In Ahriman we find again the old wrathful serpent of the Indo-Iranian period, which is the personification of evil and who in Vedism, under the name of Ahi, is regarded as an individual being. The myth of the serpent and the legends of the Avesta are mingled in Ahriman under the name of Aji Dahâka, who is said to have attacked Atar, Traêtaona, and Yima, but is himself dethroned. It is the source of the Greek myth that Apollo slays the dragon Python. The Indo-Iranian religion knows only the struggle that was carried on in the atmosphere between the fire-god and the serpent-demon Afrasiâb. And it was, according to Professor Darmesteter, the doctrine of this struggle, which, when generalized and applied to all things in the world, finally led to the establishment of dualism."

"There were two general ideas at the bottom of the Indo-Iranian religion; first, that there is a law in nature, and secondly, that there is a war in nature." (*Sacred Books of the East*, IV., p. lvii),

The law in nature proves the wisdom of Ahura, who is therefore called Mazda, the Wise. The war in nature is due to the intrusion of Ahriman into the creation of Ahura.

The fire sacrifice was accompanied by partaking of the haoma drink, a ceremony which reminds us on the one hand of the soma sacrifice of the Vedic age in India and on the other hand, of the Lord's Supper of the Christians.

We know through the sacred scriptures of the Persians that little cakes (the *draona*) covered with small pieces of holy meat (the *myazda*) were consecrated in the name of a spiritual being, a god or angel, or of some great deceased personality, and then distributed among all the worshippers that were present. But more sacred still than the draona with the myazda is the haoma drink which was prepared from the white haoma plant, also called gaokerena. Says Professor Darmesteter: "It is by the drinking of gaokerena that men, on the day of the resurrection, will become immortal." The sacrament of drinking the gaokerena was celebrated in the times of early Christianity, and was very similar to the Christian communion."

According to the Zoroastrian doctrine, after death, the soul passes the bridge or accounting, where it is judged. This bridge stretches over hell, from the peak of Judgment to the divine Mount Alborz, and becomes, according to the most common statements of the doctrine, broad to the good, and narrow to the wicked. The good person walks a broad path while the wicked walk a path no wider than a razor's edge. Evil people fall into the power of Ahriman and are doomed to hell. The good person enters the life of bliss. In an odd parallel to purgatory, those divided in their nature between good and evil remain in an intermediate state until the great judgment-day they called *âka*.

The preaching of Zoroaster consisted of a teaching regarding a great crisis at hand, which will lead to the destruction and remaking or renovation of the world. Into this new world Saviors will come. They will be born from the lineage or seed of Zoroaster. One Savior would be great in power and deed. He will resurrect the dead. He will be the "son of a virgin" and the All-conquering." His name shall be the Victorious; Righteousness made flesh, the Savior. Then the living shall become immortal, yet their bodies will be transfigured so that they will cast no shadows, and the dead shall rise, "within their lifeless bodies incorporate life shall be restored." The great battle between absolute good and absolute evil, end of the world, the newly cleansed and remade earth, the resurrection of the dead by the messiah, and life eternal, all bring the book of Revelation firmly to mind. We cannot doubt the influence of Zoroaster's religion upon Judaism and early Christianity.

But there are many Jewish ceremonies preserved to the present day, which bear a close resemblance to the ritual of ancient Mazdaism. There is, for instance, an Assyrian cylinder, which represents a worshipper standing before the idol of a god. Behind him are the tree of life and a priest carrying in his left hand a rosary, while the deity hovers above them in a similar shape to the Ahura-Mazda pictures of the Persians.

The primitive stages of Hebrew civilization are not sufficiently known to describe the changes and phases which the Israelites' idea of the Godhead had to undergo before it reached the purity of the Yahweh conception.

Jewish religion was evolving. It was leaving behind the worship of the warlike god, El, along with idol worship and human sacrifice, and embracing the protector, Yahweh. There was a feeling that Yahweh must be pure and good, since now there was a contract in force consisting of protection and guidance from Yahweh in exchange for the fidelity of the Jewish people.

The Israelites must have a demon (not unlike the Egyptian Typhon), to blame for their misfortune. This gave birth to the custom of sacrificing a goat to Azazel, the demon of the desert. The idea strongly suggests that the Israelites had absorbed the idea of dualism in which both deities were regarded as somewhat equal. If they were not equal, but god was still fully in control, sacrifice to any other deity would make no sense. One would sacrifice to God in order to persuade him to control or destroy the evil one.

Leviticus 16:
"And Aaron shall cast lots upon the two goats; one for the Lord, and the other for Azazel. And Aaron shall bring the goat upon which the Lord's lot fell, and offer him for a sin-offering. But the goat on which the lot fell for Azazel, shall be presented alive before the Lord, to make atonement with him and to let him go to Azazel in the desert."

The name *Azazel* is derived from *aziz*, which means strength, and *El*, God. Azazel is "The Strength of God." Yahweh was worshipped by the sacrifice of a goat by killing it, while the sacrifice to Azazel was to lay one's hands on a goat, called the scapegoat, and impart the sins onto the animal. Some believed the animal was released into the desert to carry the curse of the people's sin away and then die. However, it appears the animal was actually thrown over a cliff and killed, insuring the life of the animal would be payment for the sins of the people. We can see this idea in the translation of the verse: **The New English Bible:** *"one to be for the Lord and the other for the Precipice."* Lev 16:8

Azazel makes an appearance in the Book of Enoch, as one of the leaders of the Fallen Angels or Sons of God. He is considered to be the one who taught men many evil arts and traditions, and was doomed to the abyss. The Book of Enoch is later quoted and referenced by Jude and Peter in their New Testament books, and became part of Christian views and beliefs about angels and demons today.

As the scapegoat sacrifice was distanced from the demon, Azazel, and became symbolic of a "commuting of Sin," Satan became more prominent in the lore of the Jewish faith.

The belief in a God of both Good and Evil was replaced by the belief in a powerful demon. Satan, the author and originator of evil, must have been the serpent of Genesis 3:1. However, Satan was still a puppet and not equal to God. He was a tempter and troublemaker, and still a minor player in the universe.

Satan, or the Devil, is rarely mentioned in the Old Testament. The word Satan, which means "enemy" is used as a proper name, signifying the Devil, and appears only five times. One of the five events is recorded in two parallel passages. Oddly, one of the passages actually attributes the action to Yahweh in the older passage, and to Satan in the one written after it.

2 Samuel 24. 1:
"The anger of the Lord was kindled against Israel, and he moved David against them to say, Go, number Israel and Judah."

1 Chron. 21. 1:
"Satan stood up against Israel and provoked David to number Israel."

In all the Pentateuch, Satan is not mentioned at all. Acts of punishment, revenge, and temptation are performed by Yahweh himself, or by an angel at his direction. Satan was one of these malicious servants of God, who enjoys performing the functions of a tempter and avenger. The prophet Zechariah speaks of Satan as an angel whose office it is to accuse and to demand the punishment of the wicked. In the Book of Job, where the most poetical and grandest picture of the Evil One is found, he accuses God's people unjustly.

Abraham's attempted sacrifice of his son, the slaughter of the first-born in Egypt, the razing of Sodom and Gomorrah, even the evil spirit, which came upon Saul, as well as the punishments of David, the perverse spirit which made the Egyptians err (Isaiah 19. 14), the lying spirit working in the prophets of Ahab (1 Kings 22. 23; see also 2 Chron. 18. 20-22), are all the acts of God and God alone.

Satan, in the canonical books of the Old Testament, is an adversary of man, but not of God. Satan is a subject and servant of God. In the non-canonical books, his place and station are somewhat different.

As we have discussed, nations, tribes, and cultures, especially of adjacent territories borrow and mix gods and their attributes. Add to this the fact that when nations are at odds, it is common to make demons of the opponent's gods. This helps demonize the people as well. In war, whether in actual battle or in the decline of personal relationships, there are stages: Dehumanize, Demonize, Destroy without guilt.

Through this process, Beelzebub, the Phoenician god, became another name for Satan. Gehenna, the place where Moloch was worshipped in the valley of Tophet, was replaced by Sheol, the Hebrew name for hell. The idol of Moloch was made of brass, and its stomach was a furnace. According to the prophets (Is. 62: 5; Ez. 16: 20; Jer. 19: 5), children were placed in the monster's arms to be consumed by the heat of the idol. The foreign gods became the symbol of abomination among the Israelites.

When, in 586 B.C.E., the Babylonians took the nation of Israel into exile, the Israelites came into contact with new religions and cosmologies that challenged their ideas of God and the known universe. Because the Axial Age was under way and the idea of God expanded into the hearts of man, the Israelite God was no longer confined to the temple in Jerusalem. God was everywhere and within those who followed Him. As if to balance new ideas of the purity and omnipresence of God, the idea of Satan also changed.

In the writings known as the Apocrypha and those called the Midrash writings, which cover 400 B.C.E. to 200 A.D. of Jewish history, Satan takes on an expanding role of independence and autonomy. Evil separated from God, who was seen more and more as pure, holy, good, and just. No evil can survive His presence. God could no longer have anything to do with evil. Anything seen as bad, wrong, destructive, or evil was the work of Satan. Moreover, it was a very small step from viewing Satan as the purveyor of God's wrath to the origin of evil. Now, he was no longer passively tempting God's people, but actively targeting them for destruction. As Zoroastrianism was absorbed into the Jewish religion, Jews began to understand the cosmos as a divided realm of good and evil.

Nations that opposed the Jews were considered evil and were led by Satan. However, if any party or group within Israel opposed the party in power, they too were labeled evil.

At the time of Jesus, the Roman Empire occupied Jerusalem. In the Jewish community there were three groups vying for space on the religious stage: the Sadducee, the Pharisee, and the Essenes. The smallest and most radically fundamental of these were the Essenes, who believed Satan had taken control of the world through the occupying

Roman forces. The Sadducees were more liberal and did not openly oppose the Romans.

The Essences broke away from the Jewish community at large and withdrew from the areas where Romans actively lived and ruled. Their withdrawal was literally, a withdrawal from Satan's kingdom. It was also during this time that the story of Satan's fall from heaven developed, and began to be accepted as the true understanding of Satan.

The book of Enoch, written during this time, was an expansion of the story told in Genesis of the fallen angels and how they left heaven to have sex with the women on earth. Their union produced giants, monsters, nephilim, and "men of renown". They taught and produced evil and wickedness on the earth. The Book of Enoch has formed our "angelology", "demonology", and even our view of sex within the modern church, since the fall of the watchers was blamed on sex and lust.

Satan in the New Testament

Old Testament contained five passages or so directly referring to Satan. The New Testament is full of metaphors and descriptions. From Peter's description of a lion seeking to devour believers to the beast of Revelations, the New Testament is rife with passages warning the reader to beware.

Before beginning his ministry, *Jesus* was tempted by the devil after he had fasted for forty days in the wilderness. (Matthew 4:1-11, Luke 4:1-13).

As well as believing Satan to be an independent entity opposed to God and the establishment of God's kingdom on earth (Matthew 16:23), Jesus also referred to the Jewish religious leaders, or those who opposed his teaching, as "children of the devil".

"You belong to your father, the devil, and you want to carry out your father's desire. He was a murderer from the beginning, not holding to the truth, for there is no truth in him. When he lies he speaks his native language, for he is a liar and the father of lies." (John 8:44)

The Apostle Paul also spoke of Satan's ability to deceive us when he described him as an angel of light in 2 Corinthians 11:14. Christians were taught to resist and fight Satan in Ephesians 6:10-18,

James 4:7. But the personalizing and externalizing of Satan may have been the worst movement to come out of the Axial Age and the years that followed.

For 50,000 years, our ideas of god were externalized and worked out in bloody rituals and sacrifices. We blamed everything good and bad on god. We worked to appease and placate this fickle, quixotic, rash, and unpleasant deity. Then, mankind grew up and began seeing a new vision of god. We began seeking him within. We expressed our new mysticism in compassion and insight. We began to understand the inter-connected world by treating others as we wished to be treated. It was the beginning of individual responsibility.

Maybe, by breaking evil away from good, we were attempting to purify our god as well as ourselves. Maybe we were attempting to answer the question of how bad events can issue forth from perfect good. Now, by externalizing Satan as we had once externalized god, we began devolution back to blaming forces outside ourselves and thus once again sink back into lack of personal responsibility, a condition that has grown endemic in Christianity. Having an enemy who is invisible, powerful and evil, and whose sole purpose is to obstruct, tempt, and destroy us is the perfect foil to blame for our own weaknesses, shortcomings, failures and bad judgment. As much as the revelations within the Axial Age allowed us to grow, the modern view of Satan has done much to delay our spiritual growth. "The devil made me do it" and "it is the work of Satan" has become the battle cry of a dysfunctional religion and a spiritually sick society, even within our modern religious systems of Judaism and Christianity. Satan is not omnipresent, nor omniscient. Therefore, he cannot attack in more than one place at a time, or know where to be in order to successfully attack. So, our errors are not caused by some unseen adversary, but by simple fate and human weakness. We cannot control fate, however, we can control our actions and decisions, and must take responsibility for them both. The search for both good and evil leads us to look within ourselves. Our thoughts come from our own frailties and desires. It is unspeakable arrogance to think that a malevolent power from heaven would take such personal interest in you or me to spend time targeting us for some scheme to mess up our day, such as breaking our washers, dryers, or cars in order to torment us, or place sinful thoughts within our minds.

Jesus

God is born in human form. Ultimate power and authority reside in the hands of a child. Early Christians looked at their own children as they played, argued, loved, and fought and wondered what it would have been like to raise the Son of God. How would Jesus have acted as a baby, a toddler, a child, or a teenager?

How human was this "God-child," Jesus? Did he have the failings of their own children? Was he selfish and rash at the age of one? Was his stage of the "terrible twos" as horrible a stage as most? If Jesus were a normal youngster what would the outcome have been? For those who found themselves in the path of the young God's temper tantrum, devastating consequences, death or disfigurement could have followed. Questions surrounding the nature of Jesus challenged the minds of Christians from the very beginning of the faith. Did Jesus mature and grow in wisdom, as most young men should? Did he discover his path in life and his calling or was he perfect and mature from the time of his birth? The Bible reports that the child Jesus "grew strong in spirit." Did that mean he was weaker in spirit as a child? These are the questions writers of early Christianity sought to address.

The texts written by early believers struggled to make sense of the paradox of the man who is God. The scant information found in the Gospels regarding the first thirty years of his life gave rise to stories and folklore in an attempt to fill in gaps and answer questions regarding the life and times of Jesus.

Stories were told of the birth of Jesus and his early years. As he grew and began to venture out into the town to play with the other children, disagreements occurred between the strong willed deity and the children, parents, and teachers of the town. How does one discipline God?

Tales sprang from the imagination of believers about his deeds and misdeeds, his travels, and the process of maturing into the man who would save the lost.

Youth gives rise to arrogance and rash behavior, yet, age brings wisdom and self-control. With growing wisdom and guidance from his heavenly father and loving mother, Jesus began to realize his place in the universe as the compassionate rebel and the Messiah.

In the Gospel story, there is little information about the formative years of Jesus. Soon after his birth nothing more is heard of Jesus. The silence continued more than a decade. Then, at the age of twelve the Bible tells us that Jesus had grown in strength and wisdom and was capable of discussing the Torah with adults in the temple. Again the Bible falls silent for the next eighteen years. Jesus next appeared around the age of thirty, ready to start his earthly ministry, and take on the yoke of Messiah.

What happened during the periods of silence? Did Jesus simply grow up in a tiny town doing manual labor as some suggest. Did he wake up one day, lay down his hammer and become the Great Physician, or did he mature into his rightful place over time by doing what he was born to do? Did he travel, teach, and heal as a young man?

We are given virtually no reliable information about the life of Jesus. There are several books written between 150 and 400 years after his death that tell of Jesus' formative years. None of those are considered anything but fiction. The book of Luke gives us the story of Jesus.

Luke.1
[1] Forasmuch as many have taken in hand to set forth in order a declaration of those things which are surely believed among us,
[2] Even as they delivered them to us, which from the beginning were eyewitnesses, and ministers of the word;
[3] It seemed good to me also, having had perfect understanding of all things from the very first, to write to you in order, most excellent Theophilus,
[4] That you might know the certainty of those things, wherein you have been instructed.
[5] There was in the days of Herod, the king of Judaea, a certain priest named Zacharias, of the course of Abia: and his wife was of the daughters of Aaron, and her name was Elisabeth.
[6] And they were both righteous before God, walking in all the commandments and ordinances of the Lord blameless.
[7] And they had no child, because that Elisabeth was barren, and they both were now well stricken in years.
[8] And it came to pass, that while he executed the priest's office before God in the order of his course,
[9] According to the custom of the priest's office, his lot was to burn incense when he went into the temple of the Lord.
[10] And the whole multitude of the people were praying without at the time of incense.
[11] And there appeared to him an angel of the Lord standing on the right side of the altar of incense.

[12] And when Zacharias saw him, he was troubled, and fear fell upon him.
[13] But the angel said to him, Fear not, Zacharias: for your prayer is heard; and your wife Elisabeth shall bear you a son, and you shall call his name John.
[14] And you shall have joy and gladness; and many shall rejoice at his birth.
[15] For he shall be great in the sight of the Lord, and shall drink neither wine nor strong drink; and he shall be filled with the Holy Ghost, even from his mother's womb.
[16] And many of the children of Israel shall he turn to the Lord their God.
[17] And he shall go before him in the spirit and power of Elias, to turn the hearts of the fathers to the children, and the disobedient to the wisdom of the just; to make ready a people prepared for the Lord.
[18] And Zacharias said to the angel, Whereby shall I know this? for I am an old man, and my wife well stricken in years.
[19] And the angel answering said to him, I am Gabriel, that stands in the presence of God; and am sent to speak to you, and to show you these glad tidings.
[20] And, behold, you shall be dumb, and not able to speak, until the day that these things shall be performed, because you believe not my words, which shall be fulfilled in their season.
[21] And the people waited for Zacharias, and marveled that he tarried so long in the temple.
[22] And when he came out, he could not speak to them: and they perceived that he had seen a vision in the temple: for he beckoned to them, and remained speechless.
[23] And it came to pass, that, as soon as the days of his ministration were accomplished, he departed to his own house.
[24] And after those days his wife Elisabeth conceived, and hid herself five months, saying,
[25] Thus has the Lord dealt with me in the days wherein he looked on me, to take away my ridicule among men.
[26] And in the sixth month the angel Gabriel was sent from God to a city of Galilee, named Nazareth,
[27] To a virgin espoused to a man whose name was Joseph, of the house of David; and the virgin's name was Mary.
[28] And the angel came in to her, and said, Hail, you that are highly favored, the Lord is with you: blessed are you among women.
[29] And when she saw him, she was troubled at his saying, and cast in her mind what manner of salutation this should be.
[30] And the angel said to her, Fear not, Mary: for you have found favor with God.

[31] And, behold, you shall conceive in your womb, and bring forth a son, and shall call his name JESUS.

[32] He shall be great, and shall be called the Son of the Highest: and the Lord God shall give to him the throne of his father David:

[33] And he shall reign over the house of Jacob forever; and of his kingdom there shall be no end.

[34] Then said Mary to the angel, How shall this be, seeing I know not a man?

[35] And the angel answered and said to her, The Holy Ghost shall come upon you, and the power of the Highest shall overshadow you: therefore also that holy thing which shall be born of you shall be called the Son of God.

[36] And, behold, your cousin Elisabeth, she has also conceived a son in her old age: and this is the sixth month with her, who was called barren.

[37] For with God nothing shall be impossible.

[38] And Mary said, Behold the handmaid of the Lord; be it to me according to your word. And the angel departed from her.

[39] And Mary arose in those days, and went into the hill country with haste, into a city of Juda;

[40] And entered into the house of Zacharias, and saluted Elisabeth.

[41] And it came to pass, that, when Elisabeth heard the salutation of Mary, the babe leaped in her womb; and Elisabeth was filled with the Holy Ghost:

[42] And she spoke out with a loud voice, and said, Blessed are you among women, and blessed is the fruit of your womb.

[43] And whence is this to me, that the mother of my Lord should come to me?

[44] For, lo, as soon as the voice of your salutation sounded in my ears, the babe leaped in my womb for joy.

[45] And blessed is she that believed: for there shall be a performance of those things which were told her from the Lord.

[46] And Mary said, My soul does magnify the Lord,

[47] And my spirit has rejoiced in God my Savior.

[48] For he has regarded the low estate of his handmaiden: for, behold, from now on all generations shall call me blessed.

[49] For he that is mighty has done to me great things; and holy is his name.

[50] And his mercy is on them that fear him from generation to generation.

[51] He has showed strength with his arm; he has scattered the proud in the imagination of their hearts.

[52] He has put down the mighty from their seats, and exalted them of low degree.

[53] He has filled the hungry with good things; and the rich he has sent empty away.

[54] He has helped his servant Israel, in remembrance of his mercy;

[55] As he spoke to our fathers, to Abraham, and to his offspring for ever.

[56] And Mary abode with her about three months, and returned to her own house.

[57] Now Elisabeth's full time came that she should be delivered; and she brought forth a son.

[58] And her neighbors and her cousins heard how the Lord had showed great mercy upon her; and they rejoiced with her.

[59] And it came to pass, that on the eighth day they came to circumcise the child; and they called him Zacharias, after the name of his father.

[60] And his mother answered and said, Not so; but he shall be called John.

[61] And they said to her, There is none of your kindred that is called by this name.

[62] And they made signs to his father, how he would have him called.

[63] And he asked for a writing table, and wrote, saying, His name is John. And they marveled all.

[64] And his mouth was opened immediately, and his tongue loosed, and he spoke, and praised God.

[65] And fear came on all that dwelt round about them: and all these sayings were noised abroad throughout all the hill country of Judaea.

[66] And all they that heard them laid them up in their hearts, saying, What manner of child shall this be! And the hand of the Lord was with him.

[67] And his father Zacharias was filled with the Holy Ghost, and prophesied, saying,

[68] Blessed be the Lord God of Israel; for he has visited and redeemed his people,

[69] And has raised up a horn of salvation for us in the house of his servant David;

[70] As he spoke by the mouth of his holy prophets, which have been since the world began:

[71] That we should be saved from our enemies, and from the hand of all that hate us;

[72] To perform the mercy promised to our fathers, and to remember his holy covenant;

[73] The oath which he swore to our father Abraham,

[74] That he would grant to us, that we being delivered out of the hand of our enemies might serve him without fear,

[75] In holiness and righteousness before him, all the days of our life.

[76] And you, child, shall be called the prophet of the Highest: for you shall go before the face of the Lord to prepare his ways;

[77] To give knowledge of salvation to his people by the remission of their sins,

[78] *Through the tender mercy of our God; whereby the dayspring from on high has visited us,*
[79] *To give light to them that sit in darkness and in the shadow of death, to guide our feet into the way of peace.*
[80] *And the child grew, and grew strong in spirit, and was in the deserts till the day of his showing to Israel.*

Luke.2
[1] *And it came to pass in those days, that there went out a decree from Caesar Augustus, that all the world should be taxed.*
[2] *(And this taxing was first made when Cyrenius was governor of Syria.)*
[3] *And all went to be taxed, every one into his own city.*
[4] *And Joseph also went up from Galilee, out of the city of Nazareth, into Judaea, to the city of David, which is called Bethlehem; (because he was of the house and lineage of David:)*
[5] *To be taxed with Mary his espoused wife, being great with child.*
[6] *And so it was, that, while they were there, the days were accomplished that she should be delivered.*
[7] *And she brought forth her firstborn son, and wrapped him in swaddling clothes, and laid him in a manger; because there was no room for them in the inn.*
[8] *And there were in the same country shepherds abiding in the field, keeping watch over their flock by night.*
[9] *And, lo, the angel of the Lord came upon them, and the glory of the Lord shone round about them: and they were very afraid.*
[10] *And the angel said to them, Fear not: for, behold, I bring you good tidings of great joy, which shall be to all people.*
[11] *For to you is born this day in the city of David a Savior, which is Christ the Lord.*
[12] *And this shall be a sign to you; You shall find the babe wrapped in swaddling clothes, lying in a manger.*
[13] *And suddenly there was with the angel a multitude of the heavenly host praising God, and saying,*
[14] *Glory to God in the highest, and on earth peace, good will toward men.*
[15] *And it came to pass, as the angels were gone away from them into heaven, the shepherds said one to another, Let us now go even to Bethlehem, and see this thing which is come to pass, which the Lord has made known to us.*
[16] *And they came with haste, and found Mary, and Joseph, and the babe lying in a manger.*
[17] *And when they had seen it, they made known abroad the saying which was*

told them concerning this child.

[18] And all they that heard it wondered at those things which were told them by the shepherds.

[19] But Mary kept all these things, and pondered them in her heart.

[20] And the shepherds returned, glorifying and praising God for all the things that they had heard and seen, as it was told to them.

[21] And when eight days were accomplished for the circumcising of the child, his name was called JESUS, which was so named of the angel before he was conceived in the womb.

[22] And when the days of her purification according to the law of Moses were accomplished, they brought him to Jerusalem, to present him to the Lord;

[23] (As it is written in the law of the Lord, Every male that opens the womb shall be called holy to the Lord;)

[24] And to offer a sacrifice according to that which is said in the law of the Lord, A pair of turtledoves, or two young pigeons.

[25] And, behold, there was a man in Jerusalem, whose name was Simeon; and the same man was just and devout, waiting for the consolation of Israel: and the Holy Ghost was upon him.

[26] And it was revealed to him by the Holy Ghost, that he should not see death, before he had seen the Lord's Christ.

[27] And he came by the Spirit into the temple: and when the parents brought in the child Jesus, to do for him after the custom of the law,

[28] Then took he him up in his arms, and blessed God, and said,

[29] Lord, now let you your servant depart in peace, according to your word:

[30] For my eyes have seen your salvation,

[31] Which you have prepared before the face of all people;

[32] A light to lighten the Gentiles, and the glory of your people Israel.

[33] And Joseph and his mother marveled at those things which were spoken of him.

[34] And Simeon blessed them, and said to Mary his mother, Behold, this child is set for the fall and rising again of many in Israel; and for a sign which shall be spoken against;

[35] (Yea, a sword shall pierce through your own soul also,) that the thoughts of many hearts may be revealed.

[36] And there was one Anna, a prophetess, the daughter of Phanuel, of the tribe of Aser: she was of a great age, and had lived with a husband seven years from her virginity;

[37] And she was a widow of about fourscore and four years, which departed not from the temple, but served God with fastings and prayers night and day.

[38] And she coming in that instant gave thanks likewise to the Lord, and

spoke of him to all them that looked for redemption in Jerusalem.
[39] And when they had performed all things according to the law of the Lord,
they returned into Galilee, to their own city Nazareth.
[40] And the child grew, and grew strong in spirit, filled with wisdom: and the
grace of God was upon him.
[41] Now his parents went to Jerusalem every year at the feast of the Passover.

We are told, as a youth Jesus was bright and articulate. He debated with the older men and Rabbis in the city he lived. They argued about the scripture and the law. Jesus then disappears from the time he was 12 until he was about 30 years old. It is here we pick up the story.

Luke 3 English Standard Version (ESV)

John the Baptist Prepares the Way
3 In the fifteenth year of the reign of Tiberius Caesar, Pontius Pilate being governor of Judea, and Herod being tetrarch of Galilee, and his brother Philip tetrarch of the region of Ituraea and Trachonitis, and Lysanias tetrarch of Abilene, 2 during the high priesthood of Annas and Caiaphas, the word of God came to John the son of Zechariah in the wilderness. 3 And he went into all the region around the Jordan, proclaiming a baptism of repentance for the forgiveness of sins. 4 As it is written in the book of the words of Isaiah the prophet,

"The voice of one crying in the wilderness:
'Prepare the way of the Lord,
  make his paths straight.
5 Every valley shall be filled,
  and every mountain and hill shall be made low,
and the crooked shall become straight,
  and the rough places shall become level ways,
6 and all flesh shall see the salvation of God.'"
7 He said therefore to the crowds that came out to be baptized by him, "You brood of vipers! Who warned you to flee from the wrath to come? 8 Bear fruits in keeping with repentance. And do not begin to say to yourselves, 'We have Abraham as our father.' For I tell you, God is able from these stones to raise up children for Abraham. 9 Even now the axe is laid to the root of the trees. Every tree therefore that does not bear good fruit is cut down and thrown into the fire."

10 And the crowds asked him, "What then shall we do?" 11 And he answered them, "Whoever has two tunics is to share with him who has none, and whoever has food is to do likewise." 12 Tax collectors also came to be baptized and said to him, "Teacher, what shall we do?" 13 And he said to them, "Collect no more than you are authorized to do." 14 Soldiers also asked him, "And we, what shall we do?" And he said to them, "Do not extort money from anyone by threats or by false accusation, and be content with your wages."

15 As the people were in expectation, and all were questioning in their hearts concerning John, whether he might be the Christ, 16 John answered them all, saying, "I baptize you with water, but he who is mightier than I is coming, the strap of whose sandals I am not worthy to untie. He will baptize you with the Holy Spirit and fire. 17 His winnowing fork is in his hand, to clear his threshing floor and to gather the wheat into his barn, but the chaff he will burn with unquenchable fire."

18 So with many other exhortations he preached good news to the people. 19 But Herod the tetrarch, who had been reproved by him for Herodias, his brother's wife, and for all the evil things that Herod had done, 20 added this to them all, that he locked up John in prison.

21 Now when all the people were baptized, and when Jesus also had been baptized and was praying, the heavens were opened, 22 and the Holy Spirit descended on him in bodily form, like a dove; and a voice came from heaven, "You are my beloved Son; with you I am well pleased."

Luke 4English Standard Version (ESV)

The Temptation of Jesus
4 And Jesus, full of the Holy Spirit, returned from the Jordan and was led by the Spirit in the wilderness 2 for forty days, being tempted by the devil. And he ate nothing during those days. And when they were ended, he was hungry. 3 The devil said to him, "If you are the Son of God, command this stone to become bread." 4 And Jesus answered him, "It is written, 'Man shall not live by bread alone.'" 5 And the devil took him up and showed him all the kingdoms of the world in a moment of time, 6 and said to him, "To you I will give all this authority and their glory, for it has been delivered to me, and I give it to whom I will. 7 If you, then, will worship me, it will all be yours." 8 And Jesus answered him, "It is written,

Dr. Joseph Lumpkin

"'You shall worship the Lord your God,
  and him only shall you serve.'"
9 And he took him to Jerusalem and set him on the pinnacle of the temple and said to him, "If you are the Son of God, throw yourself down from here, 10 for it is written,

"'He will command his angels concerning you,
  to guard you,'
11 and

"'On their hands they will bear you up,
  lest you strike your foot against a stone.'"
12 And Jesus answered him, "It is said, 'You shall not put the Lord your God to the test.'" 13 And when the devil had ended every temptation, he departed from him until an opportune time.

Jesus Begins His Ministry
14 And Jesus returned in the power of the Spirit to Galilee, and a report about him went out through all the surrounding country. 15 And he taught in their synagogues, being glorified by all.

Jesus Rejected at Nazareth
16 And he came to Nazareth, where he had been brought up. And as was his custom, he went to the synagogue on the Sabbath day, and he stood up to read. 17 And the scroll of the prophet Isaiah was given to him. He unrolled the scroll and found the place where it was written,

18 "The Spirit of the Lord is upon me,
  because he has anointed me
  to proclaim good news to the poor.
He has sent me to proclaim liberty to the captives
  and recovering of sight to the blind,
  to set at liberty those who are oppressed,
19 to proclaim the year of the Lord's favor."
20 And he rolled up the scroll and gave it back to the attendant and sat down. And the eyes of all in the synagogue were fixed on him. 21 And he began to say to them, "Today this Scripture has been fulfilled in your hearing." 22 And all spoke well of him and marveled at the gracious words that were coming from his mouth. And they said, "Is not this Joseph's son?"

We are all familiar with the rest of the story of how Jesus chose his disciples, perfomed miricles, and taught a doctrine of love and forgiveness. His Sermon on the Mount sums up his beliefs.

Blessed are the poor in spirit,
for theirs is the kingdom of heaven.
Blessed are those who mourn,
for they will be comforted.
Blessed are the meek,
for they will inherit the earth.
Blessed are those who hunger and thirst for righteousness,
for they will be filled.
Blessed are the merciful,
for they will be shown mercy.
Blessed are the pure in heart,
for they will see God.
Blessed are the peacemakers,
for they will be called sons of God.
Blessed are those who are persecuted because of righteousness,
for theirs is the kingdom of heaven.
Blessed are you when people insult you, persecute you and falsely say all kinds
of evil against you because of me.
Rejoice and be glad, because great is your reward in heaven, for in the same
way they persecuted the prophets who were before you. (Matt. 5:1-12)

After beginning his Jewish sect, Jesus would be killed for sedition and radical teachings, which put the balance of power between the Romans and Jews in an off balanced condition.

We are told Jesus rose from the dead and continued to meet and teach his disciples until he was taken up into heaven.

In the beginning of Christianity, the religion was simply a new sect of Judaism. In a book called the Didache, written in the first century CE, we find a snapshot of the new faith. In this period of time it appears Jesus was not considered to be God, part of God, or any kind of deity.

In a time when Jewish Christianity was less refined and organized and followers were faced with defining the major elements of the emergent Christian faith, it was the Didache that offered the first textbook of worship. Importance is given to the way of life, to prophecy, to communal gatherings, to the apocalypse, and to the soon return of Jesus.

Within the teaching of the Didache, "Jesus Christ" is only mentioned once, during the rite of broken bread (9:3-4). The sharing of Eucharistic bread is not the reason for the gathering. There is no mention of the one body of Christ (1 Corinthians, 10:17). The breaking of bread is a foretaste and anticipation of the return of Christ and the perfection of self and community his return will bring, when all are united, and the "end time" brings restoration of holiness, peace, and complete harmony with God and His followers.

Christ is not mentioned during the rite of cup (9:2), neither does this title appear in the communal thanksgiving prayer, which is offered after the meal.
During the Eucharist (9:2-3, 10:2-3) Jesus is called "servant" (Greek "pais") of the Father and "Christ" (anointed) only once and his connection with the "broken bread" is referenced in 9:4.

The early Christian community believed the beginning of the "end time" and the coming apocalypse was heralded with the arrival and death of Jesus. It is the space of time between then and the return of Jesus that we deal with here.

In the Didache, the traditional Jewish custom of drinking wine, breaking bread and saying thanks after the meal was not made referring to Christ nor was the meal or thanksgiving looking to the relationship between bread and wine and the Body and Blood of the "Son of God". The love-meal (agape) was rooted in the Eucharist but became isolated only after the ritual meal of Judaism and the Eucharist were separated. At the time there were many pagan religions conducting rituals in which there was symbolic eating of the "flesh" of a sacrificial victim or "god". The ceremony was common throughout the Middle East with the mystery cults, such as Mithraism, Isis and Osiris, Greek mysteries, and other religious festivals. The rituals proposed in the Didache are not about this pagan practice but are firmly rooted in the tradition of Jewish prayer and community. Didache 10 is suggestive of the "birkat ha-mazon", a thanksgiving prayer at the end of the Jewish supper.

There is no mention that Christ is god who came in the flesh and died on the cross for our sins. This notion became the basis for the Christian Mass later.

(It should be noted, as odd as it may seem to modern Christians, that there were those who believed that Jesus was born of a virgin but still rejected his divinity. One idea does not follow the other.)

The disagreement between Eastern and Western Christianity as to the precise moment that consecration of the host happens within the Mass (both positions being without empirical proof) caused a schism between Eastern and Western Christianity. The West believes at the mention of "the Son" there is consecration (and transubstantiation), whereas the East invokes the Holy Spirit to effect the change of the substances of the Eucharist from bread to the flesh of Jesus.

There is a parallel between Didache 9:5 where a logia is mentioned and the Gospel of Thomas.

If we examine what became the Lord's Prayer we find it fairly intact.
"When you pray, say:
'Father, may Your Name be holy.
May Your rule take place.
Always give us our bread.
Forgive us our debts,
for we ourselves forgive everyone that is indebted to us.
And lead us away from a trying situation'."
Q1, logia 42-44.

The word "epiousios" (8:2) is usually translated as "daily". This translation is somewhat arbitrary but became ubiquitous and thus the accepted rendering. The word "epiousion" has "epi" and "ousia as its parts. Epi means, "it is present" or "it happens". "Ousia" means "substance or essence". It refers to the "bread". If "epiousion" is understood as a "spiritual" process happening with the bread, then this word can be read as, "Give us now our spiritual bread."

The early Christians believed that Christ would come back within their lifetime. Their liturgies served to remind them of the imminent return. The love feast or Eucharist was not part of His death as it is today.

There was no interpretation of "bread" as the "Body of Christ", nor is there a trace of the "this is My body" - "this is My blood". The meal - the Eucharist - was a gathering and a meal as a rehearsal and reminder of what communal unity and love was to come. To experience the presence of Christ by anticipating his return is evidenced in the Didache. This is the only text we have containing liturgical information about the Q-communities, of which the Essenes belonged.

The Didache shows little to no "Pauline" Christianity. Paul would have been present but his influence had not yet been fully established. It was James, the brother of Jesus, who was the "heir apparent" after the death of Jesus. James headed the Jewish Christian movement. Although Peter may have had a high status it was James who became the head of the Christian church or ministry in Jerusalem, which was considered the holiest position at the time. James wished to continue closer to the line of Judaism but Paul wished to reach out to the Pagan Gentile population. Later, the Catholic Church would view Peter as the apostle of succession and attempt to trace the papal lineage back to him, however Paul, it seems, had the greatest influence on Christianity and much of our faith today is Christianity as interpreted by Paul.

In the Book of Acts we are told Paul and Barnabas came back to Jerusalem to speak to the Apostles. The apostles, led by James, gave them a list of things to do. It was an odd list.

Acts 15:29 You are to abstain from food sacrificed to idols, from blood, from the meat of strangled animals and from sexual immorality. You will do well to avoid these things.
  Farewell.

The major problem between Jews and the Gentile converts had to do with the Gentile's continuation to worship their idols and act according to that worship instead of the Christian way. All recommendations have a connection with pagan idol worship, of which sex acts and various forms of animal sacrifice and feast were part.

Ex 20:2-6
2 I am the LORD your God, who brought you out of Egypt, out of the land of slavery.
3 You shall have no other gods before me.

4 You shall not make for yourself an idol in the form of anything in heaven above or on the earth beneath or in the waters below.
5You shall not bow down to them or worship them; for I, the LORD your God, am a jealous God, punishing the children for the sin of the fathers to the third and fourth generation of those who hate me,
6but showing love to a thousand [generations] of those who love me and keep my commandments.

Other "suggestions" are based on the 7th commandment and the Gentile's immorality. This is because such immorality was connected to idol worship.
Ex 20:14
"You shall not commit adultery.

The list of restrictions aimed at the Gentiles addressed only the major issues so the other commandments were not discussed. The Gentiles were not given license to break the other commandments. It was simply that those other offenses were not an issue.

All recommendations were based on common practices among the Gentiles who were recently converted. Gentiles couldn't consume food and drinks of close friends and relatives who sacrificed to idols.

Gentiles did not have to be circumcised to prove that they were Christians, but they had to avoid continuing certain practices. In other words, Gentile Christians should not have to become officially like their Jewish brethren through circumcision, but they should avoid identifying themselves as pagans through practices.

In the early days of Christianity the movement was considered an offshoot sect of Judaism. Soon the main trunk of the sect began to split into three major branches, although even these main branches soon began to splinter. We will first look at the main divisions and discuss the minor differences within the subdivisions later.

The Didache captures a snapshot of Christianity before it was infiltrated with the pagan religions, which surrounded the areas of Christian concentration, Jerusalem and Rome.

One of the main influences was the religion of Mithras.

Virtually all of the elements of Orthodox Christian rituals, from miter, wafer, water baptism, alter, and doxology, were adopted from the Mithras and earlier pagan mystery religions. The religion of Mithras preceded Christianity by roughly six hundred years. However, it was very active in Rome from the 1st to 4th centuries C.E.

(1) According to the Mithras myth, Mithras was born on December 25th as an offspring of the Sun. Next to the gods Ormuzd and Ahrimanes, Mithras held the highest rank among the gods of ancient Persia. He was represented as a beautiful youth and a Mediator. Reverend J. W. Lake states: "Mithras is spiritual light contending with spiritual darkness, and through his labors the kingdom of darkness shall be lit with heaven's own light; the Eternal will receive all things back into his favor, the world will be redeemed to God. The impure are to be purified, and the evil made good, through the mediation of Mithras, the reconciler of Ormuzd and Ahriman. Mithras is the Good, his name is Love. In relation to the Eternal he is the source of grace, in relation to man he is the life-giver and mediator" (Plato, Philo, and Paul, p. 15).

(2) Mithras was considered a great teacher and master. He had twelve companions and traveled with performing miracles.

(3) Mithras was called "the good shepherd, "the way, the truth and the light, redeemer, savior, Messiah." He was identified with both the lion and the lamb.

(4) The International Encyclopedia states: "Mithras seems to have owed his prominence to the belief that he was the source of life, and could also redeem the souls of the dead into the better world ... The ceremonies included a sort of baptism to remove sins, anointing, and a sacred meal of bread and water, while a consecrated wine, believed to possess wonderful power, played a prominent part."

(5) Chambers Encyclopedia says: "The most important of his many festivals was his birthday, celebrated on the 25th of December, the day subsequently fixed -- against all evidence -- Baptism and the partaking of a mystical liquid, consisting of flour and water, to be drunk with the utterance of sacred formulas, were among the inauguration acts."

(6) Prof. Franz Cumont, of the University of Ghent, writes as follows

concerning the religion of Mithras and the religion of Christ: "Followers of Mithras also held Sunday sacred, and celebrated the birth of the Sun on the 25th of December...." (The Mysteries of Mithras, pp. 190, 191).

(7) Reverend Charles Biggs stated: "The disciples of Mithra formed an organized church, with a developed hierarchy. They possessed the ideas of Mediation, Atonement, and a Savior, who is human and yet divine, and not only the idea, but a doctrine of the future life. They had a Eucharist, and a Baptism, and other curious analogies might be pointed out between their system and the church of Christ (The Christian Platonists, p. 240).

(8) In Roman catacombs a relic of Mithraic worship was preserved. It was a picture of the infant Mithras seated in the lap of his virgin mother, while on their knees before him were Persian Magi adoring him and offering gifts.

(9) He was buried in a tomb and after three days he rose again. His resurrection was celebrated every year.

(10) The Christian Father Manes, founder of the heretical sect known as Manicheans, believed that Christ and Mithras were one. His teaching, according to Mosheim, was as follows: "Christ is that glorious intelligence which the Persians called Mithras ... His residence is in the sun" (Ecclesiastical History, 3rd century, Part 2, ch. 5).

We can see from the above list that there may have been a "cross-pollination" of stories and myths between religions. We must take care not to throw out truth simply because it is mimicked in paganism. Just because a pattern occurs in another religion, it does not make the pattern in Christianity incorrect. We must simply strip off the contamination to find the original and true belief system.

Above all, to discover the unsullied core of Christianity we dare not go past the Counsel of Nicaea. The Emperor Constantine was thought to be a follower of Mithras who adopted Christianity as a matter of expediency for the purpose of uniting and controlling his subjects, the majority of whom were Christian. While forging this unity he was active in the formation of modern Christian doctrines, such as the trinity. The creed produced under his watchful eye confirms several beliefs held by the followers of Mithras, and likely held by the emperor himself. Jesus would soon be raised to the status of equal to God, God on Earth, and part of the Trinity.

The more "deified" Jesus became the more his mother, Mary, was respected and venerated. Her spiritual elevation would fill a spot in the Catholic Church that would set it apart from other Christian institutions. Mary, like the wife of El, would become the Queen of Heaven.

The Need for a Goddess Remains

A dynamic tension between the psychological need of a feminine energy, and the hesitancy to confer or concede any control to a female exists in modern Judeo-Christian religion and culture.

Carl Jung sums up the archetypes of the female as related to the stages or evolution of man's views toward women in general. To be very clear, Jung's four stages of women are the distinct stages of evolution or maturity within the male psyche and how the man views women.

Jung believed anima or life force development has four distinct levels, which he named Eve, Helen (who we also identify with Mary Magdalene), Mary, the mother of Jesus, and Sophia or Wisdom. In broad terms, the entire process of life force development in a male is about the male subject opening up to emotionality. In doing so, he obtains a broader spirituality by creating a new conscious paradigm that includes the intuitive processes, creativity and imagination, and psychic sensitivity towards himself and others where it might not have existed previously. Since religion is a reflection of the collective psyche, it is very important to examine these stages and how each influences, or have influenced, religious thought regarding women and the place of the Sacred Feminine in Christianity.

Eve

The first is *Eve*, named after the Genesis account of Adam and Eve. It deals with the emergence of a male's object of desire. This coincides with Asherah and her place as a goddess of fertility and procreation.

Helen – Mary Magdalene

The second is *Helen or Mary Magdalene*. Helen is in allusion to Helen of Troy in Greek mythology. In this phase, women are viewed as capable of worldly success and of being self-reliant, intelligent, and insightful, even if not altogether virtuous. This second phase is meant to show a strong schism in external talents (cultivated business and conventional skills) with lacking internal qualities (inability for virtue, lacking faith or imagination).

Although Mary Magdalene was not the prostitute in the biblical account, (that person was never given a name), she did have seven demons and was not considered totally virtuous. Speculation is that

117

Mary Magdalene was wealthy, being from a village that was home to wealthy ship owners and fishermen. She also supplied funds for Jesus' ministry. Luke 8: 1-4 states plainly that Jesus was supported by women, including Mary Magdalene, who "were helping to support Jesus and the Twelve with their own money." (NIRV)

Mary, The Mother
The third phase is *Mary*, named after the Christian theological understanding of the Virgin Mary (Jesus' mother). At this level, the male seems to have a perception of the female (even if in an esoteric and dogmatic way); in so much as, certain activities deemed consciously non-virtuous cannot be applied to her. We will see later how the Catholic Church has elevated Mary through all phases of Jungian feminine archetypes.

Sophia
The fourth and final phase of anima development is *Sophia*, named after the Greek word for wisdom. Complete integration has occurred, which allows females to be seen and related to as particular individuals who possess both positive and negative qualities. The most important aspect of this final level is that, as the personification "Wisdom" suggests, the anima is now developed enough that no single object can fully and permanently contain the images to which it is related. Sophia means wisdom. The name of Wisdom shows up in the Old Testament as a persona, and the consort of God. In Gnostic works, Sophia was the creative force that formed the spirit of man, and Sophia was Eve, who came down to offer knowledge to Adam.

When we look at these stages in detail, we notice that the church has created evolutionary stages within each of these archetypes as the church body works its way back to a balance of male and female forces. Let us look at each category in more detail.

Eve
Eve – her name means "Mother of All Living, Restorer, Reviver." From Eve all human life descends. She is thus the symbol of fertility and procreation. Throughout the life of the church, women have been equated with Eve and her part in the fall of mankind in the garden. In general, the state of Eve in the male psyche has been one of deep

ambivalence. There is an old saying that men hate women as a lame man hates his crutch.

Following are a few quotes from church fathers regarding women and their place in society and religion:

"Rather should the words of the Torah be burned than entrusted to a woman... Whoever teaches his daughter the Torah is like one who teaches her obscenity." *Rabbi Eliezer*

"Do you not know that you are each an Eve? The sentence of God on this sex of yours lives in this age: the guilt must, of necessity, live too. You are the Devil's gateway: You are the unsealer of the forbidden tree: You are the first deserter of the divine law: You are she who persuaded him whom the devil was not valiant enough to attack. You destroyed so easily God's image, man. On account of your desertion, even the Son of God had to die." *St. Tertullian*

"What is the difference whether it is in a wife or a mother, it is still Eve, the temptress that we must beware of in any woman......I fail to see what use woman can be to man, if one excludes the function of bearing children."
St. Augustine of Hippo

"As regards the individual nature, woman is defective and misbegotten, for the active force in the male seed tends to the production of a perfect likeness in the masculine sex; while the production of woman comes from a defect in the active force or from some material indisposition, or even from some external influence."
St. Thomas Aquinas

"If they [women] become tired or even die, that does not matter. Let them die in childbirth, that's why they are there."
Martin Luther

The status of women in the Bible has been disputed for many centuries. Beginning with Eve herself, there is a dynamic split of position and place, owing to the fact that there are two separate accounts of her creation. The traditional church sees the role of Eve as the mother of Cain and Abel, as well as the person who was deceived into sin by Satan.

119

Message Bible - Genesis 1:26-28
God spoke: "Let us make human beings in our image, make them reflecting our nature so they can be responsible for the fish in the sea, the birds in the air, the cattle, and, yes, Earth itself, and every animal that moves on the face of Earth."
27 God created human beings; he created them godlike, reflecting God's nature. He created them male and female. God blessed them: "Prosper! Reproduce! Fill Earth! Take charge!
28 Be responsible for fish in the sea and birds in the air, for every living thing that moves on the face of Earth."

Genesis 2: 21-22
God put the Man into a deep sleep. As he slept he removed one of his ribs and replaced it with flesh. God then used the rib that he had taken from the Man to make Woman and presented her to the Man. (23-25) The Man said, "Finally! Bone of my bone, flesh of my flesh! Name her Woman for she was made from Man." Therefore a man leaves his father and mother and embraces his wife. They become one flesh. The two of them, the Man and his Wife, were naked, but they felt no shame.

In the first account, Genesis 1:26, man and woman was created at the same time. In the second account, Genesis 2: 21, woman was made from man's rib. In the first account, because man and woman were created at the same time, woman was given equal status, but the prevailing ideas of the time did not allow this equality to continue. It was due to this dual storyline and the fact that women were considered inferior to man that the myth of Lilith was born. In this myth, Adam's first wife, Lilith sought to be his equal. The story illustrates the idea of equality was thought to be evil.

God created all things living, and then he created man. He created a man and a woman and gave them dominion over all things. God named the man Adam, and the woman He named Lilith. Both were formed from the dust of the earth and in both God breathed the breath of life. They became human souls and God endowed them with the power of speech.
Created at the same time, in the same way, there was no master, no leader, and only bickering between them. Lilith said, "I will not be below you, in life or during sex. I want the superior position." But Adam would not

relent and insisted God had created him to be the head of the family and in the affairs of earth. Lilith was enraged and would not submit.

Then God communed with Adam in the cool of the evening and as he entered into His presence, Adam appealed to God. As God fellowshipped with them, they reasoned together, Adam, Lilith, and the living God. But Lilith would not listen to God or Adam. Seeing that with two people of equal authority there could be no solution, Lilith became frustrated, angry, and intractable. Finally, enraged and defiant, she pronounced the holy and ineffable name of God. Corrupting the power of the name, she flew into the air, changing form, and disappeared, soaring out of sight.

Adam stood alone, confused, praying. "Lord of the universe," he said, "The woman you gave me has run away." At once, three holy angels were dispatched to bring her back to Adam. The angels overtook Lilith as she passed over the sea, in the area where Moses would later pass through. The angels ordered Lilith to come with them in the name and by the authority of the most high God, but she refused. As her rebellion increased, she changed, becoming more and more ugly and demonic.

God spoke into Lilith's heart, saying, "You have chosen this evil path, and so shall you become evil. You are cursed from now until the end of days." Lilith spoke to the angels and said, "I have become this, created to cause sickness, to kill children, which I will never have, and to torment men." With these words, she completed her demonic transformation. Her form was that of a succubus.

Confined to the night, she was destined to roam the earth, seeking newborn babes, stealing their lives, and strangling them in their sleep. She torments men even now, causing lust and evil dreams. Her rebellious and evil spirit forever traps her. Bound in the darkness of her own heart, Lilith became the mistress and lover to legions of demons. And Adam's countenance fell and he mourned, for he had loved Lilith, and he was again alone and lonely.

God said, "It is not good for man to be alone." And the Lord God caused a deep sleep to fall on him, and he slept, and He took from Adam a rib from among his ribs for the woman, and this rib was the origin of the woman. And He built up the flesh in its place, and created the woman. He awakened Adam out of his sleep. On awakening Adam rose on the sixth day, and God brought her to Adam, and he knew her, and said to her, "This is now bone of my bones and flesh of my flesh; she shall be called woman for she was taken from man, and she shall be called my wife; because she was taken from her husband."

Mary Magdalene

Mary Magdalene, the woman who the Jews considered deeply damaged by demonic possession, was set free by the man, Jesus, and she followed him to the end. She was a strong, committed, and determined woman, but she was a woman nonetheless. The apostles challenged Jesus because they believed he would be judged harshly by the masses for being too close to Mary. Recent discoveries have led scholars to believe Magdala, the city from which Mary came and whose name is derived from the place-name, was likely a woman of means. The city was known for its ships and fishing industry, and Mary possibly was part of the fishing industry and could have owned ships. Mary Magdalene was most likely bankrolling part of the ministry of Jesus.

She was a woman who followed Jesus as he ministered and preached.

Luke 8:1-3: Afterward, Jesus journeyed from one town and village to another, preaching and proclaiming the good news of the kingdom of God. Accompanying him were the Twelve and some women who had been cured of evil spirits and infirmities, Mary, called Magdalene, from whom seven demons had gone out, Joanna, the wife of Herod's steward Chuza, Susanna, and many others who provided for them out of their resources.

She was there when Jesus was crucified.

Mark 15:40: There were also some women looking on from a distance, among whom were Mary Magdalene, and Mary, the mother of James the Less and Joses, and Salome.

Matthew 27:56: Among them was Mary Magdalene, and Mary, the mother of James and Joseph, and the mother of the sons of Zebedee.

John 19:25: But standing by the cross of Jesus were His mother, and His mother's sister, Mary, the wife of Clopas, and Mary Magdalene.

She continued to believe in Jesus after he was killed.

Mark 15:47: Mary Magdalene and Mary, the mother of Joses, were looking on to see where He was laid.

Matthew 27:61: And Mary Magdalene was there, and the other Mary, sitting opposite the grave.

Matthew 28:1: Now after the Sabbath, as it began to dawn toward the first day of the week, Mary Magdalene and the other Mary came to look at the grave.

Mark 16:1: When the Sabbath was over, Mary Magdalene, and Mary, the mother of James, and Salome, bought spices, so that they might come and anoint Him.

She was the first to realize and announce the resurrection of Jesus.
John 20:1: Now, on the first day of the week, Mary Magdalene came early to the tomb, while it was still dark, and saw the stone already taken away from the tomb.

Mark 16:9: Now after He had risen early on the first day of the week, He first appeared to Mary Magdalene, from whom He had cast out seven demons.

John 20:18: Mary Magdalene came, announcing to the disciples, "I have seen the Lord," and that He had said these things to her.

Luke 24: But at daybreak on the first day of the week [the women] took the spices they had prepared and went to the tomb. They found the stone rolled away from the tomb; but when they entered, they did not find the body of the Lord Jesus. While they were puzzling over this, behold, two men in dazzling garments appeared to them. They were terrified and bowed their faces to the ground. They said to them, "Why do you seek the living one among the dead?

He is not here, but he has been raised. Remember what he said to you while he was still in Galilee, that the Son of Man must be handed over to sinners and be crucified, and rise on the third day." And they remembered his words.

Then they returned from the tomb and announced all these things to the eleven and to all the others.

The women were Mary Magdalene, Joanna, and Mary, the mother of James; the others who accompanied them also told this to the apostles, but their story seemed like nonsense and they did not believe them.

Most Gnostic Christians held to the idea of the duality of sexes playing out in multiple layers. The feminine force of Sophia became the feminine force of the Holy Spirit and was made the bride of God. The

123

gender duality continued when the feminine force of the Holy Spirit inhabited the perfect man, Jesus, making him the Messiah. The gender context is ripe for the story to be continued in the persons of Jesus and Mary Magdalene, physically shadowing the spiritual relationship of the Holy Spirit and the Supreme God, as well as Jesus and the Holy Spirit.

The concept of a married Jesus is revealed in several verses of The Gospel of Philip, such as verse 118.

"There is the Son of Man and there is the son of the son of Man. The Lord is the Son of Man, and his son creates through him. God gave the Son of Man the power to create; he also gave him the ability to have children."

If one were to examine the writings of Solomon, the play on words between the masculine and feminine, and the spiritual aspects can clearly be seen. The Gnostics simply expanded on the theme.

Song of Solomon 1 (King James Version)
1 The song of songs, which is Solomon's.
2 Let him kiss me with the kisses of his mouth: for thy love is better than wine.
3 Because of the savor of thy good ointments thy name is as ointment poured forth, therefore do the virgins love thee.
4 Draw me, we will run after thee: the king hath brought me into his chambers: we will be glad and rejoice in thee, we will remember thy love more than wine.

Song of Solomon 2
16 My beloved is mine, and I am his: he feedeth among the lilies.
17 Until the day break, and the shadows flee away, turn, my beloved, and be thou like a roe or a young hart upon the mountains of Bether.

Song of Solomon 3
1 By night on my bed I sought him whom my soul loveth: I sought him, but I found him not.
2 I will rise now, and go about the city in the streets, and in the broad ways I will seek him whom my soul loveth: I sought him, but I found him not...

Song of Solomon 5

1 I am come into my garden, my sister, my spouse: I have gathered my myrrh with my spice; I have eaten my honeycomb with my honey; I have drunk my wine with my milk: eat, O friends; drink, yea, drink abundantly, O beloved.

2 I sleep, but my heart waketh: it is the voice of my beloved that knocketh, saying, Open to me, my sister, my love, my dove, my undefiled: for my head is filled with dew, and my locks with the drops of the night.

3 I have put off my coat; how shall I put it on? I have washed my feet; how shall I defile them?

4 My beloved put in his hand by the hole of the door, and my bowels were moved for him.

5 I rose up to open to my beloved; and my hands dropped with myrrh, and my fingers with sweet smelling myrrh, upon the handles of the lock.

Song of Solomon 7
1 How beautiful are thy feet with shoes, O prince's daughter! the joints of thy thighs are like jewels, the work of the hands of a cunning workman.

2 Thy navel is like a round goblet, which wanteth not liquor: thy belly is like an heap of wheat set about with lilies.

3 Thy two breasts are like two young roes that are twins.

Due to the inherent dualism of Gnosticism, sex was a symbol, and at times, a portal to a mystical experience. Many religions are replete with sexual allegories, as was Gnosticism. Proceeding from the two points of physical metaphor in Gnostic literature and the likelihood of marriage among the population of Jewish men, controversy arose when speculation began as to whether Jesus could have married. The flames of argument roared into inferno proportions when the translation of the books of Philip and Mary Magdalene were published.

"And the companion (Consort) was Mary of Magdala (Mary Magdalene). The Lord loved Mary more than all the other disciples and he kissed her often on her mouth (the text is missing here and the word "mouth" is assumed). The others saw his love for Mary and asked him: "Why do you love her more than all of us?" The Savior replied, "Why do I not love you in the same way I love her?"
The Gospel of Philip

Peter said to Mary; "Sister we know that the Savior loved you more than all other women. Tell us the words of the Savior that you remember and know, but we have not heard and do not know. Mary answered him and said; "I will tell you what He hid from you."

The Gospel of Mary Magdalene

Mary was a sinful, damaged, redeemed, and s powerful person. It is the myth woven into the story of Mary Magdalene that endears her to us. To many, she is the captive. Possessed, enslaved, caught in the midst of crime and tragedy, she was at once redeemed, set free, and loved by God himself. (Mary was connected to the story of a prostitute, but this is not the case.) She is hope and triumph. She represents the power of truth and love to change the life of the lowest and most powerless of us. She is you and I in search of God.

Mary, The Mother of Jesus

The evolution of the status of Mary, the mother of Jesus, is the attempt by the collective psyche of the church to find the correct place for the feminine energies of God. However, since the church leaders have not reconciled the balance of masculine and feminine parts of God, Mary was chosen as a surrogate to be endowed with some of these qualities.

Rising to another level of the Sacred Feminine, *Ruak* becomes the female part of the Godhead that impregnated Mary to produce Jesus. The same spirit empowered Jesus by coming down in the visage of a dove. Mary was visited and carried this spirit within her womb. It is natural that she would come to be equated with the same mothering, nurturing, Sacred Feminine.

The Catholic Church diminished the status of women at the same time they struggled to make sense of their own female redeemer. They elevated Mother Mary by announcing the doctrine of the Immaculate Conception, and, as a result, errors in logic were exposed. If Mother Mary was conceived without sin in order to carry Jesus, who was conceived without sin, one must ask why wasn't it necessary for the mother of Mary to be conceived without sin also? This logic continues backward ad infinitum until arriving back to Eve herself. Thus, all female offspring must be sinless. Of course, the church flatly refuses this line of reasoning, saying only that certain things must be taken on faith. This is the same tactic used regarding the "Ever-Virginity" of Mother Mary, even in the face of scriptures proclaiming that the mother, sister, and brothers of Jesus had come to have audience with him.

The Greek Orthodox Church already had the answer to this dilemma. Original sin is not in their doctrine. They state only that humans are born with a pre-disposition toward sinning. This eliminates the problem of sinless birth from the beginning.

Even though the theological events of doctrine concerning Mother Mary occurred over time, they serve as an undeniable pattern of the Catholic Church as it endeavored to "purify" women and rid them of sexuality. It is within Mary that we find the complete evolution of the Sacred Feminine, but with her sexuality systematically muted and removed.

Beginning as a teenage girl, dismissed by society as a lowly female, she was, over time, elevated to a position in the Catholic Church that places her alongside, although not quite equal to, the savior himself. Some of the positions of the Catholic Church regarding Mary were not officially accepted until the mid to late nineteenth century.

In the writings of the early church fathers (Justin Martyr 165 A.D. and Irenaeus 202 A.D.), seldom mentioned Mother Mary and only then to contrast Mary's obedience with Eve's disobedience. The doctrine of Mary as Theotokos (God-bearer) probably originated in Alexandria and was first introduced by Origen. This doctrine became common in the fourth century and was accepted at the Council of Ephesus in 431 A.D.

Since the accepted Christian church continued to slip farther and farther toward the conviction that sex was evil, the doctrine of the "Ever-Virginity" of Mary was established. This was the idea that Mary conceived as a virgin, but also remained a virgin even after giving birth to Jesus and thereafter, for the rest of her life. The Catholic Church rejected the idea that Mary had other children, although the Bible speaks of the brothers and sisters of Jesus. The doctrine of "virginity" was established around 359 A.D.

St. Gregory of Tours formally developed the doctrine of the bodily Assumption of Mary around 594 A.D. This doctrine stated that Mary, the mother of Jesus, was taken up into heaven to be seated at the side of Jesus. The idea has been present in apocryphal texts since the late fourth century. The Feast of the Assumption became widespread in the sixth century, and sermons on that occasion tended to emphasize Mary's power in heaven.

Of all the doctrines regarding Mary, the doctrine of the Immaculate Conception widened the divide between the Catholic churches and other Christian churches. This doctrine took the position that Mother

127

Mary was born without the stain of original sin. Both Catholics and Orthodox Christians accept this doctrine, but only the Roman Catholic Church has named it "The Immaculate Conception" and articulated it as doctrine.

Eastern Orthodox Christians reject the western doctrine of original sin, preferring instead to speak of a tendency towards sin. They believe Mary was born without sin, but so was everyone else. Mary simply never gave in to sin.

As we see in the following statement, the doctrine was not formally accepted until 1854 A.D. "The Most Blessed Virgin Mary was, from the first moment of her conception, by a singular grace and privilege of almighty God and by virtue of the merits of Jesus Christ, Savior of the human race, preserved immune from all stain of original sin."
Pope Pius IX, Ineffabilis Deus (1854)

We will examine the four Marian dogmas, among a large number of other teachings about Mary, and how they mirror the evolution of the Scared Feminine.

Perpetual Virginity – Established in the Third Century – Proclaims that Mary was a virgin before, during, and after the birth of Jesus.

Mother of God – First Council of Ephesus in 431 A.D. - Mary is truly the mother of God, because of her unity with Christ, the Son of God.

Immaculate Conception – Pope Pius IX (1854) Mary, at her conception, was preserved immaculate from the original sin

Assumption into Heaven – Pope Pius XII (1950) - Mary, having completed the course of her earthly life, was assumed body and soul into heavenly glory.

'*Perpetual Virginity of Mary*', means that Mary was a virgin before, during and after giving birth.

Mary was a teenage unwed mother in a world where such things brought shame and death by stoning. Beginning in the general status as Eve, stressing only her lowly station as a younger woman married to an older man for the purpose of procreation and service, she is raised by the doctrine of "Ever-Virginity" to one that is a step above the norm, being without sin when it comes to her primary purpose of procreation.

This oldest Marian dogma from the Roman Catholic, Eastern Orthodox, and Oriental Orthodox Churches affirms in their doctrine that the virginity of Mary, mother of Jesus is "real and perpetual even in the act of giving birth to the Son of God made Man." According to this doctrine, Jesus was her only biological son, whose incarnation and nativity are miraculous.

In the year 107 A.D., Ignatius of Antioch described the virginity of Mary as "hidden from the prince of this world ... loudly proclaimed, but wrought in the silence of God." The Gospel of James, a text written around 120-150 A.D., was concerned with the character and purity of Mary. The text claims that Joseph had children from a marriage previous to Mary. However, the text does not explicitly assert the doctrine of perpetual virginity. The earliest such surviving reference is Origen's *Commentary on Matthew*, where he cites the *Protoevangelium* in support. By the fourth century, the doctrine was generally accepted. Athanasius described Mary as "Ever-Virgin."

In Thomas Aquinas' teaching, (*Summa Theologiae* III.28.2), Mary gave birth painlessly in miraculous fashion without opening of the womb and without injury to the hymen. *"From the first formulations of her faith, the Church has confessed that Jesus was conceived solely by the power of the Holy Spirit in the womb of the Virgin Mary, affirming also the corporeal aspect of this event: Jesus was conceived "by the Holy Spirit without human seed."*

Her corporal integrity was not affected by giving birth. The Church does not teach how this occurred physically, but insists that virginity during childbirth is different from virginity of conception. *Pope Pius XII*

Mystici Corporis: *"Within her virginal womb she brought into life Christ our Lord in a marvelous birth." This indicated the miraculous nature of the Virgin birth. In fact, this was the first act that removed the stain of sex from Mary, making her a virgin forever. She is now a woman removed from the natural cause and effect of her sexuality.*

Mary is truly the *Mother of God.*

Even though Mary was innocent of adultery, as Joseph first thought when she announced her pregnancy, and the sin of coitus was removed from her by declaring her a perpetual virgin, when it came to procreation, she remained a woman in service to men, being different from other women, but not reverenced. In this proclamation, the church elevated Mary to the heights of womanhood, announcing that she is "Theotokos," Mother-of-God, where she began to be honored.

After the Church fathers found common ground on Mary's virginity before, during, and after giving birth, this was the first specifically Marian doctrine to be formally defined by the Church. The definition *Mother of God* (in Greek: Theotokos) was formally affirmed at the Third Ecumenical Council held at Ephesus in 431 A.D. The competing view, advocated by the Patriarch of Constantinople, Nestorius of Constantinople, was that Mary should be called *Christotokos*, meaning, "Birth-giver of Christ," to restrict her role only to the mother of Christ's humanity and not his divine nature.

The holy virgin gave birth in the flesh to God, united with the flesh according to hypostasis, and for that reason, we call her *Theotokos...* If anyone does not confess that Emmanuel is, in truth, God, and, therefore, that the holy virgin is *Theotokos* (for she bore, in a fleshly manner, the Word from God become flesh), let him be anathema (banned, exiled, excommunicated)." *(Cyril's third letter to Nestorius)*

Immaculate Conception of Mary
Mary was conceived without original sin.

For Mary to be so different from other women, there must have been a divine intervention from the beginning. The answer was a miracle that kept Mary from the sin of being fully human. To be fully human, according to the church, one is born as a sinful creature. This is the first doctrine to hint that the most righteous woman could be as sinless as the most righteous man, Jesus, since both were conceived without sin.

According to the Roman Catholic Church, Immaculate Conception is the conception of a child without any stain of original sin in her mother's womb: the dogma states that, from the first moment of her existence, she (Mary) was preserved by God from the sin that afflicts mankind, and that she was instead filled with Divine Grace. It is further believed that she lived a life completely free from sin. Her immaculate conception in the womb of her mother, by normal coitus (Christian tradition identifies her parents as Joachim and Anne), should not be confused with the doctrine of the virginal conception of her son, Jesus.

Pope Sixtus IV established the feast of the Immaculate Conception, celebrated on December 8, in 1476. Pope Pius IX, in his constitution *Ineffabilis Deus*, on December 8, 1854, solemnly defined the Immaculate Conception as a dogma, a truth, not merely an implied condition, by the deposit of faith, and discerned by the Church under the infallible guidance of the Holy Spirit. However, the dogma is specifically and explicitly contained as an object of supernatural faith in the Public Revelation of the Deposit of Faith.

Mary is Mother of all Christians – 1579 A.D.

Obedience to God, perfect faith, and the church's position, which removed Mary from the sin that besets all who are "born of woman," has positioned Mary as the perfect mother. God has been born from her sinless body. She has raised and mothered God himself. In doing so, she has given birth to the church. Now she is given the status of the greatest mother in the world and is crowned as "Mother of all Christians."

The Catholic Church teaches that the Virgin Mary is mother of the Church and of all its members, namely all Christians. The Catechism of the Catholic Church states:

"The Virgin Mary . . . is acknowledged and honoured as being truly the Mother of God and of the redeemer.... She is 'clearly the mother of the members of Christ' . . . since she has by her charity joined in bringing about the birth of believers in the Church, who are members of its head." "Mary, Mother of Christ, Mother of the Church."

Mary is seen as mother of all Christians because in scripture, Christians are said to spiritually become part of the body of Christ, and Mary bore Christ in her body. Jesus adopts Christians as his "brothers and sisters." They, therefore, share the Fatherhood of God and also the motherhood of Mary with Him. To back up this stance, in the Book of John, Jesus, as he is about to die, gives the apostle John to Mary as her son, and gives Mary to John as his mother. John, as the sole remaining apostle remaining steadfast with Jesus, is taken to represent all loyal followers of Jesus from that time on.

Pope John Paul II, in his work, "Totus Tuus" was inspired by the writings of Saint Louis de Montfort on total consecration to the Virgin Mary, which he quoted:

"Now, since Mary is of all creatures the one most conformed to Jesus Christ, it follows that among all devotions that which most consecrates and conforms a soul to our Lord is devotion to Mary, his Holy Mother, and that the more a soul is consecrated to her the more will it be consecrated to Jesus Christ."

Assumption of Mary
Mary was assumed into heaven with body and soul.

As time went on, the church removed women from positions of authority and spiritual leadership. The assumption of Mary in 1950 placed a woman at the throne of God, beside her son, Jesus. She surpassed being just a mother. She is now bodily in heaven, placing her in the company of only three others: Jesus, Elijah, and Enoch, who were taken up to heaven in physical form also.

Mary, the ever virgin, mother of God, was free of original sin. The Immaculate Conception was one basis for the 1950 dogma. Another, which Pope Pius XII referred to in *Deiparae Virginis Mariae,* was the century old Church-wide veneration of the Virgin Mary as being assumed into heaven. Although the assumption of Mary was just recently defined as dogma, accounts of the bodily assumption of Mary into heaven have circulated, at least, since the 5th century. The Catholic Church itself interprets chapter 12 of the Book of Revelation as referring to it. The story appears in "The Passing of the Virgin Mary"; a late 5th century work ascribed to Melito of Sardis, tells the story of the apostles being transported by white clouds to the deathbed of Mary, each from the town where he was preaching at the hour of her death.

Theological debate about the Assumption continued until 1950 when, in the Apostolic Constitution, Munificentissimus Deus, Pope Pius XII classified it as definitive doctrine.

"We pronounce, declare, and define it to be a divinely revealed dogma: that the Immaculate Mother of God, the ever Virgin Mary, having completed the course of her earthly life, was assumed body and soul into heavenly glory."

Since the 1870 solemn declaration of Papal Infallibility by the Vatican I, this declaration by Pope Pius XII has been the only use of Papal Infallibility. While Pope Pius XII deliberately left open the question of Mary's death before her Assumption, the more common teaching of the early Fathers is that she died.

After the proclamation of the assumption of Mary, Carl Jung wrote:

"The promulgation of the new dogma of the Assumption of the Virgin Mary could, in itself, have been sufficient reason for examining the

psychological background. It is interesting to note that, among the many articles published in the Catholic and Protestant press on the declaration of the dogma, there was not one, so far as I could see, which laid anything like proper emphasis on what was undoubtedly the most powerful motive: namely the popular movement and the psychological need behind it."

Essentially, the writers of the articles were satisfied with learned considerations, dogmatic and historical, which have no bearing on the living religious process. But anyone who has followed with attention the visions of Mary, which have been increasing in number over the last few decades, and has taken their psychological significance into account, might have known what was brewing.

The fact, especially, that it was largely children who had the visions might have given pause for thought, for in such cases, the collective unconscious is always at work ...One could have known for a long time that there was a deep longing in the masses for an intercessor and mediatrix who would at last take her place alongside the Holy Trinity and be received as the 'Queen of heaven and Bride at the heavenly court.' For more than a thousand years it has been taken for granted that the Mother of God dwelt there.

I consider it to be the most important religious event since the Reformation. It is a petra scandali for the unpsycholgical mind: how can such an unfounded assertion as the bodily reception of the Virgin into heaven be put forward as worthy of belief? But the method which the Pope uses in order to demonstrate the truth of the dogma makes sense to the psychological mind, because it bases itself firstly on the necessary prefigurations, and secondly on a tradition of religious assertions reaching back for more than a thousand years.

What outrages the Protestant standpoint in particular is the boundless approximation of the Deipara to the Godhead and, in consequence, the endangered supremacy of Christ, from which Protestantism will not budge. In sticking to this point it has obviously failed to consider that its hymnology is full of references to the 'heavenly bridegroom,' who is now suddenly supposed not to have a bride with equal rights. Or has, perchance, the 'bridegroom,' in true psychologistic manner, been understood as a mere metaphor?

The dogmatizing of the Assumption does not, however, according to the dogmatic view, mean that Mary has attained the status of goddess, although, as mistress of heaven and a mediator, she is functionally on a par with Christ, the

133

King and mediator. At any rate her position satisfies a renewed hope for the fulfillment of that yearning for peace, which stirs deep down in the soul, and for a resolution of the threatening tension between opposites. Everyone shares this tension and everyone experiences it in his individual form of unrest. The more unrest he has, the less he sees any possibility of getting rid of it by rational means. It is no wonder, therefore, that the hope, indeed, the expectation of divine intervention arises in the collective unconscious and, at the same time, in the masses. The papal declaration has given comforting expression to that yearning. "How could Protestantism so completely miss the point?"

("The Answer to Job" by Carl Jung)

Mary as Mediatrix

Although this position does not make her equal to God or his son, it does acknowledge that there is now a feminine influence and energy in Heaven. With compassion and caring, the church has her whispering her counsel and wisdom into the ear of her son, the Savior.

In Catholic teachings, Jesus Christ is the only mediator between God and man, although priests may intercede. He alone reconciled, the creator and his creation through his death on the cross. Nevertheless, this does not exclude a secondary mediating role for Mary. The teaching that Mary intercedes for all believers, especially those who request her intercession through prayer, has been in the Church since early times, for example by Ephraim, the Syrian: "after the mediator, a mediatrix for the whole world." Intercession is something that may be done by all the heavenly saints, but evidently, Mary has the greatest intercessory power. The earliest surviving recorded prayer to Mary is the *Subtuum Praesidium*, written in Greek around 250 A.D.

Increasingly, Mary has been viewed as a principal dispenser of God's graces and an advocate for the people of God. She is mentioned as such in several official Church documents. Pope Pius IX used the title in the *Ineffabilis Deus* Supremi *Apostolatus*. In the first of his *Rosary Encyclicals*, (1883), Pope Leo XIII calls Our Lady, *The guardian of our peace and the dispensatrix of heavenly graces*. In his 1954 Encyclical, *Ad Caeli Reginam*, Pope Pius XII calls Mary the Mediatrix of peace.

Co-Redemptrix

This position is not doctrine, but is regarded as doctrine by many in the church. The idea was once again submitted for consideration as dogma in the late 1990's. The Catholic Church submitted that Mary is Co-Redemptrix placing her above all men, save one. She is now raised above others who are in bodily form in heaven, except Jesus himself. At this point, Mary was promoted.

Co-Redemptrix refers to the participation of Mary in the salvation process. Already, Irenaeus, the Church Father (Died 200 A.D.), referred to Mary as "causa salutis" [cause of our salvation], formally acknowledging her authority. It is teaching, which has been around since the 15th century, but never declared a dogma. The Roman Catholic view of Co-Redemptrix does not imply that Mary participates equally in the redemption of the human race, since Christ is the only redeemer. Mary, herself, needed redemption and was redeemed by Jesus Christ her son. Being redeemed by Christ implies that she cannot be his equal in the redemption process. (It seems, Mary was born without original sin in this part of the doctrine, but must have later sinned in some way in order to need redemption.)

Co-redemptrix refers to an indirect or unequal, but important, participation by Mary in the redemption process. That is, she gave free consent to give life to the redeemer, to share his life, to suffer with him under the cross and to sacrifice him for the sake of the redemption of mankind. Co-redemption is not something new.

Queen of Heaven

The doctrine that the Virgin Mary was crowned "Queen of Heaven", "the Mother of the King of the universe," and the "Virgin Mother who brought forth the King of the whole world" goes back to St. Gregory Nazianzen. The Catholic Church often sees Mary as queen in heaven, bearing a crown of twelve stars as it is written in the Book of Revelation.

The evolution of the status of Mary, the Mother of Jesus has taken eighteen hundred years to become what it is today. The king of glory now has a queen and the balance is restored in the mind of the church. But this balance is a false one and does not fulfill the reunification of the vital male and female energies in the one and only God. With Mary, there is still duality, and duality is not an acceptable answer to the unity found within one God and spirit. Yet, here we are, thousands of years later, having come back to the same place in our spiritual "sidereal" orbit to "The Queen of Heaven." Mary, impregnated by God, having given God a son, now sits in heaven and the idea of duality is established once again.

Wisdom – Sophia

Sophia has a double meaning within Christian theology owing to the split within the early church between orthodoxy and Gnosticism. Wisdom is presented as a spirit entity and consort of God within orthodox (mainstream) Christianity. The verses below reflect the reverence of wisdom within the church; however, they did not view her as an entity or the consort of God, even though the texts state that she is. Wisdom became directly connected with the "Logos" of the New Testament. Later, we will discuss the place of Sophia within lesser-known sects such as the Gnostic Church.

Proverbs 8

22) The Lord created me first of all, the first of his works, long ago.
23) I was made in the very beginning, at the first, before the world began.
24) I was born before the oceans, when there were no springs of water.
25) I was born before the mountains, before the hills were set in place,
26) Before God made the earth and its fields or even the first handful of soil.
27) I was there when he set the sky in place, when he stretched the horizon across the ocean,
28) When he placed the clouds in the sky, when he opened the springs of the ocean
29) And ordered the waters of the sea to rise no further than he said. I was there when he laid the earth's foundations.
30) I was beside him like an architect. I was his daily source of joy, always happy in his presence"
31) Happy with the world and pleased with the human race.
32) Now, young people, listen to me. Do as I say, and you will be happy.
33) Listen to what you are taught. Be wise; do not neglect it.
34) Those who listen to me will be happy" those who stay at my door every day, waiting at the entrance to my home.
35) Those who find me find life, and the Lord will be pleased with them.
36) Those who do not find me hurt themselves; anyone who hates me loves death.

The Book of Wisdom 7

(Apocrypha and Orthodox Bible)

21) I learned things that were well known and things that had never been known before,

22) because Wisdom, who gave shape to everything that exists, was my teacher.

The Nature of Wisdom

23) The spirit of Wisdom is intelligent and holy. It is of one nature, but reveals itself in many ways. It is not made of any material substance, and it moves about freely. It is clear, clean, and confident; it cannot be harmed. It loves what is good. It is sharp and unconquerable, kind, and a friend of humanity. It is dependable and sure, and has no worries. It has power over everything, and sees everything. It penetrates every spirit that is intelligent and pure, no matter how delicate its substance may be.

24) Wisdom moves more easily than motion itself; she is so pure that she penetrates everything.

25) She is a breath of God's power a pure and radiant stream of glory from the Almighty. Nothing that is defiled can ever steal its way into Wisdom.

26) She is a reflection of eternal light, a perfect mirror of God's activity and goodness.

27) Even though Wisdom acts alone, she can do anything. She makes everything new, although she herself never changes. From generation to generation she enters the souls of holy people, and makes them God's friends and prophets.

28) There is nothing that God loves more than people who are at home with Wisdom.

29) Wisdom is more beautiful than the sun and all the constellations. She is better than light itself,

30) because night always follows day, but evil never overcomes Wisdom.

Wisdom 8

1) Her great power reaches into every part of the world, and she sets everything in useful order.

Solomon's Love for Wisdom

2) Wisdom has been my love. I courted her when I was young and wanted to make her my bride. I fell in love with her beauty.

3) She glorifies her noble origin by living with God, the Lord of all, who loves her.

4) She is familiar with God's mysteries and helps determine his course of action.

137

5) Is it good to have riches in this life? Nothing can make you richer than Wisdom, who makes everything function.

6) Is knowledge a useful thing to have? Nothing is better than Wisdom, who has given shape to everything that exists.

7) Do you love justice? All the virtues are the result of Wisdom's work: justice and courage, self-control and understanding. Life can offer us nothing more valuable than these.

8) Do you want to have wide experience? Wisdom knows the lessons of history and can anticipate the future. She knows how to interpret what people say and how to solve problems. She knows the miracles that God will perform, and how the movements of history will develop.

Wisdom 9
Solomon Prays for Wisdom

1) God of my ancestors, merciful Lord, by your word you created everything.
    2) By your Wisdom you made us humans to rule all creation,
3) to govern the world with holiness and righteousness, to administer justice with integrity.
4) Give me the Wisdom that sits beside your throne; give me a place among your children.
5) I am your slave, as was my mother before me. I am only human. I am not strong, and my life will be short. I have little understanding of the Law or of how to apply it.
6) Even if someone is perfect, he will be thought of as nothing without the Wisdom that comes from you.
7) You chose me over everyone else to be the king of your own people, to judge your sons and daughters.
8) You told me to build a temple on your sacred mountain, an altar in Jerusalem, the city you chose as your home. It is a copy of that temple in heaven, which you prepared at the beginning.
9) Wisdom is with you and knows your actions; she was present when you made the world. She knows what pleases you, what is right and in accordance with your commands.
10) Send her from the holy heavens, down from your glorious throne, so that she may work at my side, and I may learn what pleases you.
11) She knows and understands everything, and will guide me intelligently in what I do. Her glory will protect me.
12) Then I will judge your people fairly, and be worthy of my father's throne. My actions will be acceptable.
13) Who can ever learn the will of God?

14) *Human reason is not adequate for the task, and our philosophies tend to mislead us,*

15) *because our mortal bodies weigh our souls down. The body is a temporary structure made of earth, a burden to the active mind.*

16) *All we can do is make guesses about things on earth; we must struggle to learn about things that are close to us. Who, then, can ever hope to understand heavenly things?*

17) *No one has ever learned your will, unless you first gave him Wisdom, and sent your holy spirit down to him.*

18) *In this way, people on earth have been set on the right path, have learned what pleases you, and have been kept safe by Wisdom.*

Proverbs 1

Wisdom Calls

20) *Listen! Wisdom is calling out in the streets and marketplaces,*

21) *calling loudly at the city gates and wherever people come together:*

22) *Foolish people! How long do you want to be foolish? How long will you enjoy making fun of knowledge? Will you never learn?*

23) *Listen when I reprimand you; I will give you good advice and share my knowledge with you.*

24) *I have been calling you, inviting you to come, but you would not listen. You paid no attention to me.*

25) *You have ignored all my advice and have not been willing to let me correct you.*

26) *So when you get into trouble, I will laugh at you. I will make fun of you when terror strikes*

27) *when it comes on you like a storm, bringing fierce winds of trouble, and you are in pain and misery.*

28) *Then you will call for wisdom, but I will not answer. You may look for me everywhere, but you will not find me.*

29) *You have never had any use for knowledge and have always refused to obey the Lord.*

30) *You have never wanted my advice or paid any attention when I corrected you.*

31) *So then, you will get what you deserve, and your own actions will make you sick.*

32) *Inexperienced people die because they reject wisdom. Stupid people are destroyed by their own lack of concern.*

33) But whoever listens to me will have security. He will be safe, with no reason to be afraid.

A small number of Christian denominations have managed to re-capture some type of balance between male and female energy within the godhead, but most have not.

An official publication of the LDS (Mormon) Church states:

"Our Father in heaven was once a man as we are now, capable of physical death. By obedience to eternal gospel principles, he progressed from one stage of life to another until he attained the state that we call exaltation or godhood. In such a condition, he and our mother in heaven were empowered to give birth to spirit children whose potential was equal to that of their heavenly parents. We are those spirit children." (Achieving a Celestial Marriage p 132)

The LDS (Mormon) Church offers courses in religion, and supplies books and manuals from which to teach. In the 3rd chapter of the manual for a course entitled, *Doctrines of the Gospel,* that is part of an advanced course for the Religion 231 and 232, we find the church addresses the nature of God. Joseph Smith's "King Follett" sermon is cited as authoritative by this official Church publication along with a statement from Spencer W. Kimball, one of the earlier church prophets:

God made man in his own image and certainly he made woman in the image of his wife-partner (Spencer W. Kimball, The Teachings of Spencer W. Kimball, p.25).

Again, we encounter the concept of the heavenly Mother, God's wife in heaven, and have the interesting assertion that women are made, not in the image of God, but in the image of God's wife-partner.

In the above quotes, we see the Church of Jesus Christ of Latter day Saints sought to fill the void of the divine or Sacred Feminine with an entity, which was the wife of God.

It is within the Christian Science Church, also called the Church of Christ Scientists, that the balance of a singular God containing all attributes of both male and female is encountered again after thousands of years.

In the church of Christ Scientists (Christian Science), God is hailed as "The Mother-Father God," vocalizing their held belief of the existence of attributes and energies of both male and female within the spirit of God.

Mary Baker Eddy defined God as "the all-knowing, all-seeing, all-acting, all-wise, all-loving, and eternal; Principle; Mind; Soul; Spirit; Truth; Love; all substance; intelligence" (Eddy 587). Very importantly, Mrs. Eddy throughout her writing also refers to God as the Father-Mother God.

Mary Baker Eddy was not the first one to perceive God as being both Father and Mother (Peel 91). Mother Ann Lee, a Shaker woman, was part of just one of many faiths that spoke of God as Mother. She wrote:

"As Father, God is the infinite Fountain of intelligence, and the Source of all power, "the Almighty and terrible in majesty"; "the high and lofty one, that inhabiteth eternity, whose name is Holy, dwelling in the high and holy place"; and "a consuming fire." But as, Mother, "God is Love" and tenderness. If all the maternal affections of all the female or bearing spirits in animated nature were combined together, and then concentrated in one individual human female, that person would be put as the type or image of our Eternal Heavenly Mother." (Peel 28).

This matches the Christian Science understanding of God's motherly aspects and serves as a helpful illustration of the maternal nature of God as Mother. God as Father is a powerful being that offers intelligence and strength; yet there is something untouchable about Him. God as Mother can be seen as our earthly mothers, tender, nurturing, maternal, and approachable.

Mary Baker Eddy produced an interpretation of the Lord's Prayer based on her understanding of the balance of male and female elements within the Godhead.

Lord's Prayer with Spiritual Interpretation by Mary Baker Eddy
Our Father which art in heaven,
Our Father-Mother God, all-harmonious,
Hallowed be Thy name.
Adorable One.
Thy kingdom come.
Thy kingdom is come; Thou art ever-present.
Thy will be done in earth, as it is in heaven.
Enable us to know – as in heaven, so on earth – God is omnipotent, supreme.
Give us this day our daily bread;
Give us grace for today; feed the famished affections;
And forgive us our debts, as we forgive our
debtors.

And Love is reflected in love;
And lead us not into temptation, but deliver us
from evil;
And God leadeth us not into temptation, but delivereth
us from sin, disease, and death.
For Thine is the kingdom, and the power, and the
glory, forever.
For God is infinite, all-power, all Life, Truth, Love, over all, and All.

Having seen some of the attempts of the modern churches to understand and rectify the lack of recognition or understanding of the Sacred Feminine, it is necessary to ask, "What happened to the Sacred Feminine of Genesis? What initiated the lack of recognition or denial of the female side of God? "

The feminine side of God was erased with the change of language from the Hebrew feminine word "Ruak" into the Greek word "Pneuma" and into the Latin word "Spiritus." Both words, Spiritus and Pneuma mean "breath," but the word used in Latin is a masculine word and in Greek the word has no gender at all. Thus the feminine side of God simply disappeared into a linguistic void and was forgotten; never to be recognized for her nurturing and brooding nature until centuries later. Since the church was almost completely controlled by men at the time, they either did not notice or they did not care that the feminine spirit of God vanished and was replaced with a translation that rendered the spirit of God either neuter or masculine.

Although it is understood that God is a singular being, our psyches still call out for some manifestation of the female force. We long for a mother as well and a father. We search the Bible for the Sacred Feminine. In its pages we find no less than three distinct feminine archetypal forms within God: Ruak, Shikina, and Sophia (Wisdom).

Let us first look at the feminine forces of Ruak, Shikhinah, and Sophia (Wisdom).

Ruak, Ruach, or Rawach:

We have already seen that Ruak was the spirit that hovered and brooded over the earth like a mother hen broods over her chicks. In the Ten Commandments, we are taught to "honor your father and your mother" and that doing so would make "your days long upon the land which Yahweh your God is giving you." There seems to be no obvious connection in the temporal sense, except that by not honoring your parents you could be stoned. However, if Yahweh is actually speaking of our spiritual father and mother, that is Yahweh and His Holy Spirit, then it all makes sense. Yahweh is the Creator, Provider, Protector, and ultimate Authority. These are all "male" traits. Ruak Qodesh or Holy Spirit is the maternal aspect of God. She is the Caregiver, Counselor, and Comforter.

Shekinah, Shechinah, Shekhina, or Shechina.

In the Hebrew language this word means the glory or radiance of God. The Glory of God rests or resides in his house or Tabernacle amongst his people. Thus, the word is derived from the Hebrew word 'sakan', which means 'to dwell'.

The Shekhina is defined, in traditional Jewish writings, as the "female aspect of God." It is part of the feminine "presence" of the infinite God in the world. She is introduced in early rabbinical commentaries as the "immanence" or "indwelling" of the living God. Her purpose is to animate or impart life force. She is certainly not the 'Canaanite' Mother Goddess, Asherah. Around 622 BCE, King Josiah removed the Asherah from the Jerusalem temple and destroyed the shrines.

While she does not appear by name in the five books of Moses, her presence is seen in interpreting the text. For example, when Moses encounters the burning bush, he is told to remove his shoes and prepare himself to receive the Shekhina.

A Talmudic verse said: "Let them make Me a sanctuary that I may dwell (*ve'shakhanti*) among them." In a later version, the translation said, "Let them make Me a Sanctuary so that My Shekhina will dwell among them."

A Talmudic quotation from the end of the 1st century BCE: " ...while the Children of Israel were still in Egypt, the Holy One, blessed be He, stipulated that He would liberate them from Egypt only in order that they built him a Sanctuary so that He can let His Shekhina dwell among them ... As soon as the Tabernacle was erected, the Shekhina descended and dwelt among them."

Another quotation from early 3rd century says: "On that day a thing came about which had never existed since the creation of the world. From the creation of the world and up to that hour, the

Shekhina had never dwelt among the lower beings. But from the time that the Tabernacle was erected, she did dwell among them."

Although the language of the text may lead us to view "her" as a separate entity, the Shekhina is a specific way the Spirit of God is manifesting. She gives life, restores and revives life.. This is the most powerful of female attributes.

Another tradition claimed that she had always dwelt among her people, but their sins drove her, on and off, into heaven. However, she was drawn back to her children and tried to save them, over and over. This viewpoint is more in line with the New Testament idea of the Holy Spirit.

Keeping with the idea of the Shekhina returning to the people, when the Jews were exiled to Babylonia, she transferred her seat there, and appeared alternately in two major synagogues.

Jewish tradition and teaching tells us that as the Jews dispersed throughout the world, the Shekhina comforted the poor and the suffering. She drew the sinner back to God by enlivening their spirit and conscience. She caused sinners to repent and then accepted and comforted them as if they had never sinned. Spiritually, she carried aloft the suffering and those whose hearts were broken and whose spirit was low. They were seated next to the Shekhina. "When their spirits were healed, the Shekhina walked with them every day...."

Since we are limited in our understanding, the idea of a single entity, even a spirit, being in two places at once was disconcerting for the people. The paradox of dwelling in one place, and being other places with many people at the same time, had to be resolved.

The Talmud attempted to explain the paradox within a simple and well-known anecdote. "The Emperor said to Raban Gamaliel: 'You say that wherever ten men are assembled, the Shekhina dwells among them'."

Still, we continued to worry over the fact that God is at once in heaven and on the earth, manifesting as Shekhina. An interesting medieval teaching shows the Shekhina as a total separate entity, in her most important role - interceding on behalf of her children.

Another story shows her being equated to an intercessor. "The Shekhina comes to the defense of sinful Israel by saying first to Israel: 'Be not a witness against thy neighbor without a cause' and then thereafter saying to God: 'Say not: I will do to him as he hath done to me.' This is obviously a conversation taking place among three distinct entities - Israel, God, and the Shekhina.

Another significant passage from the 11th century, describes Rabbi Akiva (a second century sage) saying: "When the Holy One, blessed be He, considered the deeds of the generation of Enoch and that they were spoiled and evil, *He removed Himself and His Shekhina* from their midst and ascended into the heights with blasts of trumpets..."

Talmud reports that the Shekhina is what caused prophets to prophesy and King David to compose his Psalms. The Shekhina manifests herself as a form of joy, connected with prophecy and creativity. (Talmud Pesachim 117a)

The Shekhina is associated with the transformational spirit of God regarded as the source of prophecy:

"After that thou shalt come to the hill of God, where is the garrison of the Philistines; and it shall come to pass, when thou art come thither to the city, that thou shalt meet a band of prophets coming down from the high place with a psaltery, and a timbrel, and a pipe, and a harp, before them; and they will be prophesying.

And the spirit of the LORD will come mightily upon thee, and thou shalt prophesy with them, and shalt be turned into another man." (1 Samuel 10:5-6 JPS).

The 16th century mystic, Rabbi Isaac Luria, wrote a famous Shabbat hymn about the Shekhina or Glory of God. In it we see how this part of God is directly equated with a bride:

"I sing in hymns to enter the gates of the Field of holy apples.

A new table we prepare for Her, a lovely candelabrum sheds its light upon us.

Between right and left the Bride approaches, in holy jewels and festive garments..."

Zohar states: "One must prepare a comfortable seat with several cushions and embroidered covers, from all that is found in the house, like one who prepares a canopy for a bride. For the Shabbat is a queen and a bride. This is why the masters of the Mishna used to go out on the eve of Shabbat to receive her on the road, and used to say: '*Come, O bride, come, O bride!*' And one must sing and rejoice at the table in her honor ... one must receive the Lady with many lighted candles, many enjoyments, beautiful clothes, and a house embellished with many fine appointments..." The tradition of the Shekhina as the Shabbat Bride continues to this day as a powerful and moving symbol of the Sacred Feminine.

Sophia (Wisdom)

Although the mainstream Christian church forgot about Sophia, the Gnostic Christians would not. In their unorthodox theology they fought to understand the duality of the world and the Sacred Feminine. The Gnostic movement started before second century A.D., but was condemned by the emerging powers of the Orthodox Church probably because they could not control the people through Gnostic theology, which taught the individual transmission of knowledge from God to the individual without the help or interference of priests or church.

In the Gnostic text called, The Apocryphon of John, Sophia is quoted:

"I entered into the midst of the cage which is the prison of the body. And I spoke saying: 'He who hears, let him awake from his deep sleep.' Then Adam wept and shed tears. After he wiped away his bitter tears he asked: 'Who calls my name, and from where has this hope arose in me even while I am in the chains of this prison?' And I (Sophia) answered: 'I am the one who carries the pure light; I am the thought of the undefiled spirit. Arise, remember, and follow your origin, which is I, and beware of the deep sleep.'"

As the myth evolved, Sophia, after animating Adam, became Eve in order to assist Adam in finding the truth. She offered it to him in the form of the fruit of the tree of knowledge. To Gnostics, this was an act of deliverance. Sophia would later become equated to the Holy Spirit as it awakened the comatose soul.

In other stories, Sophia becomes the serpent in order to offer Adam a way to attain the truth. In either case, the friut represented the hard sought truth, which was the knowledge of good and evil, and through that knowledge Adam could become a god. Later, the serpent became a feminine symbol of wisdom, probably owing to the connection with Sophia. Eve, being Sophia in disguise, became the mother and sacred feminine of us all. As Gnostic theology began to coalesce, Sophia was considered a force or conduit of the Holy Spirit, due, in part, to the fact that the Holy Spirit was believed to be a feminine and creative force from the Supreme God. The Gospel of Philip echoes this theology in verse six as follows:

146

39. Wisdom (Sophia) is barren. She has no children but she is called Mother. Other are found (adopted) by the Holy Spirit, and she has many children.

Most Gnostics were suppressed or killed. The last great Gnostic movement came from the Cathars. Catharism represented total opposition to the Catholic Church, which they basically viewed as a large, pompous, and fraudulent organization that had lost its integrity and "sold out" for power and money in this world, a world that the Gnostics viewed as evil.

As time went on and the mainstream church became established in its power base, they could more effectively fight their enemies. The Inquisition was proof of this. Catharism, one of the last great sects of Gnosticism, vanished from the stage of history by the end of the 14th century. Many well-preserved Gnostic texts were found in 1945 in Nag Hammadi, Egypt.

The Nature of Jesus

Christians believe that Jesus represents the pinnacle of the Axial Age. No matter what one may think about his nature or divinity, his teachings convey everything positive resulting from the Axial Age. He addresses the heart and mind of man and asserts that it is the mental, subjective, inner world of mankind that brings either peace or violence – heaven or hell.

Recently, scholars, academics, and theologians have argued and speculated on how Christians of the first century viewed Jesus. Was he divine or not? Did the first Christians believe he was god or just a teacher? I believe the question itself is incorrect, leading to a false premise from which false conclusions arise. Jesus was not yet taken off the cross before differences as to who or what he was appeared between followers. Christianity in the first century was even more diverse than it is today. Different factions viewed Jesus through the lens of their prior religious backgrounds and beliefs, exactly as we do today.

The first Christians were converted Jews. They were expecting a messiah sent from God, not God himself. The job of this savior was to bridge the gap between God and man, and bring harmony and communion back between Yahweh and his people. This is quite clear if one were simply to read the way God and the readers are addressed within the New Testament.

Romans 1:7 To all that be in Rome, beloved of God, called to be saints: Grace to you and peace from **God our Father, and the Lord Jesus** Christ...

Romans 4:24 But for us also, to whom it shall be imputed, if we believe on him that raised up **Jesus our Lord** from the dead...

Romans 5:1 Therefore being justified by faith, we have **peace with God through our Lord Jesus** Christ...

Romans 5:11 And not only so, but we also **joy in God through our Lord Jesus** Christ, by whom we have now received the atonement...

Hebrews 13:20 Now **the God of peace,** that brought again from the dead our Lord Jesus, that great shepherd of the sheep, **through the blood of the everlasting covenant**...

1 Peter 1:2 Elect according to the foreknowledge of **God the Father, through sanctification of the Spirit, unto obedience and sprinkling of the blood of Jesus** Christ: Grace unto you, and **peace**, be multiplied…

2 Peter 1:2 Grace and peace be multiplied unto you **through the knowledge of God, and of Jesus our Lord**…

There are many other such passages, but we shall not belabor the point. The salutations of these epistles acknowledge God as God and Jesus as Lord. The salutations also imply that Jesus is the Christ, the messiah, and the mediator, but not God or even a God. Let me put this in perspective. Lord was a formal way of addressing a superior. In the Spanish translations of the Bible the word is correctly rendered, "señor." The definition is, "Title used as a courtesy title before the surname, full name, or professional title of a man in a Spanish-speaking area. Used as a form of polite address for a man in a Spanish-speaking area." This word, translated, "lord" is:

κύριος , kurios , *koo'-ree-os* From κυ ρος kuros (*supremacy*); *supreme* in authority, that is, (as noun) *controller*; by implication *Mr.* (as a respectful title). It is not the "Lord" rendered from the name, Yahweh.

Since we no longer used the word, it takes on a greater meaning than was intended. This is an example of the American Christian filtering ideas through his or her background. Early Christians had these filters also. Some came from a background influenced by Plato, who believed the world was the creation of an insane angel, thus all matter was corrupt. It was impossible for the holy God even to contact earthly matter, as it would be contrary to his nature of holiness and purity. For these people, the idea of divinity inhabiting human flesh was unthinkable. Jesus could not have been God in human form.

Historically speaking, the fate of the Jews who followed Jesus is one of the puzzles of history. Centuries of Christian anti-Semitism, and Jewish resentment of Christianity have obscured the history of Jewish Christians. Pieces of history have been removed, distorted, or simply left unreported. There was an argument between James and Paul about how much, if any, of the Jewish law and custom such converts to Christianity should keep. Some Jewish converts wondered how the self-sacrifice of Jesus related to the animal sacrifices in the law, and believed that the law and customs should be continued, while others believed that Jesus was the sacrifice, once and for all, encouraging

149

followers to give up the law and Jewish religious customs. Both sides were previously taught by Jewish custom to hate the Gentiles and now did not know what to do with the Gentile believers.

Proto-orthodox authors clearly agree that the Ebionites were Jewish followers of Jesus. They were not the only group of Jewish-Christians known to have existed at the time, but they were the group that generated some of the greatest opposition. The Ebionite Christians, about whom we are most informed, believed that Jesus was the Jewish Messiah sent from the Jewish God to the Jewish people in fulfillment of the Jewish Scriptures. They also believed that in order to belong to the people of God, one needed to be Jewish. They observed the Sabbath, kept the kosher, and circumcised their male children. These were the people that opposed Paul in Galatia. The Ebionite Christians were their spiritual descendants.

Bart Ehrman points out; the Ebionites had a foundation, even during the time of Paul. In the book of Galatians, we see Paul arguing and writing against people who held similar beliefs to the Ebionites. Therefore, the Ebionites may not have been established as late as modern day Christians purport. Rather, Ebionites could very well be the very same descended, first century followers mentioned in the book of Galatians, and not only a first century group but a group appearing 30-50 years after Jesus' death!

Their insistence on staying (or becoming) Jewish should not seem especially peculiar from a historical perspective, since Jesus and his disciples were Jewish. But the Ebionites' "Jewish-ness" did not endear them to most other Christians who believed that Jesus allowed them to bypass the requirements of the Law for salvation. The Ebionites, however, maintained that the original disciples authorized their views, especially Peter and Jesus' own brother, James, head of the Jerusalem church after the resurrection.

(Bart, Ehrman, Lost Christianities. Oxford University Press, 2003. PP. 100)

Another aspect of the Ebionites' Christianity that set it apart from most other Christian groups was their understanding of who Jesus was. The Ebionites did not subscribe to the notion of Jesus' pre-existence or his virgin birth. These ideas were originally distinct from each other. The two New Testament Gospels that speak of Jesus being conceived of a virgin (Matthew and Luke) do not indicate that he existed *prior* to his birth. For them, Jesus was the Son of God, not because of his divine nature or virgin birth, but because of his adoption by God to be his son. Although the New Testament was not around at this time, we can now see this view expressed in the scene when Jesus was Baptized, and the voice of God was heard saying, "This is My Son -- the Beloved; hear ye him;" Luke 9:35. This kind of Christology is, consequently, called "adoptionist." To express the matter more fully, the Ebionites believed that Jesus was a real flesh-and-blood human like the rest of us, born as the eldest son of the sexual union of his parents, Joseph and Mary. What set Jesus apart from all other people was that he kept God's law perfectly, and therefore was the most righteous man on earth.

Keeping in mind that the New Testament was a long way from existing as we know it, and keeping in mind that Paul was simply a Jewish Rabbi insisting that a person is made right with God apart from keeping the Law, in the minds of the Ebonites, Paul was a heretic, a religious snob and an intellectual bully, who led people astray.

So according to the Ebionites, Jesus was not divine, he was a man like everyone else, yet what made him special and set him apart was that he was the Jewish Messiah, and that he perfectly followed the law. The Ebionites summarily dismissed Paul, his ideas, and his writings. They considered him an apostate of the Law.

The doctrines of this sect are said by Irenaeus to be like those of Cerinthus and Carpocrates. They denied the Divinity and the virginal birth of Christ; they clung to the observance of the Jewish Law; they regarded St. Paul as an apostate, and used only a Gospel according to St. Matthew
(Adv. Haer., I, xxvi, 2; III, xxi, 2; IV, xxxiii, 4; V, i, 3).

According to several sources, it was the Ebionite theology that influenced the development of the Islamic faith. We will discuss this in greater detail later.

Besides the Ebionites, there existed a later Gnostic development of the same heresy. These Ebionite Gnostics differed widely from the main schools of Gnosticism, in that they absolutely rejected any distinction between Jehovah the Demiurge (maker of the physical world) and the Supreme Good God. They believed the universe was divided into two realms, good and evil. The Son of God rules over the realm of the good, and to him is given the world to come, but the Prince of Evil is the prince of this world (cf. John 14:30; Ephesians 1:21; 6:12). This Son of God is the Christ, a middle-being between God and creation, not a creature, yet not equal to, nor even to be compared with, the Father.

Their belief in salvation is different than what became orthodox. Man is saved by knowledge (*gnosis*), by believing in the supreme God, the Teacher, and by being baptized unto remission of sins. At this point, the initiated person receives knowledge and strength to observe all the precepts of the law.

Another divergence from orthodox belief is Marcionism. The sect originated from the teachings of a man named Marcion, a Christian theologian, and son of a Christian Bishop. Marcion began to formulate his theology around the year 144. This was well before an official Bible and most of what the latter church power dictated as doctrine.

Marcion could not reconcile the God of the Jewish Bible with the God of the New Testament. The Old Testament God commanded genocide, and mass murder, as well as the slaughter of thousands of animals at a time. He regarded the God of the Old Testament as an evil "lesser god," much like the Gnostic regarded the god who made the physical world. Subsequently, Marcion rejected the Jewish Bible and its god.

Zephaniah 2:12
You Ethiopians will also be slaughtered by my sword," says the LORD. And the LORD will strike the lands of the north with his fist. He will destroy Assyria and make its great capital, Nineveh, a desolate wasteland, parched like a desert. The city that once was so proud will become a pasture for sheep and cattle. ...

Ezekiel 9:5
Then I heard the LORD say to the other men, "Follow him through the city and kill everyone whose forehead is not marked. Show no mercy; have no pity! Kill them all - old and young, girls and women and little children...

Deuteronomy 3:6
6 And we utterly destroyed them, as we did unto Sihon king of Heshbon, utterly destroying the men, women, and children, of every city...

Marcion saw a different God, in the New Testament. It was a God of love, mercy, grace, and forgiveness.

Bart Erhman, a major New Testament scholar, writes about the Marcionites in *Lost Christianities:*

"Living at the same time and also enjoying the unwanted attention of the proto-orthodox opponents, though standing at just the opposite end of the theological spectrum, were a group of Christians known as the Marcionites. In this instance, there is no question concerning the origin of the name. These were followers of the second century evangelist/theologian Marcian, known to later Christianity as one of the arch heretics of his day, but by all accounts one of the most significant Christian thinkers and writers of the early centuries. The Marcionites on the other hand, had a highly attractive religion to many pagan converts, as it was avowedly Christian with nothing Jewish about it. In fact, everything Jewish was taken out of it. Jews, recognized around the world for customs that struck many pagans as bizarre at best, would have difficulty recognizing the Marcionite religion as an offshoot of their own. Not only were Jewish customs rejected, so, too, were the Jewish scriptures and the Jewish God. From a historical perspective, it is intriguing that any such religion could claim direct historical continuity with Jesus."

"I should say a word about the theology Marcion developed, which was seen as distinctive, revolutionary, compelling, and therefore dangerous. Among all Christian texts and authors at his disposal, Marcion was especially struck by the writings of the apostle Paul, and in particular the distinction Paul drew in Galatians and elsewhere between the Law of the Jews and the gospel of Christ. As we have seen, Paul claimed that a person is made right with God by faith in Christ, not by doing the works of the Law. This distinction became fundamental to Marcion, and he made it absolute. The Gospel is good news of deliverance; it involves love, mercy, grace, forgiveness, reconciliation, redemption, and life. The Law, however, is the bad news that makes the gospel necessary in the first place; it involves harsh commandments, guilt, judgment, enmity, punishment, and death. The Law is given to the Jews. Christ gives the gospel."

Marcion concluded that there must in fact be two Gods; the God of the Jews, as found in the Old Testament, and the God of Jesus, as found in the writings of Paul.

Once Marcion arrived at this understanding, everything else naturally fell into place. The God of the Old Testament was the God who created this world and everything in it, as described in Genesis. The God of Jesus, therefore, had never been involved with this world but came into it only when Jesus appeared from heaven. The God of the Old Testament was the God who called the Jews to be his people and gave them his law. The God of Jesus did not consider the Jews to be his people (for him; they were the chosen of the other God), and he was not a God who gave laws.

The God of Jesus came into this world in order to save people from the vengeful God of the Jews. He was previously unknown to this world and had never had any previous dealings with it. Hence Marcion sometimes referred to him as God the stranger. Not even the prophecies of the future Messiah come from this God, for these refer not to Jesus but to a coming Messiah of Israel, to be sent by the God of the Jews, the creator of this world and the God of the Old Testament. Jesus came completely unexpectedly and did what no one could possibly have hoped for: He paid the penalty for other people's sins, to save them from the wrath of the Old Testament God.

Marcion's New Testament consisted of eleven books. Most of these were the letters of his beloved Paul, the one predecessor whom Marcion could trust to understand the radical claims of the gospel. Why, Marcion asked, did Jesus return to earth to convert Paul by means of a vision? Why did he not simply allow his own disciples to proclaim his message faithfully throughout the world? According to Marcion, it was because Jesus' disciples were followers of the Jewish God and readers of the Jewish Scriptures and never did correctly understand their master. Confused by what Jesus taught them, wrongly thinking he was the Jewish Messiah, even after his death and resurrection they *continued* not to understand, interpreting Jesus' words, deeds, and death in light of their understanding of Judaism. Jesus then had to start afresh, and he called Paul to reveal to him 'the truth of the gospel.' That is why Paul had to confront Jesus' disciple Peter and his earthly brother James, as seen in the letter to the Galatians. Jesus had revealed the truth to Paul, and these others simply never understood.

Marcion returned to Asia Minor to propagate his version of faith, and he was fantastically successful in doing so. We cannot be sure exactly why, but Marcion experienced an almost unparalleled success on the mission field, establishing churches wherever he went, so that within a few years, one of his proto-orthodox opponents, the apologist and theologian in Rome, Justin, could say that he was teaching his heretical views to many people of every nation." *(Apology 1.26). (Bart, Ehrman. Lost Christianities. Oxford University press, 2003. PP. 103-109)*

Then, there are the Gnostics. They flourished in the second and third century, but their root can be traced back the oldest Christian sects from 30 to 120 C.E., such as the Simonians, Ophites, Naassenes,

Cerinthians, and others. The Gnostics, as a group, were so diverse in their beliefs, it is difficult to label one belief Gnostic and one not.

Many believed that the world was not compatible with the divine nature of God, thus if Jesus was from God, he could not have a mortal body. He was a spirit tricking us in to believing he was a man. He did not die on the cross. It was part of the illusion.

Some believed that Jesus had a divine nature trapped within his body. He came to show us this fact so that we could find our divine nature and escape the corrupt world. In the Gospel of Judas (available from Fifth Estate Publishing), we see this play out as Jesus appoints Judas to the special task of making sure Jesus is killed and can be released from his body, thereby again becoming one with the supreme God.

The common thread of all Gnostics seems to be the belief that there was knowledge that passed to the believer, which allowed him or her to be saved. This knowledge ignites the Christ spirit, which was in each of us from the beginning, but has been lost or forgotten. Jesus came to show us this by letting us see the seed of God within him that we all have within us. They believed that sin was the lack of knowledge about yourself and your divine spark. When you became one with God within yourself, you became one with all that is. This is salvation. There was no original sin, only ignorance of our own purpose and divine nature.

However, this doctrine had no place for institutional control. If salvation is left to the individual to follow the template laid down by Jesus himself, where and how could the emerging church gain control? It could not, so the idea of man's divine spirit was deemed heresy by the church, and all but stamped out, surviving only among a few sects and teachers throughout the subsequent centuries, and ending, for the most part, in the great slaughter of the Cathers (the last great Gnostic sect) by the Roman church in 1290 A.D.

If Jesus came to show us the way to become messiahs ourselves, saying to us, "Greater things than me will you do...", there would be no place for organized religion, so the church tried to kill the idea, and when they could not do that, they killed the people.

The diverse views of God and his Messiah, Jesus, are most astounding. Was Jesus a man or a spirit? Was he God, a god, the God, a servant, a man...? Christianity was not united on these fronts. We were not in harmony even in our basic doctrines.

If one were to rule a people, the people must be in harmony. The church wished to rule, and the King wished to rule. These desires would come to a head in Nicaea

In A.D. 312, Constantine won control of the Roman Empire in the battle of Milvian Bridge. Attributing his victory to the intervention of Jesus Christ. He had seen a vision of a cross and heard a voice telling him to conquer. Because of his vision he made Christianity the religion of the empire. "One God, one Lord, one faith, one church, one empire, one emperor" became his motto.

The new emperor soon discovered that there was no "one faith and one church." Instead there were factions split by theological disputes, especially the differing understandings of the nature of Christ. Arius, a priest of the church in Alexandria, asserted that God created Christ before the beginning of time. Therefore, the divinity of Christ was similar to the divinity of God, but not of the same essence.

Bishop Alexander and his successor, Athanasius affirmed that the divinity of Christ, the Son, is of the same substance as God, the Father. Otherwise Christians would be guilty of polytheism. It would imply that knowledge of God in Christ was not final knowledge of God. They must have forgotten that when Jesus was asked about the end of the world, he replied that he did not know. Only God knew.

Constantine convened a council in Nicaea in A.D. 325 and demanded the rift be settled. There were threats and commands until a creed reflecting some compromise was produced and signed by a majority of the bishops. There were actually more than just these two sides, but the others were removed from the church, excommunicated, or done away with. The remaining parties continued to battle each other until A.D. 381, when a second council met in Constantinople. It adopted a revised and expanded form of the A.D. 325 creed, now known as the Nicene Creed.

The evolution of God is now firmly in the hands of man. We shall qualify and quantify what is and is not God. We shall do so with measuring sticks of our own making. Two of these rods are canon of Scripture and doctrine. With these measuring rules in hand those in power will make the world conform to their standards. Belief or doctrine limits the accepted canon. In turn, canon will support doctrine as we turn to the scriptures to prove our point.

Gnosticism

Gnosticism has been mentioned several times. Let us now define and explore the sect of Christianity called Gnosticism.

"Gnosticism: A system of religion mixed with Greek and Oriental philosophy of the 1st through 6th centuries A.D. Intermediate between Christianity and paganism, Gnosticism taught that knowledge rather than faith was the greatest good and that through knowledge alone could salvation be attained."

Webster's Dictionary

The word Gnostic is based on the Greek word "Gnosis," which means "knowledge." The "Gnosis" is the knowledge of the ultimate, supreme God and his spirit, which is contained within us all. It is this knowledge that allows one to transcend this material world with its falsities and spiritual entrapments and ascend into heaven to be one with God.

For centuries, the definition of Gnosticism has been a point of confusion and contention within the religious community. This is due, in part, to the ever-broadening application of the term and the fact that various sects of Gnosticism existed as the theology evolved and began to merge into what became mainstream Christianity.

Even though Gnosticism continued to evolve, it is the theology at the time the Gnostic Gospels were written that will be examined here.

We will look at religious concepts, history, people, and cosmology of the time related the this sect of Christianity. These areas are not separate, but are continually interacting.

The roots of Gnosticism may pre-date Christianity. Similarities exist between Gnosticism and the wisdom and mystery cults found in Egypt and Greece. Gnosticism contains the basic terms and motifs of Plato's cosmology, as well as the mystical qualities of Buddhism. Plato was steeped in Greek mythology, and the Gnostic creation myth has elements owing to this. Both cosmology and mysticism within Gnosticism present an interpretation of Christ's existence and teachings, thus, Gnostics are considered to be a Christian sect. Gnostic followers are urged to look within themselves for the truth and the Christ spirit hidden, asleep in their souls. The battle cry can be summed up in the words of the Gnostic Gospel of Thomas, verse 3:

157

Jesus said: If those who lead you say to you: Look, the Kingdom is in the sky, then the birds of the sky would enter before you. If they say to you: It is in the sea, then the fish of the sea would enter ahead of you. But the Kingdom of God exists within you and it exists outside of you. Those who come to know (recognize) themselves will find it, and when you come to know yourselves you will become known and you will realize that you are the children of the Living Father. Yet if you do not come to know yourselves then you will dwell in poverty and it will be you who are that poverty.

Paganism was a religious traditional society in the Mediterranean region leading up to the time of the Gnostics. Centuries after the conversion of Constantine, mystery cults worshipping various Egyptian and Greco-Roman gods continued. These cults taught that through their secret knowledge, worshippers could control or escape the mortal realm. The Gnostic doctrine of inner knowledge and freedom may have part of its roots here. The concept of duality and inner guidance taught in Buddhism supplemented and enforced Gnostic beliefs.

The belief systems of Plato, Buddha, and paganism melted together, spread, and found a suitable home in the mystical side of the Christian faith as it sought to adapt and adopt certain Judeo-Christian beliefs and symbols.

Like modern Christianity, Gnosticism had various points of view that could be likened to Christian denominations of today. Complex and elaborate creation myths took root in Gnosticism, being derived from those of Plato. Later, the theology evolved and Gnosticism began to shed some of its more unorthodox myths, leaving the central theme of inner knowledge or gnosis to propagate.

The existence of various sects of Gnosticism, differing creation stories, along with the lack of historical documentation, has left scholars in a quandary about exactly what Gnostics believed. Some have suggested that the Gnostics represented a freethinking and idealistic movement much like that of the "Hippie" movement active in the United States during the 1960's.

Just as the "Hippie" movement influenced political thought, some early sects of Gnostics exerted direct influence on the Christian church and its leadership.

Although it appears that there were several sects of Gnosticism, we will discuss the more universal Gnostic beliefs along with the highlights of the major sects.

Gnostic cosmology, (which is the theory of how the universe is created, constructed, and sustained), is complex and very different from orthodox Christianity cosmology. In many ways, Gnosticism may appear to be polytheistic or even pantheistic.

To understand some of the basic beliefs of Gnosticism, let us start with the common ground shared between Gnosticism and modern Christianity. Both believe the world is imperfect, corrupt, and brutal. The blame for this, according to mainstream Christianity, is placed squarely on the shoulders of man himself. With the fall of man (Adam), the world was forever changed to the undesirable and harmful place in which we live today. However, Gnostics reject this view as an incorrect interpretation of the creation myth.

According to Gnostics, the blame is not in ourselves, but in our creator. The creator of this world was himself somewhat less than perfect and in fact, deeply flawed and cruel, making mankind the child of a lesser God. The Gnostic view of creation is presented to us in great detail in the book, *The Apocryphon of John*.

Gnosticism teaches that, in the beginning, a Supreme Being called The Father, The Divine All, The Origin, The Supreme God, or The Fullness, emanated the element of existence, both visible and invisible. His intent was not to create, but just as light emanates from a flame, so did creation shine forth from God. This creation was Barbelo, who is the Thought of God, manifested as the primal element needed for creation.

The Father's thought performed a deed and she was created from it. It is she who had appeared before him in the shining of his light. This is the first power which was before all of them and which was created from his mind. She is the Thought of the All and her light shines like his light. It is the perfect power, which is the visage of the invisible. She is the pure, undefiled Spirit who is perfect. She is the first power, the glory of Barbelo, the perfect glory of the kingdom (kingdoms), the glory revealed. She glorified the pure, undefiled Spirit and it was she who praised him, because thanks to him she had come forth.
The Apocryphon of John

It could be said that Barbelo is the creative emanation, and like the Divine All, is both male and female. It is the "agreement" of Barbelo and the Divine All, representing the union of male and female that created the Christ Spirit and all the Aeons. In some renderings the word "Aeon" is used to designate an ethereal realm or kingdom. In other versions "Aeon" indicate the rulers of the realm. One of these rulers was called Sophia or Wisdom. Her fall began a chain of events that led to the introduction of evil into the universe.

Seeing the Divine Flame of God, Sophia sought to know its origin. She sought to know the very nature of God. Sophia's passion ended in tragedy when she managed to capture a divine and creative spark, which she attempted to duplicate with her own creative force, without the union of a male counterpart. It was this act that produced the Archons, beings born outside the higher divine realm. In the development of the myth, explanations point to the fact that Sophia carried the divine essence of creation from God within her, but chose to attempt creation by using her own powers. It is unclear if this was in an attempt to understand the Supreme God and his power, or an impetuous act that caused evil to enter the cosmos in the form of her creations.

The realm containing the Fullness of the Godhead and Sophia is called the pleroma or Realm of Fullness. This is the Gnostic heaven. The lesser Gods created in Sophia's failed attempt were cast outside the pleroma and away from the presence of God. In essence, she threw away and discarded her flawed creations.

"She cast it away from her, outside the place where no one of the immortals might see it, for she had created it in ignorance. And she surrounded it with a glowing cloud, and she put a throne in the middle of the cloud so that no one could see it except the Holy Spirit who is called the mother of all that has life. And she called his name Yaldaboth."
Apocryphon of John

The beings that Sophia created were imperfect and oblivious to the Supreme God. Her creations contained deities even less perfect than herself. They were called the Powers, the Rulers, or the Archons. Their leader was called the Demiurge, but his name was Yaldaboth. It was the flawed, imperfect, spiritually blind Demiurge (Yaldaboth), who became the creator of the material world and all things in it. Gnostics considered Yaldaboth to be the same as Jehovah (Yahweh), who is the Jewish creator God. These beings, the Demiurge and the Archons, would later equate to Satan and his demons, or Jehovah and his angels, depending on which Gnostic sect is telling the story. Both are equally evil.

In one Gnostic creation story, the Archons created Adam, but could not bring him to life. In other stories Adam was formed as a type of worm, unable to attain personhood. Thus, man began as an incomplete creation of a flawed, spiritually blind, and malevolent god. In this myth, the Archons were afraid that Adam might be more powerful than the Archons themselves. When they saw Adam was incapable of attaining the human state, their fears were put to rest, thus, they called that day the "Day of Rest."

Sophia saw Adam's horrid state and had compassion, because she knew she was the origin of the Archons and their evil. Sophia descended to help bring Adam out of his hopeless condition. It is this story that set the stage for the emergence of the sacred feminine force in Gnosticism that is not seen in orthodox Christianity. Sophia brought within herself the light and power of the Supreme God. Metaphorically, within the spiritual womb of Sophia was carried the life force of the Supreme God for Adam's salvation.

In the Apocryphon of John, Sophia is quoted:
"I entered into the midst of the cage which is the prison of the body. And I spoke saying: 'He who hears, let him awake from his deep sleep.' Then Adam wept and shed tears. After he wiped away his bitter tears he asked: 'Who calls my name, and from where has this hope arose in me even while I am in the chains of this prison?' And I (Sophia) answered: 'I am the one who carries the pure light; I am the thought of the undefiled spirit. Arise, remember, and follow your origin, which is I, and beware of the deep sleep.'"

Sophia would later equate to the Holy Spirit as it awakened the comatose soul.

As the myth evolved, Sophia, after animating Adam, became Eve in order to assist Adam in finding the truth. She offered it to him in the form of the fruit of the tree of knowledge. To Gnostics, this was an act of deliverance.

In other stories, Sophia becomes the serpent in order to offer Adam a way to attain the truth. In either case, the fruit represented the hard sought truth, which was the knowledge of good and evil, and through that knowledge Adam could become a god. Later, the serpent became a feminine symbol of wisdom, probably owing to the connection with Sophia. Eve, being Sophia in disguise, became the mother and sacred feminine of us all. As Gnostic theology began to coalesce, Sophia was considered a force or conduit of the Holy Spirit, due, in part, to the fact that the Holy Spirit was believed to be a feminine and creative force from the Supreme God. The Gospel of Philip echoes this theology in verse six as follows:

In the days when we were Hebrews we were made orphans, having only our Mother. Yet when we believed in the Messiah (and became the ones of Christ), the Mother and Father both came to us.
Gospel of Philip

As the emerging orthodox church became more and more oppressive to women, later even labeling them "occasions of sin", the Gnostics countered by raising women to equal status with men, saying Sophia was, in a sense, the handmaiden or wife of the Supreme God, making the soul of Adam her spiritual offspring.

In Gnostic cosmology, the "living" world is under the control of entities called Aeons, of which Sophia is head. These means the Aeons influence or control the soul, life force, intelligence, thought, and mind. Control of the mechanical or inorganic world is given to the Archons. They rule the physical aspects of systems, regulation, limits, and order in the world. Both the ineptitude and cruelty of the Archons are reflected in the chaos and pain of the material realm.

The lesser God that created the world, Yaldaboth began his existence in a state that was both detached and remote from the Supreme God in both spiritual and physical aspects. Since Sophia had misused her creative force, which passed from the Supreme God to her, Sophia's creation, the Demiurge (Yaldaboth), contained only part of the original creative spark of the Supreme Being. He was created with an imperfect nature caused by his distance in lineage and spirit from the Supreme God. It is because of his imperfections and limited abilities the lesser God is also called the "Half-Maker."

The Creator God, the Demiurge, and his helpers, the Archons took the stuff of existence produced by the Supreme God and fashioned it into this material world. Since the Demiurge (Yaldaboth) had no memory of how he came to be alive, he did not realize he was not the true creator. The Demiurge believed he somehow came to create the material world by himself. The Supreme God allowed the Demiurge and Archons to remain deceived.

The Creator God (the Demiurge) intended the material world to be perfect and eternal, but he did not have it in himself to accomplish the feat. What comes forth from a being cannot be greater than the highest part of himself, can it? The world was created flawed and transitory and we are part of it. Can we escape? The Demiurge was imperfect and evil. So was the world he created. If it was the Demiurge who created man and man is called upon to escape the Demiurge and find union with the Supreme God, is this not demanding that man becomes greater than his creator? Spiritually, this seems impossible, however, since many children become greater than their parents, man is expected to become greater than his maker, the Demiurge. This starts with the one fact that the Demiurge denies: the existence and supremacy of the Supreme God.

Man was created with a dual nature as the product of the material world of the Demiurge with his imperfect essence, combined with the spark of God that emanated from the Supreme God through Sophia. A version of the creation story has Sophia instructing the Demiurge to breath into Adam that spiritual power he had taken from Sophia during his creation. It was the spiritual power from Sophia that brought life to Adam.

It is this divine spark in man that calls to its source, the Supreme God, and which causes a "divine discontent," that nagging feeling, that keeps us questioning if this is all there is. This spark and the feeling it gives us keep us searching for the truth.

The Creator God (the Demiurge) sought to keep man ignorant of his defective state by keeping him enslaved to the material world. By doing so, he continued to receive man's worship and servitude. He did not wish man to recognize or gain knowledge of the true Supreme God. Since he did not know or acknowledge the Supreme God, he views any attempt to worship anything else as spiritual treason.

The opposition of forces set forth in the spiritual battle over the continued enslavement of man and man's spiritual freedom set up the duality of good and evil in Gnostic theology. There is a glaring difference between the orthodox Christian viewpoint and the Gnostic viewpoint. According to Gnostics, the creator of the material world was an evil entity and the Supreme God, who was his source, was the good entity. Christians quote John 1:1, "In the beginning was the Word, and the Word was with God, and the Word was God."

According to Gnostics, only through the realization of man's true state or through death, can he escape captivity in the material realm. This means the idea of salvation does not deal with original sin

163

or blood payment. Instead, it focuses on the idea of awakening to the fullness of the truth.

According to Gnostic theology, neither Jesus nor his death can save anyone, however, the truth that he came to proclaim can allow a person to save his or her own soul. It is the truth, or realization of the lie of the material world and its God that sets one on a course of freedom.

To escape the earthly prison and find one's way back to the pleroma (heaven) and the Supreme God, is the soteriology (salvation doctrine) and eschatology (judgment, reward, and doctrine of heaven) of Gnosticism.

The idea that personal revelation leads to salvation may be what caused the mainline Christian church to declare Gnosticism a heresy. This fact, along with the divergent interpretation of the creation story, which placed the creator God, Yaldaboth or Jehovah, as the enemy of mankind, was too much for the church to tolerate. Reaction was harsh. Gnosticism was declared to be a dangerous heresy.

Gnosticism may be considered polytheistic because it espoused many "levels" of Gods, beginning with an ultimate, unknowable, Supreme God and descending as he created Sophia, and Sophia created the Demiurge (Creator God); each becoming more inferior and limited.

There is a hint of pantheism in Gnostic theology due to the fact that creation occurs because of a deterioration of the Godhead and the dispersion of the creative essence, which eventually devolves into the creation of man.

In the end, there occurs a universal reconciliation after being realizes the existence of the Supreme God and renounces the material world and its inferior creator.

Combined with its Christian influences, the cosmology of the Gnostics may have borrowed from the Greek philosopher, Plato, as well as from Buddhism. There are disturbing parallels between the creation myth set forth by Plato and some of those recorded in Gnostic writings.

Plato lived from 427 to 347 B.C. He was the son of wealthy Athenians, a student of the philosopher, Socrates, and the mathematician, Pythagoras. Plato himself was the teacher of Aristotle.

In Plato's cosmology, the Demiurge was an artist who imposed form on materials that already existed. The raw materials were in a chaotic and random state and the Demiurge arranged them into a visible form which was put together much like a puzzle is constructed.

This later idea gave way to a philosophy, which stated that all things in existence could be broken down into a small subset of geometric shapes.

The name, Demiurge, may be the Greek word for "craftsman" or "artisan", or, according to how one divides the word, initiates nature. It could also be translated as "half-maker."

In the tradition of Greek mythology, Plato's cosmology began with a creation story. The philosopher, Timaeus of Locris, a fictional character of Plato's making, narrated the story. In his account, a creator deity, called the "Demiurge" sought to create the cosmos modeled on his understanding of the supreme and original truth. In this way, he created the visible universe based on invisible truths. He set rules of process in place such as birth, growth, change, death, and dissolution. This was Plato's "Realm of Becoming." It was his Genesis. Plato stated that the internal structure of the cosmos had innate intelligence and therefore, was called the World Soul. The cosmic super-structure of the Demiurge was used as the framework on which to hang or fill in the details and parts of the universe. The Demiurge then appointed his underlings to fill in the details, which allowed the universe to remain in a working and balanced state. All phenomena of nature resulted from an interaction and interplay of the two forces of reason and necessity.

Plato represented reason as constituting the World Soul. The material world was a necessity in which reason acted out its will in the physical realm. The duality between the will, mind, or reason of the World Soul and the material universe and its inherent flaws set in play the duality of Plato's world and is seen reflected in the beliefs of the Gnostics.

In Plato's world, the human soul was immortal; each soul was assigned to a star. Souls that were just or good were permitted to return to their stars upon their death. Unjust souls were reincarnated to try again. Escape of the soul to the freedom of the stars and out of the cycle of reincarnation was best accomplished by following the reason and goodness of the World Soul and not the physical world, which was set in place only as a necessity to manifest the patterns of the World Soul.

Although in Plato's cosmology, the Demiurge was not seen as evil, in Gnostic cosmology, he was considered not only to be flawed and evil, but was also the beginning of all evil in the material universe, having created it to reflect his own malice. Following the path of Plato's cosmology, some Gnostics left the possibility of reincarnation open, if a person had not reached the truth before his death.

Most Gnostics were suppressed or killed. The last great Gnostic movement came from the Cathars. Catharism represented total opposition to the Catholic Church, which they basically viewed as a large, pompous, and fraudulent organization that had lost its integrity and "sold out" for power and money in this world, a world that the Gnostics viewed as evil.

As time went on and the mainstream church became established in its power base, they could more effectively fight their enemies. The Inquisition was proof of this. Catharism, one of the last great sects of Gnosticism, vanished from the stage of history by the end of the 14th century. Nevertheless, many well-preserved Gnostic texts were found in 1945 in Nag Hammadi, Egypt.

In the year 13 A.D., Roman annals record the visit of an Indian king named Pandya or Porus. He came to see Caesar Augustus carrying a letter of introduction in Greek. A monk, who burned himself alive in the city of Athens to prove his faith in Buddhism, accompanied him. Nicolaus of Damascus described the event as, not surprisingly, causing a great stir among the people. This is considered the first transmission of Buddhist teaching to the masses.

In the second century A.D., Clement of Alexandria wrote about Buddha: "*Among the Indians are those philosophers also who follow the precepts of Boutta (Buddha), whom they honour as a god on account of his extraordinary sanctity.*" (Clement of Alexandria, "*The Stromata, or Miscellanies*" Book I, Chapter XV).

"*Thus philosophy, a thing of the highest utility, flourished in antiquity among the barbarians, shedding its light over the nations. And afterwards it came to Greece.*" (Clement of Alexandria, "*The Stromata, or Miscellanies*").

To clarify what "philosophy" was transmitted from India to Greece, we turn to the historians Hippolytus and Epiphanius who wrote of Scythianus, a man who had visited India around 50 A.D. They report; "He brought 'the doctrine of the Two Principles.'" According to these writers, Scythianus' pupil Terebinthus called himself a Buddha. Some scholars suggest it was he that traveled to the area of Babylon and transmitted his knowledge to Mani, who later founded Manichaeism.

Adding to the possibility of Eastern influence, we have accounts of the Apostle Thomas' attempt to convert the people of Asia-Minor. If the Gnostic gospel bearing his name was truly written by Thomas, it was penned after his return from India, where he also encountered the Buddhist influences.

Ancient church historians mention that Thomas preached to the Parthians in Persia, and it is said he was buried in Edessa. Fourth century chronicles attribute the evangelization of India (Asia-Minor or Central Asia) to Thomas. The texts of the Gospel of Thomas, which some believe predate the four gospels, has a very "Zen-like" or Eastern flavor.

Since it is widely held that the four gospels of Matthew, Mark, Luke, and John have a common reference in the basic text of Mark, it stands to reason that all follow the same general insight and language. If The Gospel of Thomas was written in his absence from the other apostles or if it was the first gospel written, one can assume it was written outside the influences common to the other gospels. Although the codex found in Egypt is dated to the fourth century, most Biblical scholars place the actual construction of the text of Thomas at about 70–150 A.D. Most agree that the time of writing was in the second century A.D.

Following the transmission of the philosophy of "Two Principals," both Manichaeism and Gnosticism retained a dualistic viewpoint. The black-versus-white dualism of Gnosticism came to rest in the evil of the material world and its maker, versus the goodness of the freed soul and the Supreme God with whom it seeks union.

Oddly, the disdain for the material world and its Creator God drove Gnostic theology to far-flung extremes in attitude, beliefs, and actions. Gnostics idolize the serpent in the "Garden of Eden" story. After all, if your salvation hinges on secret knowledge, the offer of becoming gods through the knowledge of good and evil sounds wonderful. So powerful was the draw of this "knowledge myth" to the Gnostics that some sects linked the serpent to Sophia. This can still be seen today in our medical and veterinarian symbols of serpents on poles, conveying the ancient meanings of knowledge and wisdom.

Genesis 3 (King James Version)
1 Now the serpent was more subtil than any beast of the field which the LORD God had made. And he said unto the woman, Yea, hath God said, Ye shall not eat of every tree of the garden?
2 And the woman said unto the serpent, We may eat of the fruit of the trees of the garden:

167

3 But of the fruit of the tree which is in the midst of the garden, God hath said, Ye shall not eat of it, neither shall ye touch it, lest ye die.
4 And the serpent said unto the woman, Ye shall not surely die:
5 For God doth know that in the day ye eat thereof, then your eyes shall be opened, and ye shall be as Gods, knowing good and evil.

It is because of their vehement struggle against the Creator God, and the search for some transcendent truth that Gnostics held the people of Sodom in high regard since the people of Sodom sought to "corrupt" the messengers sent by their enemy, the Creator God. Anything done to thwart the Demiurge and his minions was considered valiant.

To modern Christians, the idea of admiring the serpent, which we believe was Satan, may seem unthinkable. Supporting the idea of attacking and molesting the angels sent to Sodom to warn of the coming destruction seems appalling; but to Gnostics the real evil was the malevolent entity, the Creator God of this world. To destroy his messengers would impede his mission. They believed that by obtaining the knowledge of good and evil, as was offered by the serpent in the garden, the captives would be set free.

To awaken the inner knowledge of the true God was the battle. The material world was designed to prevent the awakening by entrapping, confusing, and distracting the spirit of man. The aim of Gnosticism was the spiritual awakening and freedom of man.

Gnostics, in the age of the early church, would preach to converts (novices) about this awakening, saying the novice must awaken the God within himself and see the trap that was the material world. Salvation came from the recognition or knowledge contained in this spiritual awakening.

Not all people are ready or willing to accept the Gnosis. Many are bound to the material world and are satisfied to be only as and where they are. These have mistaken the Creator God for the Supreme God, and do not know there is anything beyond the Creator God or the material existence. These people know only the lower or earthly wisdom and not the higher wisdom above the Creator God. They are referred to as "dead."

Gnostic sects are split primarily into two categories. Both branches held that those who were truly enlightened could no longer be influenced by the material world. Both divisions of Gnosticism believed that their spiritual journey could not be impeded by the material realm, since the two were not only separate, but in opposition. Such an attitude influenced some Gnostics toward Stoicism, choosing to abstain from the world, and others toward Epicureanism, choosing to indulge.

Major schools fell into two categories; those who rejected the material world of the Creator God, and those who rejected the laws of the Creator God. For those who rejected the world the Creator God had spawned, overcoming the material world was accomplished by partaking of as little of the world and its pleasures as possible. These followers lived very stark and ascetic lives, abstaining from meat, sex, marriage, and all things that would entice them to remain in the material realm.

Other schools believed it was their duty to simply defy the Creator God and all laws that he had proclaimed. Since the Creator God had been identified as Jehovah, God of the Jews, these followers set about to break every law held dear by Christians and Jews.

As human nature is predisposed to do, many Gnostics took up the more wanton practices, believing that nothing done in their earthly bodies would affect their spiritual lives. Whether it was excesses in sex, alcohol, food, or any other assorted debaucheries; the Gnostics were safe within their faith, believing nothing spiritually bad could come of their earthly adventures.

Early Church leaders mention the actions of the Gnostics. One infamous Gnostic school is actually mentioned in the Bible.

The world was out of balance, inferior, and corrupt. The spirit was perfect and intact. It was up to the Gnostics to tell the story, explain the error, and awaken the world to the light of truth. The Supreme God had provided a vehicle to help in their effort. He had created a teacher of light and truth.

Since the time of Sophia's mistaken creation of the Archons, there was an imbalance in the cosmos. The Supreme God began to re-establish the balance by producing Christ to teach and save man. That left only Sophia, now in a fallen and bound state, along with the Demiurge, and the Archons to upset the cosmic equation. In this theology, one might loosely equate the Supreme God to the New Testament Christian God, Demiurge to Satan, the Archons to demons, the pleroma to heaven, and Sophia to the creative or regenerative force of the Holy Spirit. This holds up well except for one huge problem. If the Jews believed that Jehovah created all things, and the Gnostic believed that the Demiurge created all things, then to the Gnostic mind, the Demiurge must be Old Testament god, Jehovah, and that made Jehovah their enemy.

For those who seek that which is beyond the material world and its flawed creator, the Supreme God has sent Messengers of Light to awaken the divine spark of the Supreme God within us. This part of us will call to the True God as deep calls to deep. The greatest and most perfect Messenger of Light was the Christ. He is also referred to as The Good, Christ, Messiah, and The Word. He came to reveal the Divine Light to us in the form of knowledge.

According to the Gnostics, Christ came to show us our own divine spark and to awaken us to the illusion of the material world and its flawed maker. He came to show us the way back to the divine Fullness (The Supreme God). The path to enlightenment was the knowledge sleeping within each of us. Christ came to show us the Christ spirit living in each of us. Individual ignorance or the refusal to awaken our internal divine spark was the only original sin. Christ was the only Word spoken by God that could awaken us. Christ was also the embodiment of the Word itself. He was part of the original transmission from the Supreme God that took form on the earth to awaken the soul of man so that man might search beyond the material world.

One Gnostic view of the Incarnation was "docetic," which is an early heretical position that Jesus was never actually present in the flesh, but only appeared to be human. He was a spiritual being and his human appearance was only an illusion. Of course, the title of "heretical" can only be decided by the controlling authority of the time. In this case, it was the church that was about to emerge under the rule of the Emperor Constantine.

Most Gnostics believed that the Christ spirit indwelt the earthly Jesus at the time of his baptism by John, at which time Jesus received the name, and thus the power, of the Lord or Supreme God.

The Christ spirit departed from Jesus' body before his death. These two viewpoints remove the idea of God sacrificing himself as atonement for the sins of man. The idea of atonement was not necessary in Gnostic theology since it was knowledge and not sacrifice that set one free.

Since there was a distinction in Gnosticism between the man Jesus and the Light of Christ that came to reside within him, it is not contrary to Gnostic beliefs that Mary Magdalene could have been the consort and wife of Jesus. Neither would it have been blasphemous for them to have children.

Various sects of Gnosticism stressed certain elements of their basic theology. Each had its head teachers and its special flavor of beliefs. One of the oldest types was the Syrian Gnosticism that existed around 120 A.D. In contrast to other sects, the Syrian lacked much of the embellished mythology of Aeons, Archons, and angels.

The fight between the Supreme God and the Creator God was not eternal, though there was strong opposition to Jehovah, the Creator God. He was considered to have been the last of the seven angels who created this world out of divine material, which emanated from the Supreme God. The Demiurge attempted to create man, but only created a miserable worm, which the Supreme God had to save by giving it the spark of divine life. Thus man was born.

According to this sect, Jehovah, the Creator God, must not be worshiped. The Supreme God calls us to his service and presence through Christ his Son. They pursued only the unknowable Supreme God and sought to obey the Supreme Deity by abstaining from eating meat and from marriage and sex, and by leading an ascetic life. The symbol of Christ was the serpent, which attempted to free Adam and Eve from their ignorance and entrapment to the Creator God.

Another Gnostic school was the Hellenistic or Alexandrian School. These systems absorbed the philosophy and concepts of the Greeks, and the Semitic names were replaced by Greek names. The cosmology and myth grew out of proportion and appear to be unwieldy. Yet, this school produced two great thinkers, Basilides and Valentinus. Though born at Antioch, in Syria, Basilides founded his school in Alexandria around the year A.D. 130, where it survived for several centuries.

Valentinus first taught at Alexandria and then in Rome. He established the largest Gnostic movement around A.D. 160. This movement was founded on an elaborate mythology and a system of sexual duality of male and female interplay, both in its deities and its savior.

Tertullian wrote that between 135 A.D. and 160 A.D. Valentinus, a prominent Gnostic, had great influence in the Christian church. Valentinus ascended in church hierarchy and became a candidate for the office of bishop of Rome, the office that quickly evolved into that of Pope. He lost the election by a narrow margin. Even though

Valentinus was outspoken about his Gnostic slant on Christianity, he was a respected member of the Christian community until his death, and was probably a practicing bishop in a church of lesser status than the one in Rome.

The main platform of Gnosticism was the ability to transcend the material world through the possession of privileged and directly imparted knowledge. Following this doctrine, Valentinus claimed to have been instructed by a direct disciple of one of Jesus' apostles, a man by the name of Theodas.

Valentinus is considered by many to be the father of modern Gnosticism. G.R.S. Mead summarizes his vision of the faith in the book "Fragments of a Faith Forgotten."

"The Gnosis in his hands is trying to embrace everything, even the most dogmatic formulation of the traditions of the Master. The great popular movement and its incomprehensibilities were recognized by Valentinus as an integral part of the mighty outpouring; he laboured to weave all together, external and internal, into one piece, devoted his life to the task, and doubtless only at his death perceived that for that age he was attempting the impossible. None but the very few could ever appreciate the ideal of the man, much less understand it. " (Fragments of a Faith Forgotten, p. 297)

Gnostic theology vacillated from polytheism to pantheism to dualism to monotheism, depending on the teacher and how he viewed and stressed certain areas of their creation myths. Marcion, a Gnostic teacher, espoused differences between the God of the New Testament and the God of the Old Testament, claiming they were two separate entities. According to Marcion, the New Testament God was a good true God while the Old Testament God was an evil angel. Although this may be a heresy, it pulled his school back into monotheism. The church, however, disowned him.

Syneros and Prepon, disciples of Marcion, postulated three different entities, carrying their teachings from monotheism into polytheism in one stroke. In their system, the opponent of the good God was not the God of the Jews, but Eternal Matter, which was the source of all evil. Matter, in this system, became a principal creative force. Although it was created imperfect, it could also create, having the innate intelligence of the "world soul."

Of all the Gnostic schools or sects the most famous is the Antinomian School. Believing that the Creator God, Jehovah, was evil, they sat out to disrupt all things connected to the Jewish God. This included his laws. They considered it their duty to break any law of morality, diet, or conduct given by the Jewish God, who they considered the evil Creator God. The leader of the sect was called Nicolaites. The sect existed in apostolic times and is mentioned in the Bible.

Revelation 2 (King James Version)
5 Remember therefore from whence thou art fallen, and repent, and do the first works; or else I will come unto thee quickly, and will remove thy candlestick out of his place, except thou repent.
6 But this thou hast, that thou hatest the deeds of the Nicolaitanes, which I also hate.

Revelation 2 (King James Version)
14 But I have a few things against thee, because thou hast there them that hold the doctrine of Balaam, who taught Balac to cast a stumbling block before the children of Israel, to eat things sacrificed unto idols, and to commit fornication.
15 So hast thou also them that hold the doctrine of the Nicolaitanes, which thing I hate.
16 Repent; or else I will come unto thee quickly, and will fight against them with the sword of my mouth.

One of the leaders of the Nocolaitanes, according to Origen, was Carpocrates, whom Tertullian called a magician and a fornicator. Carpocretes taught that one could only escape the cosmic powers by discharging one's obligations to them and disregarding their laws. The Christian church fathers, St. Justin, Irenaeus, and Eusebius wrote that the reputation of these men (the Nicolaitanes), brought infamy upon the whole race of Christians.

Although Gnostic sects varied, they had certain points in common. These commonalities included salvation through special knowledge, and the fact that the world was corrupt because it was created by an evil God. According to Gnostic theology, nothing can come from the material world that is not flawed. Because of this, Gnostics did not believe that Christ could have been a corporeal being. Thus, there must be some separation or distinction between Jesus, as a

173

man, and Christ, as a spiritual being born from the Supreme, unrevealed, and eternal God.

To closer examine this theology, we turn to Valentinus, the driving force of early Gnosticism, for an explanation. Valentinus divided Jesus Christ into two very distinct parts; Jesus, the man, and Christ, the anointed spiritual messenger of God. These two forces met in the moment of Baptism when the Spirit of God came to rest on Jesus and the Christ power entered his body.

Here Gnosticism runs aground on its own theology, for if the spiritual cannot mingle with the material, then how can the Christ spirit inhabit a body? The result of the dichotomy was a schism within Gnosticism. Some held to the belief that the specter of Jesus was simply an illusion produced by Christ himself to enable him to do his work on earth. It was not real, not matter, not corporeal, and did not actually exist as a physical body would. Others came to believe that Jesus must have been a specially prepared vessel, and was the perfect human body formed by the very essence of the plumora (heaven). It was this path of thought that allowed Jesus to continue as human, lover, and father.

Jesus, the man, became a vessel containing the Light of God, called Christ. In the Gnostic view, we all could and should become Christs, carrying the Truth and Light of God. We are all potential vehicles of the same Spirit that Jesus held within himself when he was awakened to the Truth.

The suffering and death of Jesus then took on much less importance in the Gnostic view, as Jesus was simply part of the corrupt world and was suffering the indignities of this world as any man would. Therefore, from their viewpoint, he could have been married and been a father without disturbing Gnostic theology in the least.

The Gnostic texts seem to divide man into parts, although at times the divisions are somewhat unclear. The divisions alluded to may include the soul, which is the will of man; the spirit, which is depicted as wind or air (pneuma) and contains the holy spark that is the spirit of God in man; and the material human form, the body. The mind of man sits as a mediator between the soul, or will, and the spirit, which is connected to God.

Without the light of the truth, the spirit is held captive by the Demiurge, which enslaves man. This entrapment is called "sickness." It is this sickness that the Light came to heal so that we may be set free. The third part of man, his material form, was considered a weight, an anchor, and a hindrance, keeping man attached to the corrupted earthly realm.

As we read the text, we must realize that Gnosticism conflicted with traditional Christianity. Overall theology can rise and fall upon small words and terms. If Jesus was not God, his death and thus his atonement meant nothing. His suffering meant nothing. Even the resurrection meant nothing, if one's view of Jesus was that he was not human to begin with, as was true with some Gnostics. For those Gnostics, resurrection of the dead was unthinkable since flesh, as well as, all matter is destined to perish. According to Gnostic theology, there was no resurrection of the flesh, but only of the soul. How the soul would be resurrected was explained differently by various Gnostic groups, but all denied the resurrection of the body. To the enlightened Gnostic, the actual person was the spirit who used the body as an instrument to survive in the material world but did not identify with it. This belief is echoed in the Gospel of Thomas.

29. Jesus said: If the flesh came into being because of spirit, it is a marvel, but if spirit came into being because of the body, it would be a marvel of marvels. I marvel indeed at how great wealth has taken up residence in this poverty.

Owing to the Gnostic belief of the separation of spirit and body, the Christ spirit within the body of Jesus departed the body before the crucifixion. Others said the body was an illusion and the crucifixion was a sham perpetrated by an eternal spirit on the men that sought to kill it. Lastly, some suggested that Jesus deceived the soldiers into thinking he was dead. The resurrection under this circumstance became a lie, which allowed Jesus to escape and live on in anonymity, hiding, living as a married man, and raising a family until his natural death.

Think of the implications to the orthodox Christian world if the spirit of God departed from Jesus as it fled and laughed as the body was crucified. This is the Gnostic interpretation of the death of Jesus when he cries out, "My power, my power, why have you left me," as the Christ spirit left his body before his death. What are the ramifications to the modern Christian if the Creator God, the Demiurge, is more evil than his creation?

Although, in time, the creation myth and other Gnostic differences were swept under the rug. It was this division between Jesus and the Christ spirit that put them at odds with the emerging orthodox church.

175

At the establishment of the doctrine of the trinity, the mainline church firmly set a divide between themselves and the Gnostics.

To this day there is a battle raging in the Christian world as believers and seekers attempt to reconcile today's Christianity to the sect of the early Christian church called, "Gnostics."

The Trinity

The Trinity, the doctrine that many hold so dear, is never mentioned in the Bible, and was not discussed nor considered by the early church. The doctrine was crafted in a political effort to unite the church in order that it might be more easily ruled and controlled.

Adolf von Harnack (May 7, 1851–June 10, 1930), a German theologian and prominent church historian, affirms that the early church view of Jesus was as Messiah, and after his resurrection he was 'raised to the right hand of God' but not considered as God. (See Mark 16:19). This was the baseline view by the church in the first century. From this point of view, an evolution of infiltration began that would culminate in the doctrine of the trinity.

Bernard Lonergan, a Roman Catholic priest and Bible scholar, explains that the educated Christians of the early centuries believed in a single, supreme God. This was the same basic view as held by the Jewish believers of the time.

As for the Holy Spirit, McGiffert tells us that early Christians considered the Holy Spirit "not as a separate entity, but simply as the divine power, working in the world and particularly in the church." It is the power or will of God working in the world.

Durant articulated the evolution of early Christianity when he said: "In Christ and Peter, Christianity was Jewish; in Paul it became half Greek; in Catholicism it became half Roman" (Caesar 579).

The Christian church has always been in turmoil. In the days of the Apostles the church was far from unified. Throughout his book "Orthodoxy and Heresy in Earliest Christianity", the German New Testament scholar, and early Church historian, Walter Bauer, explores the fact that Gnosticism influenced many early Christians forming heresies here and there throughout the budding Christendom.

In his work 'The Greek Fathers," James Marshall Campbell, a Greek professor, explains that the fear of Gnosticism was prevalent in the early church. Sects of Gnosticism varied in their Greek influence but the seeds were primarily of Greek origin and carried within it the mythos and theosophy of Plato and the Greeks that divided the universe into opposing realms of matter and spirit. In this world-view the body was a prison for the captive spirit like that of the "iron maiden" torture device of years to come.

The late Professor Arthur Cushman McGiffert interprets some of the early Christian fathers as believing Gnosticism to be "identical to" in all intents and purposes with Greek polytheism. Gnosticism had a mixed influence on the early Christian writers, sending them in various directions in their Christology. That these philosophies of the Greek, Romans, and Gnostics affected Christianity is a historical fact.

What did these philosophers teach about God? In Plato's Timeus, 'The Supreme Reality appears in the trinitarian form of the Good, the Intelligence, and the World-Soul'. R.D. Laing attributes elaborate trinitarian theories to the Neoplatonists, and considers Neoplatonic ideas as 'one of the operative factors in the development of Christian theology'. One of the questions posed in the book is simply, " What is real in Christianity." What would Christianity be if we were to find and eliminate most outside influences?

Durant ties in philosophy with Christianity when he states that the second century Alexandrian Church, from which both Clement and Origen came, 'wedded Christianity to Greek philosophy'; and finally, Durant writes of the famed pagan philosopher, Plotinus, that 'Christianity accepted nearly every line of him...'

As the apostles died, various writers undertook the task of defending Christianity against the persecutions of the pagans. The problem was that they were so tainted due to education and environment that some of the defenders did more harm than good.

The most famous of these Apologists was Justin Martyr (c.107-166). He was born a pagan, became a pagan philosopher, then a Christian. He believed that Christianity and Greek philosophy were related. As for the Trinity, McGiffert asserts, "Justin insisted that Christ came from God; he did not identify him with God." Justin's God was "a transcendent being, who could not possibly come into contact with the world of men and things." The Church was divided by Gnosticism, enticed by philosophy, and corrupted by paganism, but there were geographic divisions also, with East and West differing greatly.

As a reminder, sects of Gnosticism were differing combinations of Christianity and the Greek teachings, most centering around those of Plato. To the Gnostic Christians the material world and the spiritual world were very much at odds and could not coexist. Due to the increasing influence of Platoism and Gnosticism, the relationship between spirit and flesh as viewed by the church was shifting quickly. The body, once viewed as the vehicle and temple of the spirit and inseparable from it, was now viewed as a flesh prison for the spirit and opposed in nature to it. These views would turn the dancing and joyous Jewish celebration of life into repression and sorrow.

Changes would echo through time in various forms, ending in the stoicism of the sexual abstinence of priests and finally the self-flagellation of some monks. (Self-flagellation seems to have taken root in the dark ages during the plague when monks thought it would appease God if they punished themselves by beating themselves with whips.) In the early church the changes would be seen in the struggle to articulate the relationship between the various forms of the newly emerging Godhead. The Father was a spirit. The Holy Ghost was obviously a spirit, since it was the will of God who was pure spirit. It was the existence of Jesus and His position and state within the spiritual and material worlds that gives pause within the various sects of the early church.

The Eastern Church, centered in Alexandria, Egypt, and the Western Church, centered in Rome, Italy, grew in divergence. The Eastern Church was inquisitive and had an environment of free thought as a reflection of the surrounding Greek culture. The theological development of the East is best represented in Clement and Origen.

Clement of Alexandria (c.150-220) was trained in the "Catechetical School of Alexandria," a place of training for Christian theologians and priests. Even though Clement was trained here, Gnosticism influenced his views. If one were to wish for a single focused statement explaining the Greek influence on the Christian Church, it would likely be the following by McGiffert; "Clement insists that philosophy came from God and was given to the Greeks as a schoolmaster to bring them to Christ as the law was a schoolmaster for the Hebrews." McGiffert further states that Clement considered "God the Father revealed in the Old Testament" separate and distinct from the "Son of God incarnate in Christ," with whom he identified the Logos.

Campbell continues this line of explanation when he says; "[with Clement the] philosophic spirit enters frankly into the service of Christian doctrine, and with it begins... the theological science of the future." However, it was his student, Origen, who "achieved the union of Greek philosophy and Christianity."

To sum up this bit of church history; Clement believed that just as the law was given to the Jews as a schoolmaster to bring them into the understanding that they needed a savior, philosophy was given

179

to the Greeks to enable them to bring reason and a scientific approach to Christianity to establish its theology.

Campbell considered Origen (c.185-253) to be the founder of theology", the greatest scholar of the early church and the greatest theologian of the East. Durant adds "with [Origen] Christianity ceased to be only a comforting faith; it became a full-fledged philosophy, buttressed with scripture but proudly resting on reason." However, the reason it rested on was directed and disciplined by the Greek style and content of thought. This is why in Origen the church experiences a changing view of God.

According to Pelikan"s Historical Theology, Origen was the "teacher of such orthodox stalwarts as the Cappadocian Father's, (Cappadocian was an area stretching from Mount Taurus to the Black Sea), but also the "teacher of Arius' and the "originator of many heresies."" Centuries after his death, he was condemned by councils at least five times; however, both Athanasius and Eusebius had great respect for him.

Origen turned his attention to the trinity, beginning with what he called the "incomprehensible God." He applied Stoic and Platonic philosophies in true Greek style. Origen believed the Father and Son were separate "in respect of hypostasis" (substance), but "one by harmony and concord and identity of will." If we stop at this point and poll members of most major denominations we are likely to find this to be the understanding of the majority, for how can a God who is pure spirit be of the same substance as Jesus, who is flesh and blood? Origen then went on to claim the Son was the image of God, probably drawing on the scripture where Christ proclaimed, "If you have seen me you have seen the father." In this he seems to contradict himself, anthropomorphizing to the point of endowing God with the limits of a human body made of a substance differing from that of which Jesus was made.

Keeping in mind that Gnosticism, as well as certain Greek philosophies, tend to divide the universe into realms of the spiritual and material, Origen, seeing those realms in opposition, maintained that there was a difference between "the God" and "God." He attempted to explained that "the God" [God himself] was a unity to himself and not associated with the world but, "Whatever else, other than him who is called is also God, is deified by participation, by sharing in his divinity, and is more properly to be called not "the God" but simply "God"'" (Quotes are mine for clarification.) With such theological hair-splitting we enter into confusion and error.

As Origen and others introduced more and more Greek influences into the Eastern Church, it became more mystical, philosophical, and at times obtuse. This line of thought brought us from the Jewish proclamation of, Deuteronomy 6:4 "Hear, O Israel: The LORD our God, the LORD is one" and placed us into the first stage of the trinity by dividing God in twain. The simple and direct teaching of Christ to love God and treat others with dignity gave way to the complex, sophisticated, and often convoluted arguments as men found their self-importance in their ability to divide, and persuade.

It was Tertullian (c.160-230) who first coined the term trinitas from which we derive our English word "trinity." Tertullian writes, "...the unity makes a trinity, placing the three in order not of quality but of sequence, different not in substance but in aspect, not in power but in manifestation." Tertullian did not consider the Father and Son co-eternal. He considered God the creator of all. God must, therefore, pre-date everything that exists, even the first creative impulse, which would have created the pre-incarnate Christ. To clarify his belief Tertullian wrote, "There was a time when there was neither sin to make God a judge, nor a son to make God a Father." Tertullian also rejected the idea of God and Christ being co-equal. He reasoned that God was and contains everything, thus the Son cannot contain everything. He explains, "For the Father is the whole substance, whereas the Son is something derived from it." Another way to see his point is to say that all things are contained in or are part of God, thus Christ is in or part of God. The fullness of God could not be physically contained in Christ. (This statement flew in the face of Col. 2:9, which states that the fullness of the deity lives in Christ.) The idea of Trinitas is the beginning of the Trinitarian discussion in earnest, but it will take time to grow and develop into the full doctrine of the Trinity established under the political pressure of Constantine.

The world around the early Church was changing. The Roman Empire began to crumble and Constantine came to power. He wished to unify the Empire, and although he was a pagan, living in a society of polytheists, he chose Christianity, as a vehicle to work his will. What better way to unite a nation than through the growing monotheistic faith? But Christianity was far from unified; so to unify the empire the king had to unify the faith.

181

In 318 A.D., controversy over the matter of the Trinity had blown up again between Arius, a deacon, and Alexander, the bishop of the church in Alexandria, Egypt. Bishop Alexander of Alexandria and his deacon, Athanasius, believed there were three persons in one god.

This time Emperor Constantine involved himself. The emperor began to send letters encouraging them to put aside what the emperor called their "trivial" disputes regarding the nature of God and the "number" of God. As a polytheist, the emperor saw the argument over the semantics of whether one worshiped a single god, three gods or "three gods in one" as trivial and inconsequential. Arius, Presbyter in Alexandria, and Eusebius, Bishop of Nicomedia believed in only one indivisible god. According to the concept of homo-ousion, Christ the Son was consubstantial, that is to say the Son shares the same substance with the Father. Arius and Eusebius disagreed. Arius thought the Father, Son, and Holy Spirit were materially separate and different. He believed that the Father created the Son. Arius and his followers, the Arians, believed if the Son were equal to the Father, there would be more than one God. If one were to sum up the heart of the matter within the debate, it would be over the status of the Son as compared to the Father.

To exemplify the points of contention, an essay by Wright regarding Arius reports; "Arius was a senior presbyter in charge of Baucalis, one of the twelve "parishes" of Alexandria. He was a persuasive preacher, with a following of clergy and ascetics, and even circulated his teaching in popular verse and songs. Around 318 A.D., he clashed with Bishop Alexander. Arius claimed that Father alone was really God; the Son was essentially different from his father. He did not possess by nature or right any of the divine qualities of immortality, sovereignty, perfect wisdom, goodness, and purity. He did not exist before he was begotten by the father. The father produced him as a creature. Yet as the creator of the rest of creation, the son existed "apart from time before all things." Nevertheless, he did not share in the being of God the Father and did not know him perfectly. Wright concludes that before the 3rd century the "three were separate in Christian belief and each had his or it's own status."

The dispute became louder and more strident until it spilled over once again into the Christian community, causing division and controversy within the church body. The emperor's plan to unify the faith in order to unify the nation was being placed in jeopardy. In 325 A.D. the church faced two serious points of strife. The date of observance of the Passover on Easter Sunday had become an issue, and the concept of the Trinity was in full debate. Serious questions were being raised as to whether the church would remain intact. Letters from Constantine failed to settle the dispute, so the emperor called the "Council of Nicea."

Constantine chose leaders, who would represent each major division within the church and invited these bishops to join him in the seaside village of Nicea (Nicaea). There they formed a council, which Constantine hoped could unify the church. McGiffert tells us about the council. There were three main groups represented at this council: Eusebius of Nicomedia, who represented the Arian view of the Trinity, Alexander of Alexandria presenting the Athanasian version, and a very large party led by Eusebius of Cesarea. The Cesarea contingent was made up of those who wanted unity and peace. Their theological stance was not one so immovable and intractable that it would interfere with their desire for peace. It should be noted that Alexander of Alexandria was the bishop who was involved in the "discussion" with Arius, which began the final fray. He was so self-assured that he would not move on his idea of the Trinity. It is amazing that any man could be so self-assured about his knowledge of the mind and substance of God. It is presumption.

There is a general rule of negotiations. If you are sitting at the table with your enemies, the one who moves first loses. The moment a line is drawn or a position is articulated, it sets a limit on the discussion. If the 'negotiation is about price, the price stated would serve only as a limit from which to work. It was the mistake of Eusebius of Nicomedia to submit the Arian creed first. This served only to set a stage from which the other groups could spring. Their creed was summarily rejected. Then the more amicable of Eusebius of Cesarea submitted their creed, known as the Cesarean baptismal creed. Now the Alexandrian group knew where both parties stood. They would use this information to institute a brilliant political maneuver. Instead of submitting a creed of their own, the Alexandrian group modified the creed from Eusebius. The changes were not substantial enough to change the deeper intent of the creed. Eusebius was compelled to sign the creed. Now two of the three parties were united and the Arians were out of the negotiations. The majority of Eastern bishops sided with Arius in that they believed Christ was the Son of God 'neither consubstantial nor co-eternal' with his Father, but it no longer mattered.

183

Constantine saw well over two-thirds of the church in one accord, at least on paper. He now began to pressure all bishops to sign. Arians refusing to sign were exiled. Constantine exiled the excommunicated Arius to Illyria. Constantine's friend Eusebius, who eventually withdrew his objection, but still wouldn't sign the statement of faith, and a neighboring bishop, Theognis, were also exiled to Gaul. Constantine would reverse his opinion about the Arian heresy, and have both exiled bishops reinstated three years later, in 328 A.D. At the same time, Arius would also be recalled from exile; but for now, it was political blackmail.

The pressure from the emperor was so great and his reactions so feared that attendees justified their signatures thusly; Apuleius, wrote "I pass over in silence… those sublime and Platonic doctrines understood by very few of the pious, and absolutely unknown to every one of the profane." "The soul is nothing worse for a little ink."

Abu Al-Hassan Al-Nadwi reported that out of the 2030 attendees, only 318 readily accepted this creed ("Al-Seerah Al-Nabawiyya", p. 306). Only after returning home did other attendees such as Eusebius of Nicomedia, Maris of Chaledon and Theognis of Nicaea summon the courage to express to Constantine in writing how much they regretted having put their signatures to the Nicene formula, **"We committed an impious act, O Prince," wrote Eusebius of Nicomedia, "by subscribing to a blasphemy from fear of you."**

Thus Constantine had his unified Church, which was not very unified. McGiffert asserts that Eusebius of Cesarea was not altogether satisfied with the creed because it was too close to Sabellianism (Father, Son, and Holy Spirit are three aspects of one God). Lonergan shows just how much of the creed Eusebius took exception to as the words were explained. "Out of the Father's substance" was now interpreted to show that the Son is "out of the Father", but "not part of the Father's substance." "Born not made" because "made" refers to all other creatures "which come into being through the Son", and "consubstantial" really means that the Son comes out of the Father and is like him.

Lonergan goes on to explain that the language of debate on the consubstantiality of the Father and the Son has made many people think that the "Church at Nicea had abandoned the genuine Christian doctrine, which was religious through and through, in order to embrace some sort of hellenistic ontology." Nicene dogma marked

the "transition from the prophetic Oracle of Yahweh... to Catholic dogma."

The evolution of the Trinity can be seen in the words of the Apostles' Creed, Nicene Creed, and the Athanasian Creed. As each of the creeds became more wordy and convoluted, the simple, pure faith of the Apostolic church became lost in a haze. Even more interesting is the fact that as the creeds became more specific (and less scriptural) the adherence to them became stricter, and the penalty for disbelief harsher.

In stark contrast, is the simple oneness of the Hebrew God. After the Council of Chalcedon in 451, debate was no longer tolerated and those opposing the Trinity were considered to commit blasphemy. Sentences ranged from mutilation to death. Christians now turned on Christians, maiming and slaughtering thousands because of this difference of belief.

The reign of Constantine marks the time of the transformation of Christianity from a religion into a political system; and though, in one sense, that system was degraded, in another it had risen above the old Greek mythology. The maxim holds true in the social as well as in the mechanical world, that, when two bodies strike, the form of both is changed. Paganism was modified by Christianity; Christianity by Paganism. In the Trinitarian controversy, the chief point in discussion was to define the position of "the Son."

After the divisions regarding the Trinity had subsided, the church continued to narrow its tolerance and tighten its grip.

Oddly, it is the doctrine of the Trinity that so enrages ardent Muslims that they would attack and kill Christians for being polytheists. So it continues that in Islam the Christian doctrine of the Trinity is considered to be the most grievous heresy.

Killing In the Name of God

After doctrine and control are established one may go about the business of ridding the world of those who do not agree with you. This slows religious change and evolution to a crawl by eliminating most who have differing ideas and thoughts. It does however keep the established rulers, priests and popes in power. That is after all the goal of any religion, to remain in power, to grow, spread, and to become exclusive. Thus was the approach of the Catholic Church, and many other religions before and after.

To eliminate someone there is a general path followed psychologically. First the enemy must be demonized. They must be made to look evil. Then they must be de-humanized. They must become less than fully human in the eye of the killers. Then they may be killed without regret or guilt. This is what the church did, first to its own people, then to those of other faiths.

The Catholic Church first warned those people who did not comply with church laws and teaching of excommunication and the resulting hellfire. If they continued to live outside control of the church they would be killed. If the problem was a group or sect of Christians the first order of business was the extermination of the sect. Thus was the case with the last remaining Gnostics. The church had been killing those deemed as heretics for a thousand years, but there was a large surviving Gnostic community living in France.

According to Time Magazine, in an article titled, "Religion: Massacre of the Pure" Friday, Apr. 28, 1961

"These heretics are worse than the Saracens!" exclaimed Pope Innocent III, and on March 10, 1208, he proclaimed a crusade against a sect in southern France that became one of the bloodiest blots in European history.

The heretics called Cathari (from the Greek word for pure), or Albigenses, from the town of Albi, one of their centers in Languedoc, were stamped out in 35 ruthless years of fire and sword. But as the centuries rolled on, they have had a measure of revenge against the Roman Catholic Church. The hatred generated by the crusade prepared the way for Protestantism. And in modern France, where popular apostasy from Catholicism is today wider and deeper than anything Pope Innocent could have imagined, the ancient heresy of Catharism is enjoying a remarkable revival of interest.

The long-lived tradition of anticlericalism in southern France, which recruited the Huguenots in the 16th century and fueled Communism in the 20th, is finding a new outlet in a spreading bush fire of enthusiasm for the vanished sect whose 750-year-old lost cause against the church gave anticlericalism its biggest beachhead in France. Some 30 books have been published during the last 15 years about their beliefs and practices and their slaughterous persecution-most of them highly favorable to the heretics and critical of the church. Several plays have been written about them, and literary reviews have published long articles. Hundreds of weekenders are climbing the 4,000-ft. rock atop which stands Montségur, the holy citadel of Catharism, where 300 soldiers and 200 unarmed, pacifist Cathari stood off an army of 10,000 for ten months before being burned at one huge stake for their "pure Christian" beliefs.

Catharism was not an isolated phenomenon. It was part of an ancient heresy that flowed like an underground stream beneath the surface of Christianity and burst forth in many forms during the church's first 1,000-odd years. Gnosticism, Manichaeanism, Paulicianism, Bogomilism and the Albigenses all had basic characteristics in common. There was rejection of the world of matter as a trap imprisoning the divine "spark." There was the concept of the Savior as a heavenly being merely masquerading as human to bring salvation to the elect, who often have to conceal themselves from the world, and who are set apart by their special knowledge and personal purity (sexual intercourse is usually forbidden as serving the ends of the evil creator-god).

Thanks to recent research, an increasing amount is known about Catharism. It began to spread through southern France and northern Italy in the 11th century; as early as 1022 in Orléans, 13 Cathari (ten of them canons of the church) were condemned to the stake. The heresy was aided by the corruption of the clergy of the time-against whose wenching and venality the puritanism of the "Pure" was an attractive contrast. The inner circle of Cathari were the "perfect," who had received the "consolation"-a rite performed by another "perfect" in the laying on of hands and the placing of the Gospel of John on the head of the candidate. The "perfect" eschewed sexual intercourse, taking oaths, practicing war, owning property, eating meat or dairy products (since they are the products of the act of reproduction). Some of them carried their asceticism as far as the endura-suicide by self-starvation. Most of the Cathari, however, remained among the "believers," free to live ordinary lives in the world in the hope of salvation without the rigor of living as a "perfect."

The Cathari built no churches; they worshiped in private houses without the sacraments (being material, they were evil) or the cross (because Christ had no real body and died no real death). They read the Scriptures-especially the Gospel of John-listened to a sermon, said the Lord's Prayer (in native Languedoc dialect rather than Latin) and shared a common meal. The clergy wore black robes-until Pope Innocent's crusade began.

In July 1209, an army of crusaders marched down from northern France into Languedoc and besieged the city of Beziers. When the city fathers refused to hand over 222 Cathari heretics, the crusaders broke in and massacred every man, woman and child-priests included-of Béziers' 20,000 inhabitants. Before the massacre one of the crusaders is said to have asked his leader, Abbe Arnaud Amalric, head of the Cistercian monastic order, how to distinguish between the heretics and the faithful. "Kill them all," was the abbot's alleged reply. "God will recognize his own!" From then on, the crusade became a war without mercy, in which almost any southern Frenchman was assumed to be a heretic. Historians estimate the total number of casualties at 1,000,000."

End of citation.

The massacre of the Gnostics was just another arm of the Christian Crusades. It was a secondary aim of the crusades to purge those who did not believe as the established church commanded. The main goal of the crusades was to capture Jerusalem and the Holy Land from the Muslims, however, those who took up the cross were also motivated by their own interests which were not necessarily religious or spiritual in nature. Many Crusaders were driven by the opportunity to gain land, wealth and power, while the Roman Catholic Church saw an opportunity to establish its dominance in the Holy Land.

The main crusades were a series of military expeditions undertaken by the Christians in Europe against the Muslims in the Holy Land between the end of the 11th century and the end of the 13th century. The main objective of the crusades was to "free" the Holy Land from the Muslims although the Crusaders were also driven by other motives including economic, social and political. The Christian holy wars, however, were also deployed in Europe against heretics and pagans, and even political enemies.

In 1095 Pope Urban II at the Council of Clermont in 1095 asked for military aid against the Seljuk Turks. The Byzantine Emperor Alexios I Komnenus urged the Western Christendom to help their fellow Christians in the east in their assault to take Jerusalem. The response resulted in huge numbers of men ready to do battle in the name of God.

The first skirmish in 1096 resulted in the Seljuk Turks soundly defeating the inexperienced and poorly equipped peasant bands. The so-called People's Crusade thus came to an end before the European princes arrived in the Byzantine capital.

The first Crusade involving actual warriors (1096 - 1099) under the command of the European princes - Godfrey of Boullon and his brother Baldwin, Raymond IV of Toulouse, Robert Guiscard's son Bohemond of Taranto, Tancred, Hugh of Vermandois and Robert of Normandy were completing their last preparations when the peasant bands in Asia Minor were annihilated by the Seljuk Turks. They were supposed to meet in Constantinople in 1096 and launch a joined military expedition against the Muslims. However, they took different routes and the First Crusade was launched in spring of 1097.

Before the Crusaders shipped off to Asia Minor, the Byzantine Emperor feared the Crusaders would take the captured territories for themselves, so he forced them to take an oath of fealty and promise to return the conquered lands to Constantinople. The Crusaders broke their oaths and the First Crusade ended with the conquest of Jerusalem in July 1099 and creation of four crusader states. The Principality of Antioch, Kingdom of Jerusalem, County of Edessa and County of Tripoli carved out for the leaders of the expedition. Godfrey of Boullon took the Kingdom of Jerusalem, his brother Baldwin became Count of Edessa (and later King of Jerusalem), Bohemond of Taranto gained the Principality of Antioch, while Raymond IV of Toulouse was made Count of Tripoli. This was the end of the first Crusade.

The Second Crusade took place between 1147 and 1149. In 1144, the County of Edessa was captured by Zengi, ruler of Mosul. The fall of

Edessa did not bother the other crusader states but when the news reached Europe, a number of preachers started calling for a new crusade. Bernard of Clairvaux convinced Conrad III of Germany and Louis VII of France to amass troopes. They arrived in the Holy Land in 1147 and 1148. Their siege on Damascus in 1148 ended in failure for the German King and he left the Holy Land. Louis VII followed him one year later. The Second Crusade ended as a failure.

Jerusalem fell to Sultan Saladin of Egypt in 1187 and began the third Crusade (1189 - 1192). Frederick I (Barbarossa) of Germany, Richard I of England and Philip II of France responded to the Pope's call for the military expedition to recapture Jerusalem from the Muslims. However, Frederick I Barbarossa who set out first, died on his way to the Holy Land, while the rivalry between Richard and Philip resulted in the departure of the latter from the Holy Land. The English king managed to capture the city of Acre, which was besieged from 1189 shortly after Philip's departure in 1191 and defeated Saladin in the Battle of Arsuf. By the end of year 1191, he was only a few miles from Jerusalem but he was forced to withdraw. Before he departed from the Holy Land, however, he concluded a truce with Saladin by which he negotiated Jaffa and a narrow strip of coast, and a free access to the Holy Sepulcher for the Christians. With Richard's withdrawal in 1192, the Third Crusade came to an end without achieving its goal - recapture of Jerusalem.

One decade after the end of the Third Crusade, Pope Innocent III raised another crusader army. This was the Fourth Crusade (1202 - 1204). This Crusade was troubled by lack of financial resources. The Crusaders agreed to capture the city of Zara on the Adriatic coast for Venice in payment for their transportation by sea. The crusaders were contacted by Alexios IV Angelos who asked them for military assistance to conquer and kill his uncle Alexios III Angelos and restore his father Isaac II Angelos to the Byzantine throne. In return, they would be paid a large sum of money and provided with supplies for the crusade. The money and supplies allowed the Crusaders to capture Constantinople and restored Isaac II Angelos as the Byzantine Emperor who, however, failed to keep his son's promise. With the lack of promised money and supplies the Fourth Crusade ended with the fall of Constantinople to the Crusaders, who turned on their ungrateful benefactor. The

Crusaders established states on the territory of the Byzantine Empire. The Crusaders never made it to the Holy Land.

The church can fall prey to its own mythos at times No idea was more foolish than the Children's Crusade (1212). The idea was that God would help innocent children succeed where their sinful elders failed due to their impiety and impurity. The Children's Crusade ended tragically with children Crusaders sold into slavery. Those that were not made slaves died from starvation and diseases while trying to reach the Italian ports.

The successor of Pope Innocent III, Pope Honorius III pursued his predecessor's policy and the Fifth Crusade was launched (1217 - 1221). Andrew II of Hungary and Duke Leopold VI of Austria responded but they did not set out to the Holy Land but Egypt instead. In 1219, the Crusaders captured Damietta. In their arrogance they refused the offer of Ayyubid Sultan of Egypt, Al-Kamil who offered them all holy cities and the western part of the Kingdom of Jerusalem in return for their withdrawal from Egypt. The expedition to Cairo, however, ended as a disaster and forced the Crusaders to return home empty-handed.

Pope Gregory IX demanded Fredrick II to launch a crusade. Fredrick drug his feet a bit too long and was excommunicated one year earlier for postponing his promise to take up the cross. The Sixth Crusade (1228 - 1229) was undertaken by Frederick II, Holy Roman Emperor. Frederick's crusade involved little military action. Almost immediately after his arrival to the Holy Land, he entered negotiations with the Egyptian Sultan Al-Kamil and managed to win Jerusalem, Jaffa, Nazareth and Bethlehem for the Christians, and had himself crowned the King of Jerusalem. His gains, however, were lost in 1244 when the Egyptian Muslims and their Turkish allies recaptured Jerusalem.

The Seventh Crusade (1248 - 1254) was launched by Louis IX of France who made a vow to God to take up the cross and restore the Muslim controlled Palestine to the Christians if God would heal him from an illness. He decided to launch a campaign in Egypt. But just like the leaders of the Fifth Crusade, he failed to capture Cairo and was taken captive. He was released after a ransom had been paid. He returned to France after he received the news of his mother's death.

After nearly two decades, Louis IX of France launched the Eight Crusade (1270). The campaign began in Tunis but ended in failure. Louis died on August 25, 1270, most likely from dysentery, while his brother Charles of Anjou concluded a peace treaty with the Tunisian caliph and returned home.

The Ninth Crusade (1271 - 1272) was undertaken by the future King of England, Edward I who was on the way to Tunis when Louis IX died. Edward wintered in Sicily and landed in Acre in 1271 hoping to win support for the Christian cause. Men were weary and had little interest for another crusade. Edward received the news of his father's illness and returned to England with nothing accomplished.

For a while, after the crusades medieval Europe and the Middle East were able to exchange ideas and change the course of science, literature, medicine, architecture, invention, trade, commerce and transportation. Men began to think of knowledge and independence. Feudal systems weakened as nations strengthened in Europe. Men began to identify with nationalism instead of tribalism. However, due to the battles in the Middle East, the breach between the Eastern and Western branches of Christianity became wider. The Christian and the Muslim worlds would forever hold each other at arm's distance and mistrust.

Islam

Dues to the rise in terrorism since 9/11/2001 it seemed appropriate to take an extended look into Islam and why this religion has produced such chaos and destruction in the world over the last two decades.

At the writing of this book there is such a wide gap and great chasm between moderate and fundamental Muslims it is difficult to reconcile the two within the same religion. Fundamentalism is defined as a movement emphasizing the literal interpretation of the scripture of a religion. This literal interpretation is applied to ones beliefs and actions. Since Muslims attempt to emulate the life and beliefs of Mohammed as written in the Quran this became problematic since Mohammed was a warlord living in an age where modern laws and cultural sensibilities did not apply. Thus, we begin this chapter with a caveat. Not all Muslims are fundamentalists. Many, like their Christian brothers, are simply seeking to extract the best parts from their faith and its teachings.

Beginning as the faith of a small community of believers in Arabia in the seventh century, Islam rapidly became one of the major world religions. The core of this faith is the belief that Mohammed (c. 570-632), a businessman living in Mecca, a commercial and religious center in western Arabia, received revelations from God. These revelations have been preserved perfectly and without error in the Quran. The heart of the revelations is that "there is no god but Allah (The God), and Mohammad is the messenger of God." The message is one of monotheism meant to guide the believer back on to the path of the great religious forefathers, Abraham, and Jesus.

Jesus, or Isa, is mentioned 59 times in the Quran. 25 times by name, 11 times as messiah, and 23 as son of Mary. Abraham (Ibrahim) is mentioned 69 times, Moses is mentioned 136 times. Mohammed is mentioned 4 times in the Quran.

The term Islam comes from the Arabic word-root s-l-m, which has a general reference to peace and submission. Specifically, Islam means submission to the will of God, and a Muslim is one who makes that submission. But do not confuse the idea of submission to god and the peace this submission is expected to bring with the idea of peace toward one's fellow man. There is a great difference between these two ideas.

This submission or act of Islam means living a life of faith and practice as defined in the Quran and participating in the life of the community of believers like oneself. This homogenous belief system becomes important when one understands there are various branches of Islam, somewhat like the different denominations within Christianity and like Catholics and Protestants of the past, the various branches of Islam are now at war and killing one another.

Muslims believe that Islam is the same monotheistic faith proclaimed by Abraham, the prophets and Jesus, down through history. The Quran is thought to provide the complete and final record of the message from Allah, which began with Abraham and was passed down to Jesus through the earlier prophets, ending with Mohammed. Islam begins with Mohammed in the city of Mecca.

The first and most important thing to realize is that Islam is not like any other religion. The Quran is not read or interpreted like the bible. The bible is a number of books collected into a single volume written by many authors, all bringing individual viewpoints. Christians are told when interpreting the bible to do so, "line upon line and precept upon precept." That is to say, balance and integrate the various knowledge, wisdom, and points of view of the included authors and arrive at a reasonable position on various subjects. It is also understood that the bible represents two distinct eras or dispensations consisting of the Old Testament, where there is a legalistic and punitive period and the New Testament, which focuses on love, mercy, and forgiveness.

Muslims believe the Quran is a single book, written by a single author, containing shifting points of view as Mohammed experienced life and its obstacles and received revelations from Allah. We will see later that this belief is not based in fact. Muslims are instructed that although there may be different instructions and viewpoints presented in the Quran, whatever Mohammed last spoke regarding a topic is the final and lasting edict. This is the most important piece of information to remember when attempting to understand Islam. It is called, "The Rule of Abrogation". All Muslims do not follow the Rule of Abrogation. Many attempt to understand the times and situations in which it was written and take from it the teachings of peace. However, those who wish to kill non-believers all over the world are raising the Rule of Abrogation as a standard of interpretation.

All laws (Sharia Laws) and the moral, ethical, and social codes held in Sharia Law, issue from the Quran and the example set and shown by the life, teachings, and words of Mohammed, who preached in the beginning of the 7th century C.E. The morality, ethics, religious codes and laws reflect the outlook and understanding of a 7th century Middle Eastern culture and the example set by Mohammed, who practiced murder, pedophilia, polygamy, slavery and other horrific acts. Owing to the staunch belief that the Quran is perfect and timeless, the laws cannot be changed, updated, or altered. Sharia Law places the followers back into the bloody, violent time of the 7th century where women had no rights, slavery was a way of life, the spoils of war included people, and sex was forced upon anyone who was taken captive.

There is never separation of church and state in Islam because Islam is a self contained legal, political, and religious system. To live in a perfect Islamic state, such as that which ISIS is attempting to craft, is to covert or be killed or made a slave.

Islam is built upon five principles or Pillars. The Five Pillars of Islam are:
Declaration of faith, Obligatory prayer, Compulsory giving, Fasting in the month of Ramadan, Pilgrimage to Mecca.

Because Mohammed began preaching Islam in Mecca as a peaceful and tolerant man, teaching a religion of monotheism and tolerance, and ended his life as a warlord preaching death to infidels and conversion by the sword, and because the Quran is not written in chronological order it would be easy to misunderstand Islam and its intent but it is only the final stage and position that matters, and this position is one of violence and forced conversion by the sword or death to those who refuse to convert. This means the pious Muslims, those who attempt to follow the teachings of Mohammed as closely as possible, must seek to carry out his last commands. Essentially, this is the reason ISIS and al-Qaeda believe it is their obligation to conquer and kill.

What drove Mohammed to change from a man who married one woman and preached peace, monotheism and tolerance to a man who became a warlord and a polygamist who married a six-year-old girl, we may never know. The differences between the mythical life of Mohammed and the historical life of Mohammed have grown so divergent over time it is difficult to discern the truth. But before we plunge headlong into the religion of Islam it would be good to try to learn about the man behind the movement.

Islam and the Golden Rule

There will be religions based on the old concepts of laws, judgment, punishment, blood, animal sacrifice, cruelty, and killing in an attempt to please God. There will be religions based on grace, love, peace, meditation, and a mystical interior journey to commune with God. Spiritually, for religious systems and for each person, these are our choices and this sets the stage for conflict, both internally and externally on a global scale.

An internal or post-Axial Age religion seeks a relationship with the source, God, or inner self that deepens ones compassion, humanity, and connection with one's source, god, and fellow man. One seeks to connect personally with god or inner self in such a way as to know within one's soul what is right, and to treat all others in accordance with that universal love and respect. .

An external or pre-Axial Age religion is one that follows a set of rules and laws precisely in order to please a punitive, angry, and judgmental god and stay his judgment or glean his favor. Another important mark of a pre-Axial Age religion is the idea that the believer should kill for their god, as if their god needed men to defend god's honor or word. Islam is among a very few religions that continue to do animal sacrifice, cutting the throats of animals and performing rituals to evoke the blessings of their god. Prayers, alms, rituals and sacrifice are all part of being Muslim. Killing in the name of Allah places those radical believers firmly in the pre-Axial Age position. Although they are not the only modern religion that demands the death of innocent animals as well as non-believers, they are among a small and vanishing number.

Islamic Text on the Golden Rule

The Quran:
"Serve God, and join not any partners with Him; and do good- to parents, kinsfolk, orphans, those in need, neighbors who are near, neighbors who are strangers, the companion by your side, the wayfarer

(ye meet), and what your right hands possess [the slave]: For God loveth not the arrogant, the vainglorious" (Q:4:36)

(In fact the Quran goes beyond saying the Golden Rule by stating in more than four places that "Return evil with Kindness." (13:22, 23:96, 41:34, 28:54, 42:40))
Other quotes are found in Sahih Muslim, a collection of hadith compiled by Imam Muslim ibn al-Hajjaj al-Naysaburi (rahimahullah).

"None of you have faith until you love for your neighbor what you love for yourself" (Sahih Muslim)
"Whoever wishes to be delivered from the fire and to enter Paradise" should treat the people as he wishes to be treated." (Sahih Muslim)
"None of you truly believes until he wishes for his brother what he wishes for himself"(Forty Hadith-Nawawi)

(The Hadith is a collection of teachings from Mohammed, which came down by hearsay. It is a collection of statements recording what people supposedly heard the prophet say.)

"None of you is a believer if he eats his full while his neighbor hasn't anything." (Musnad)
"Do unto all men as you would wish to have done unto you; and reject for others what you would reject for yourselves." (Abu Dawud)
"Hurt no one so that no one may hurt you." (Farewell Sermon)
"There should be neither harming nor reciprocating harm." (Ibn-Majah)

The above statements depict the golden rule in Islam, and if Mohammed would have died within this time frame Islam may have become a force of peace in the world, but sadly this is not how events transpired.

In order to attract followers Mohammed taught things that people like and could easily identify as good. Once he became accepted as a prophet and spiritual leader he began to change his teachings. Due to the Quran being interpreted through abrogation, that is the rule that says whatever the prophet utters last supersedes everything that was said before, it was easy to change the golden rule to the rule of law.

The difference between a true spiritual teacher and a despot is in their consistency of selflessness and compassion. The problem with the good teachings of Mohammed is that they are reserved for fellow Muslims. When the hadith says "None of you [truly] believes until he wishes for his brother what he wishes for himself,." it is talking about the fellow Muslims. The brotherhood in Islam does not extend to everyone. The Quran (9:23) states that the believers should not take for friends and protectors (awlia) their fathers and brothers if they love Infidelity above Islam. That is to say if a friend, guardian, lover or parent is an infidel (non-believer) you should leave them behind and not count them as part of your life. In fact there are many verses that tell the Muslims to kill the unbelievers and be harsh to them. A clear example that Islam is not based on the Golden Rule is the verse (48:29): "Mohammed is the messenger of Allah; and those who are with him are strong (harsh) against Unbelievers, but compassionate with each other."

In "Islam and the Golden Rule" Robert Spencer writes:
"The Quran tells Muslims to slay the unbelievers wherever they find them (2:191), do not befriend them (3:28), fight them and show them harshness (9:123), smite (cut off) their heads (47:4), etc. "These teachings, because they came later in the life of Mohammed, take precedence and authority over previous more compassionate verses and are not compatible with the Golden Rule. According to Muslims it is not the Golden Rule that defines what is good or bad, but the words or deeds of Mohammed that defines good and evil and what is compatible with the deeds or words of Mohammed is defined as good. Islam is the only doctrine that calls upon its believers to do evil to others for the simple fact that they do not believe as Muslim believers. They believe that what is good for Islam is the highest virtue and what is bad for Islam is the ultimate evil. This is the definition of good and evil in Islam.

An example of this reversal of tone can be found between the following chapters:
Verse 41:34 is a Meccan verse where Mohammed and his followers were greatly outnumbered and the religion was just getting started. In this verse Muslims were the underdogs. Here he preached patience and said repel evil with good so your enemy becomes a friend. These orders changed when Mohammed came to power. In Medina Mohammed banished and massacred entire populations just because he suspected

that they might not be friendly to him. 28:54 is a repetition of 23:96 and 42:40 says whoever forgives and amends, he shall have his reward from Allah. However, Mohammed never forgave those who mocked him. Oqba used to mock Mohammed when he was in Mecca. When Oqba was captured in the Battle of Badr, Mohammed ordered his decapitation. When asked why Mohammed was going to do such a thing Mohammed replied, "Because of your enmity to God and to his prophet." "And my little girl!" cried Oqba, in the bitterness of his soul, "Who will take care of her?" — "Hellfire!", "and persecutor! Unbeliever in God, in his prophet, and in his Book! I give thanks unto the Lord that has slain you, and comforted mine eyes thereby." And with that Oqba was decapitated."

These actions and words should be compared to those of Jesus when he was slighted, beaten, mocked, and killed. His dying words were, "father forgive them. They do not know what they are doing..."

How do you reconcile the claim that Mohammed in his farewell sermon said, "Hurt no one so that no one may hurt you." With the fact that on his deathbed he said, "No two religions are allowed in Arabia" and ordered the forced conversion, expulsion or ethnic cleansing of the Jews and Christian and the murder of Pagans?

The Golden Rule does not exist unless it is applied equally throughout the family of mankind, without respect to gender, race, or religion.

In "Islam and the Golden Rule" Robert Spencer writes:
        "The chapter (sura) 9, which are among the last words of Mohammed, is a manifesto of discrimination and human right abuses. Mohammed declared non-believers to be the worst of all creatures, worthy of eternal punishment and with these words he diminished the humanity of non-Muslims to a point incompatible with the Golden Rule, which relies totally on the idea of equality and universal love of mankind. Sura (chapter) 9 is referred to as the Verse of the Sword. The words were uttered so late in the life of the prophet and were so contrary to previous teaching they set aside in part or totally over 100 verses and rewrote the attitude of Islam into a violent and warlike religion. It deserves repeating that the Quran cannot be read in its

entirety and synthesized, as one would read the Gita, Tao Te Ching, Bible, Dhammapada or other holy books.

The rules of interpretation for the Quran are simple.
1)   Find out what timeframe each verse was written in.
2)   Read and understand the verses and what they are dealing with.
3)   On each subject and belief, the last word stands uncontested.
Even though the attitudes, laws, rules, and beliefs are based on 7th century ideas, they cannot be altered or adapted. These are the rules that Islamic fundamentals live by."

In the Quran the last words written on a subject ABROGATES all verses that came before. This is called the rule or doctrine of Abrogation. Not understanding the rule of abrogation has led many non-Muslims to believe that fundemental Islam is a religion of peace. It is not. All Muslims do not hold to the doctrine of abrogation, all terrorists do. It provides a clear reason for violence against non-Muslims. More liberal Muslims may ignore abrogation and attempt to ferret out the peaceful parts of the Quran and limit their practice to that, making them seekers of peace and tolerance, but if the rule of abrogation is observed there will be violence against anyone who dares to not convert to Islam.

Christianity went through its violent stage during the crusades between 1095 – 1291 CE. Islam is a younger faith and continues in its violent phase even now. For 1400 years Islam has been at war. At first, they killed non- believers. Then they began killing other Muslims over differences in leadership and prayers. Now Islam is at war with the western world, blaming Christians, Jews, and western society for their woes. Fundamental Muslims blame the United States for their sins and lack of progress, although the U.S. has existed for only a little over two hundred years. We are not the ones causing them to cut off the hands of their people nor are we causing the stoning or beating of Muslims who transgress in some way their Sharia law. We are not the ones raping their women and children. Yet, like some great scapegoat or ancient sin eater, all sin is conveyed upon the west and upon Israel. Now they must kill us in a misguided attempt of propitiation to free themselves of the violence still living inside the Islam of fundamentalist and terrorists. It is a violence and evil uncontained and uncontrolled.

Finding the Baseline

According to a Pew Research Center, June, 2013 study, "There are an estimated 1.6 billion Muslims around the world, making Islam the world's second-largest religious tradition after Christianity, according to the December 2012 Global Religious Landscape report from the Pew Research Center's Forum on Religion & Public Life.
Although many people, especially in the United States, may associate Islam with countries in the Middle East or North Africa, nearly two-thirds (62%) of Muslims live in the Asia-Pacific region, according to the Pew Research analysis. In fact, more Muslims live in India and Pakistan (344 million combined) than in the entire Middle East-North Africa region (317 million)."

The Washington Examiner, February 13, 2016 reports,
Of the 1.2 billion Muslims they estimate as a world population, "Not all of them are radicals! The majority of them are peaceful people. The radicals are estimated to be between 15 to 25 percent, according to all intelligence services around the world. That leaves 75 percent of them peaceful people.
But when you look at 15 to 25 percent of the world's Muslim population, you're looking at 180 million to 300 million people dedicated to the destruction of Western civilization. That is as big [as] the United States.
So why should we worry about the radical 15 to 25 percent? Because the radicals are the ones who kill. Because it is the radicals that behead and massacre."

According to counterjihadreport.com, January 2016, Matt Barber wrote,
"We need only look to the many polls to affirm the alarmingly high percentages of Muslims (hundreds-of-millions in number) who seek, through the most violent means imaginable, Islamic world domination. Again, here are but a few:
83 percent of Palestinian Muslims, 62 percent of Jordanians and 61 percent of Egyptians approve of jihadist attacks on Americans. World Public Opinion Poll (2009).

1.5 Million British Muslims support the Islamic State, about half their total population. ICM (Mirror) Poll 2015.

Two-thirds of Palestinians support the stabbing of Israeli civilians. Palestinian Center for Policy and Survey Research (2015).

38.6 percent of Western Muslims believe 9/11 attacks were justified. Gallup(2011).

45 percent of British Muslims agree that clerics preaching violence against the West represent "mainstream Islam." BBC Radio (2015).

38 percent of Muslim-Americans say Islamic State (ISIS) beliefs are Islamic or correct. (Forty-three percent disagree.) The Polling Company CSP Poll (2015).

One-third of British Muslim students support killing for Islam. Center for Social Cohesion (Wikileaks cable).

78 percent of British Muslims support punishing the publishers of Mohammed cartoons. NOP Research.

80 percent of young Dutch Muslims see nothing wrong with holy war against non-believers. Most verbalized support for pro-Islamic State fighters. Motivation Survey (2014).

Nearly one-third of Muslim-Americans agree that violence against those who insult Mohammed or the Quran is acceptable. The Polling Company CSP Poll (2015).

68 percent of British Muslims support the arrest and prosecution of anyone who insults Islam. NOP Research.

51 percent of Muslim-Americans say that Muslims should have the choice of being judged by Sharia courts rather than courts of the United States (only 39 percent disagree). The Polling Company CSP Poll (2015).

81 percent of Muslim respondents support the Islamic State (ISIS). Al-Jazeera poll (2015)."

The Rubic Center Research in International Affairs, February 13, 2016 estimated probable conflict intensity in connection with Islamic State terrorism (IS, formerly known as ISIS and ISIL). Based on Pew data, covering 2/5 of the global Muslim population, it is estimated that 17.38 percent of Muslims worldwide openly express terror sympathies (there were five terrorism support indicators used). Quantitative estimates on terror support rates for a number of additional countries are also provided, based on European Social Survey (ESS) data and their statistical relationship to Pew data.

The number of radical Muslims appears to be anyone's guess. While the Rubic Center placed the percentage at about 17 percent, Representative Loretta Sanchez of California thinks as many as 20 percent of Muslims want to establish an Islamic caliphate by any means necessary. Sanchez added that this 5 to 20 percent "are willing to use and they do use terrorism."

Speaking on PoliticKING With Larry King, the Democrat asserted: "We know that there is a small group, and we don't know how big that is — it can be anywhere between 5 and 20 percent, from the people that I speak to — that Islam is their religion and who have a desire for a caliphate and to institute that in any way possible."
President Barack Obama has repeated his guess several times, saying 99 percent of Muslims are peaceful people. It is a guess that most people dismiss outright as false.

Applied to the global Muslim population of over 1.6 billion, Loretta Sanchez's estimate of 5 – 20 percent of radicalization would imply a pro-caliphate, pro-terrorist contingent of 80 - 320 million people worldwide.

Sanchez did not give a source for these figures, other than "the people she speaks to." A recent Pew survey found minorities of Muslims supporting ISIS in several countries (including 20 percent of Nigerian Muslims, the highest figure), though in Lebanon, for example, ISIS' unfavorable status stood at 100 percent.

In the midst of all of this hatred and killing, where are the "Moderate Muslims"? Some believe there really is not such a person. Islam demands what Islam demands and a Muslim believing otherwise is not a true Muslim. They are apostate, cowards, lukewarm, westernized, or have simply sold out to the west. This is the rhetoric radicalized Muslims - or devout Muslims, as they would label themselves – are spewing against those Muslims who would interpret the Quran and Islam in a peaceful light.

USA News and World Report, December 18, 2015, in the article, "Pressing a Muslin Reformation", Mary Kate Cary wrote,

"A small group of Muslim men and women launched the Muslim Reform Movement here in Washington. Led by Dr. Zuhdi Jasser, who is a medical doctor and a former U.S. naval officer, the group held a press conference at the National Press Club, issued a statement of their principles, and – in a move reminiscent of the famous "95 Theses" that Martin Luther posted on a church door in 1517, sparking the Protestant Reformation – affixed their precepts to the door of the Islamic Center in the heart of D.C.'s Embassy Row."

▪ We reject interpretations of Islam that call for any violence, social injustice and politicized Islam. We invite our fellow Muslims and neighbors to join us.

▪ We reject bigotry, oppression and violence against all people based on any prejudice, including ethnicity, gender, language, belief, religion, sexual orientation and gender expression.

▪ We are for secular governance, democracy and liberty.

▪ Every individual has the right to publicly express criticism of Islam. Ideas do not have rights. Human beings have rights.

▪ We stand for peace, human rights and secular governance. Please stand with us!

This is exactly what we've all been waiting to hear. But while The Washington Post reported beforehand that the event would be taking place, once it did, the Post didn't even send a reporter. Instead, the Post editors ran a Religion News Service report and only posted it online – it didn't make the regular paper. As far as I can tell, The New York Times didn't run a story at all. Neither did the evening news broadcast that night on ABC, NBC and CBS."

The obvious problems are that their types of groups are too few, too quiet, and too small. There is a greater and more immoveable issue, it is one of perceived legitimacy. Even clerics have denounced the ongoing killing and radical movements. Some of these are high-ranking clerics. But, the problem with fundamentalism in any religion is that if anyone, no matter their station or rank, disagrees with them, that person is considered in error, apostate, sinful, and hell bound. It is a closed loop.

Those who agree unite and fight. Those who do not agree are labeled apostate and fought against. The logic is inescapable and the minds are closed.

What does that mean? Assuming the worst-case numbers, simply put, there are 1.6 billion Muslims on earth and 300 million are would be terrorists seeking to bring down western civilization and they are not listening to alternative beliefs. The only thing that will stop them are moderate Muslims who are willing to find them and report them before Islam itself is declared an enemy of the free world.

The media and the Muslim communities attempt to chastise the wary U.S. public for being "Islamophobic," but if the information regarding the numbers and percentages of radical or fundamental Muslims is true, then out of every ten Muslims in the world, one or two will seek to destroy any society that is not based on Islam and kill anyone who is not Muslim. It seems foolish to be blind to such disconcerting odds. If a game of chance had a one in ten chance of ending in death, would you place a bet or spin the wheel?

So, how did this all start? Who was the man that founded such a faith? What do we know about him? How did Islam get to this point?

Mohammed

Mohammed was born 570 AD in the town of Mecca in Arabia. His father Abd-Allah, from the tribe of Hashim in Mecca, died before he was born. His mother Amina, from the tribe of Naggar in Medina, died five years later. Mohammed lived in Mecca with his pagan father's parents and was cared for by an Ethiopian Christian woman named "Baraka," whom he called his "Mom". From childhood, Mohammed suffered epileptic seizures. "The Hadith (Islamic tradition) describes the half-abnormal ecstatic condition with which Mohammed was overcome." (The Shorter Encyclopedia of Islam by Cornell University)

At age ten Mohammed began working on a caravan for his uncle, Abu-Talib. He traveled in Israel and Syria on trading missions. On his journeys, Mohammed enjoyed talking to Christian Monks in the monasteries that were located in Arabia along the route of the caravans. The monasteries served as "Rest Areas" on the route of caravans. (The Detailed Encyclopedia in the History of Arabs Prior to Islam by Dr. Jawad Ali, published by The Iraqi Scientific Association)

At age 25, Mohammed worked on a caravan owned by Khadija, a forty-year-old Christian widow. Mohammed was attracted to Khadija, and her help gave him status in the community. They married and Mohammed went to live with her. Khadija's cousin, Waraka Bin Nofel, was the priest of a Christian sect called the Ebionites -- founded in Arabia in the 7th century. The Ebionites believed that the Messiah was just a prophet, not God manifested in human flesh. Islamic sources indicate that Bin Nofel was working on an Arabic translation of a book, The Hebrew Gospel of Matthew. The translation is lost to history, but its traces can be found in the Quran.

After marrying Khadija, Mohammed was exposed to and studied Ebionism for 15 years. Ebonites do not believe in the godhead, divinity, or virgin birth of Jesus, but they do believe Jesus was a prophet. It is this heretical Christian sect that may have formed the basis of Islam.

The formation of Islam began with Mohammed having a vision that frightened him greatly. He felt he had encountered a demon. His wife convinced him it was not a demon but it was the angel Gabriel. He would accept this interpretation of his vision and move forward to be a religious leader.

When he was 40, Mohammed felt himself selected by God to be a prophet, based on a vision he had revealing that there was only one God. Up to this pint the Arabs, unlike other nations, had no prophet. In the cave of Mt. Hira, north of Mecca, he had a vision in which he was commanded to preach. Throughout his life he continued to have revelations, many of which were collected and recorded in the Quran.

The central points of his message were,
There is one God; people must submit to Him; nations have been and will be punished for rejecting God's prophets; heaven and hell are real and they are waiting; the world will come to an end with a great judgment. He included as religious duties frequent prayer and almsgiving, and he forbade usury (making money on loans).

In his first years Mohammed was preaching in Mecca, a city of Jews and polytheists. The polytheistic people of the city and the surrounding area saw their gods as protectors and the reason their city was prosperous. Much of the city's revenues depended on its pagan shrine, the Kaaba, a huge cube-like structure in the center of town that displayed as many 360 pagan gods. An attack on the existing religion was an attack on the prosperity of Mecca. The system worked and the people had no reason to change. Certainly the Jews were not going to change. They held to their religion and enjoyed the fruits of the trade route, which Mecca was on. Still, Mohammed preached. He made few converts but many enemies. His first converts were Khadija, Ali (who became the husband of Fatima, Mohammed's youngest daughter), and Abu Bakr, a man who would become a driving force in Islam, after Mohammed's death.

Mohammed continues to preach and push the idea that he was the last prophet in the line of Abraham and Jesus. His message was rejected and from about 620 AD on, Mecca became actively hostile.

For 12 years, from 610 AD to 622 AD, Mohammed tried to gain followers in Mecca. He was so frustrated that he resorted to deception to try to convince people to follow him. He claimed that the djins / jinns (genies) and fairies, who Arabs believed inhabited the trees, rocks and water of Arabia, believed in him. (See Quran 72)

72. Surah Al-Jinn (The Jinn)
In the Name of Allah, The Most Gracious, Most Merciful

1. Say (O Mohammed): "It has been revealed to me that a group (from three to ten in number) of jinns listened (to this Quran). They said: 'Verily! We have heard a wonderful Recital (this Quran)!
2. 'It guides to the Right Path, and we have believed therein, and we shall never join (in worship) anything with our Lord (Allah).
3. 'And exalted be the Majesty of our Lord, He has taken neither a wife, nor a son (or offspring or children).
4. 'And that the foolish among us [i.e. Iblis (Satan) or the polytheists amongst the jinns] used to utter against Allah that which was wrong and not right.
5. 'And verily, we thought that men and jinns would not utter a lie against Allah.
6. 'And verily, there were men among mankind who took shelter with the masculine among the jinns, but they (jinns) increased them (mankind) in sin and disbelief.
7. 'And they thought as you thought, that Allah will not send any Messenger (to mankind or jinns).
8. 'And we have sought to reach the heaven; but found it filled with stern guards and flaming fires.
9. 'And verily, we used to sit there in stations, to (steal) a hearing, but any who listens now will find a flaming fire watching him in ambush.
10. 'And we know not whether evil is intended for those on earth, or whether their Lord intends for them a Right Path.
11. 'There are among us some that are righteous, and some the contrary; we are groups each having a different way (religious sect, etc.).
12. 'And we think that we cannot escape (from the punishment of) Allah in the earth, nor can we escape (from the punishment) by flight.
13. 'And indeed when we heard the Guidance (this Quran), we believed therein (Islamic Monotheism), and whosoever believes in his Lord shall have no fear, either of a decrease in the reward of his good deeds or an increase in punishment for his sins.

Mohammed's teaching was failing in his hometown but it was faring better farther way. In the town of Yathrib, Islam was gaining a foothold. As it would turn out, Islam would live or die in Yathrib.

As Mecca begin to turn against Mohammed and people began to whisper about killing the troublemaker he began to fear for his life. In the summer of 622 AD Mohammed fled from Mecca as an attempt was being prepared to murder him. He and his followers escaped the city in the night and made their way to Yathrib. From this event, the flight, or Hegira, of the prophet (622), the Islamic calendar begins. There was a reason Mohammed chose Yathrib as his destination. He had been in negotiations with the leaders of the town to come there as a type of judge or arbitrator. The city fathers of Yathrib could not seem to settle disputes by bickering factions, which threatened to tear the town apart. It was not a pleasant task but Mohammed had little to lose.

Mohammed spent the rest of his life at Yathrib. That city is now called Medina, the City of the prophet. At Medina he built his model theocratic state and from there ruled his rapidly growing empire. It was Mohammed's harsh judicial methods and decisions at Medina over the next 10 years that set in place the laws of Islam.

Medina sits on the caravan and trade route north of Mecca. Caravans were constantly making their way to and from, carrying goods and money. Mohammed would send his men to raid the caravans and steal what they could. They tormented the Meccans. The Meccans could not tolerate the fact that Mohammed's men were plundering the caravans and planned to fight back. Skirmishes occurred on a regular basis but a major battle occurred at Badr between Mohammed's men and the Meccans. The Muslim raiders were victorious. Since the Muslims were of an inferior force from the poorer city and won over the men of Mecca, the Muslims claimed it was divinely inspired and thus they gained prestige in southwest portion of Arabia. A year later Muslim raiders were active in the Eastern Empire, in Persia, and in Ethiopia.

Mohammed had become absolutely convinced that he was the successor of Abraham and Jesus and was the last in the line of prophets. Mohammed expected the Jews and Christians would agree and accept his position and revelations. It was not to be.

Medina had a large Jewish population and the Jewish history was replete with stories of Jews withstanding conversion. The Jews were not about to give up their ancient faith. They controlled the wealth of the city and they stood in unity against Mohammed. But Mohammed was empowered by his position in Medina. After heated discussions, from which Mohammed left unsatisfied, he simply took their property by force. He then turned to one of the nearest Jewish enclaves and begin to exact his anger on them. In 628 Mohammed and his men raided and conquered the mostly Jewish city, the oasis of Khaibar. The Christians were no easier to convince of his calling and they too refused to convert. Mohammed became equally resentful and distrustful of Christians.

His renown increased, and he made a pilgrimage to Mecca.

Amidst growing fame as a warlord and religious leader, in 629 he returned to Mecca with an army to conquer the city. He did so without interference. Once in Mecca, he pulled down all of the idols and statues of the pagan gods, including a moon god referred to as Allah. Allah is a general name for god, probably indicating it was the main god of the area. This could very possibly be the origin of the term used for the Islamic god and for the symbol of the moon used in Islam. The pagan gods were displayed on the top of a black cube, called the kaaba. Karen Armstrong speculates there were 360 statues on the top of the Kaaba, one god for every day of the year. The kaaba still stands and all Muslims performing the hajj or pilgrimage to Mecca circle this same kaaba and kiss it. Mohammed would later tell his followers the kaaba was rebuilt by Abraham. Stories differ as to its origins. Some say angels and some say Adam built it.

In Mecca Mohammed won valuable converts, including Amr and Khalid (who had fought him at Uhud). In 630 he marched against Mecca, which fell without a fight. Arabia was won.

Myth and miracle are mixed with fact, so it is very difficult to know details about the founder of a world religion. In the case of Mohammed, Muslim literary sources for his life only begin around 750-800 CE, some four to five generations after his death, and very few Islamicists (specialists in the history and study of Islam) these days assume them to be straightforward historical accounts.

There is no doubt that Mohammed existed. His neighbors in Byzantine Syria got to hear of him within two years of his death. A Greek text written during the Arab invasion of Syria between 632 and 634 mentions that "a false prophet has appeared among the Saracens" and dismisses him as an impostor on the ground that prophets do not come "with sword and chariot". It thus conveys the impression that he was actually leading the invasions and the occupants did not accept a warlord as a prophet. An Armenian document probably written shortly after 661 identifies him by name and gives a recognizable account of his monotheist preaching. Sources dating from the mid-8th century preserve a document drawn up between Mohammed and the inhabitants of Medina (Yathrib), which is accepted as authentic.

Mohammed's death is normally placed in 632, but there is the possibility that it should be placed two or three years later. The Muslim calendar was instituted after Mohammed's death, with a starting-point of his emigration (hijra) to Medina ten years earlier. Some Muslims, however, seem to have correlated this point of origin with the year which came to span 624-5 in the Gregorian calendar rather than the canonical year of 622.

We can be reasonably sure that the Quran is indeed a collection of sayings uttered by Mohammed as he believed Allah revealed them to him. The book does not preserve all the messages he claimed to have received. We have evidence from several witnesses that indicate verses were lost, forgotten, and not remembered correctly. To add to the confusion regarding the Quran, the arrangement of the verses is not in the order they were revealed or dictated by Mohammed. They were collected after his death, and seem to be arranged from largest to smallest.

Even though the Quran is constructed by verses uttered by Mohammed, it cannot be used as a historical source. The source does not reveal much about the historical Mohammed and the language used to write the earliest versions of the Quran is too "fluid." There are also unresolved questions as to how the Quran reached its present, codified and classical form. The earliest versions of the Quran offer only the consonantal skeleton of the text. No vowels are marked and no diacritical marks, so that many consonants can also be read in a number of ways. This is reminiscent of Hebrew before the vowel marks were used. It was essentially a written language with no vowels.

Modern scholars usually assure themselves that since the Quran was recited from the start, we can rely on the oral tradition to supply us with the correct reading. But there is often considerable disagreement in the traditions. To prove the point, the disagreements usually have to do with vowelling, but sometimes involving consonants as well and always over the correct way in which a word should be read. This rarely affects the overall meaning of the text, but it does affect the details that are so important for historical reconstruction. There were, in the very beginning, at least four versions of the Quran written down from several reciters and none of them were exactly the same.

Sometimes the Quran uses expressions that were unknown even to the earliest exegetes. There are words that do not seem to fit in some sentences, so the meaning must be inferred or guessed. Sometimes it seems to give us fragments detached from context making the meaning vague or uncertain.

The prophet could have formulated his message in the liturgical language in which he grew up and was adapting and imitating ancient texts such as hymns and prayers, which had been translated from another Semitic language.

Patricia Crone was professor of Islamic history at the Institute for Advanced Study, Princeton until her death in July 2015.
In the June 2008 publication Open Democracy, Patricia Crone wrote, "The Quran does not give us an account of the prophet's life. It focuses on his psyche as God is speaking to him, telling him what to preach, how to react to people who poke fun at him, what to say to his supporters, and so on. We see the world through his eyes, and the allusive style makes it difficult to follow what is going on. Add to that the fact the Quran is not in chronological order so verses must be artificially placed in a sequence in which they were assumed to occur." (The allusive style refers to expressions designed to call something to mind without mentioning it explicitly.)
    Crone continues, "Events are referred to, but not narrated. Disagreements are debated without being explained. People and places are mentioned, but rarely named. Supporters are simply referred to as believers; opponents are condemned as unbelievers, polytheists, wrongdoers, hypocrites, all with only the barest information on who they were or what they said or did.

One thing seems clear however, all the parties in the Quran are monotheists worshipping the God of the Biblical tradition, and all are familiar – if rarely directly from the Bible itself – with Biblical concepts and stories. This is true even of the so-called polytheists, traditionally identified with Mohammed's tribe in Mecca. The Islamic tradition says that the members of this tribe, known as Quraysh, were believers in the God of Abraham whose monotheism had been corrupted by pagan elements. Modern historians would be inclined to reverse the relationship and cast the pagan elements as older than the monotheism, but some kind of combination of Biblical-type monotheism and Arabian paganism is indeed what one encounters in the Quran. "

Those who hold to the monotheistic Abrahamic God, such as Jews and Christians are called, "Children of the Book." Although, it seems the jury is now out on Christians. Due to the doctrine of the Trinity, some Muslims now consider Christians polytheists.

Most polytheists in Arabia believed in one creator God who could be approached through prayer and ritual. These gods usually had helpers and messengers such as angels, and even though Islam holds fast to their belief in jinns or genies, which are themselves supernatural creatures, Mohammed denounced all of these religions as totally polytheistic. One highly respected Islamic source named Ibn al-Kalbi cast the pagans as "naive worshippers of stones and idols of a type that may very well have existed in other parts of Arabia."

Crone continues, "What then are the big issues dividing the prophet and his opponents? Two stand out. First, time and again he accuses the polytheists of the same crime as the Christians – deification of lesser beings. The Christians elevated Jesus to divine. The polytheists elevated the angels to the same status and compounded their error by casting some of them as females. Just as the Christians identified Jesus as the son of God, so the polytheists called the angels sons and daughters of God, apparently implying some sort of identity of essence. "

Indeed, it is the main source of division and killing of Christians by Muslims today that some Muslims consider Christians to be polytheists because of the Christian doctrine of the Trinity.

Much of the vitriol of Muslims toward Christians comes from the misunderstanding of the Trinity and a refusal to entertain the possibility of any other expression of God in any other form since this would lead to a type of polytheism. Thus the concept of a single God being expressed as a Father image, and /or a messiah, and/or a spirit led Muslims to label Christians as polytheists, which in turn, according to the Quran, gave Muslims permission, if not the command, to kill Christians as they were wont to do with any polytheist who did not convert to Islam. This continues to be part of the battle cry by fundamentalist Muslims today that all polytheists and all those who will not convert must be destroyed. It was the first purpose of Islam and will likely be its last that only those fitting a fixed theological and monotheistic mold should be allowed to live.

The polytheists further claimed that the angels were helpers and messengers between god and man. Christians also saw angels as messengers and helpers. To Christians, Jesus was the only intercessor between God and man. Mohammed took exception to this since to him it spoke of Jesus having a shared power or essence as God.

The angels were seen by some pagans as manifestations of God himself rather than simply his servants. Christians see Jesus as the manifestation of God on earth in the form of the Son of God. All of the above opens these non-Muslims up to accusations of polytheism. This flew in the face of the primary message of Islam, that God is one and alone, without children and shared in his divinity, essence or power with no one.

Muslims believe in the resurrection of the dead. Mohammed preached of a bodily resurrection, after which they would be judged. Many sects of pagan did not agree with him. Some saw the end as a spiritual resurrection. Some did not believe the dead would come back in any form. The Quran speaks to this subject.

"Verily, those who believe Our Signs and treat them with arrogance, for them the gates of heaven will not be opened, and they will not enter Paradise until the camel goes through the eye of the needle. Thus do We recompense the criminal sinners." (Quran 7:40)

"And the Trumpet will be blown, and all who are in the heavens and all who are on the earth will swoon away, except him whom God wills." (Quran 39:68)

"And the Trumpet will be blown (the second blowing) and behold! From the graves they will come out quickly to their Lord." (Quran 36:51)

"As We began the first creation, We shall repeat it." (Quran 21:104)

In the verses above we see, in the comments about trumpets being blown and "a camel passing through the eye of a needle", a Christian or New Testament influence in Islam. Islam also has an obvious Old Testament influence. Moses is mentioned in the Quran more than any other person. Israelites are mentioned 43 times. Like Judaism, Islam has a body of laws. Both have oral and written traditions. Other sources likely contributed but are difficult to pinpoint due to the limited historical information about Mohammed or his exposure to other religions. Religions are blended and terms are redefined for the purpose of Islam but little of this process is recorded or described. Adding to the problem of having no direct history of Mohammed's life is the fact that the place where Islam originated was somewhat inaccessible. There were trade routes within the area in which goods and money flowed, but the center of the Arabia peninsula was not easily accessible, leaving many of the exact towns and places mentioned in the Quran open to interpretation.

Patricia Crone wrote, "Inhabitants of the Byzantine and Persian empires wrote about the northern and the southern ends of the peninsula, from where we also have numerous inscriptions; but the middle was terra incognita. This is precisely where the Islamic tradition places Mohammed's career. We do not know what was going on there, except for what Islamic tradition tells us.

It yields no literature to which we can relate the Quran – excepting poetry, for which we are again dependent on the Islamic tradition. Not a single source outside Arabia mentions Mecca before the conquests. In sum, we have no context for the prophet and his message. It is difficult not to suspect that the tradition places the prophet's career in Mecca for the same reason that it insists that he was illiterate, to drill home the fact that out of nowhere God raised up an illiterate man to be his prophet and so everything he knew or said came from God. Mecca was supposed to be a virgin territory; it had neither Jewish nor Christian communities. The facts seem to be quite different. The area had both Christian and Jewish inhabitance. And there is a very great chance Mohammed knew how to read and write, due to the fact that he ran a business and was married to a well to do older lady, who would not have married a man who was illiterate.

The suspicion that the location is doctrinally inspired is reinforced by the fact that the Quran describes the polytheist opponents as agriculturalists who cultivated wheat, grapes, olives, and date palms. Wheat, grapes and olives are the three staples of the Mediterranean; date palms take us southwards, but Mecca was not suitable for any kind of agriculture, and one could not possibly have produced olives there.

In addition, the Quran twice describes its opponents as living in the site of a vanished nation, that is to say a town destroyed by God for its sins. There were many such ruined sites in northwest Arabia. The prophet frequently tells his opponents to consider their significance and on one occasion remarks, with reference to the remains of Lot's people, that "you pass by them in the morning and in the evening". This takes us to somewhere in the Dead Sea region."

Sources say that the Quraysh traded in southern Syria, Yemen, Iraq, and Ethiopia. The Quraysh were a powerful merchant tribe that controlled Mecca and its Ka'aba (Kaaba). They traded in leather goods, wool, and frankincense for which they exchanged for goods from India and South Asia. Routes and journeys of the caravan are part of biblical and quranic stories. It was within these caravans and trade routes that converts spread Christianity and Islam.

Hidden Context

One of the most perplexing problems in understanding the Quran is that the stories and people are spoken of without context or background. The early expansion of Islam is a patchwork of snapshots seen outside firm context, due to a lack of historical knowledge of the time and place Mohammed lived and preached.
We attempt to glean knowledge from the Quran, the hadith, and from archeology.

The Quran, like many religious texts, is slanted in its historical depiction and silent regarding stories which paint the religion in a negative light. It is practically silent when it comes to the details of the life of its prophet and tends only to reveal certain qualities of his thought process and disposition.

To learn about Mohammed and to place things in context we must rely on outside or second hand sources. Two of these are the hadith and the sira.

The sira literature includes a variety of materials, containing stories of military expeditions undertaken by Mohammed and his followers. The stories are intended as historical accounts and used for veneration. The fact that they were written to be used for veneration tells us they cannot be fully relied on as historically accurate.

The sira also includes a number of written documents, such as speeches, sermons, and political treaties, such as the Treaty of Hudaybiyyah or Constitution of Medina. They also include military enlistments, assignments of officials as well as documents going to and from foreign rulers. The version or collection of sira by Hassan ibn Thabit is considered the most accurate, or authentic.

The hadith is a collection of second hand reports of the words and deeds, and ideas of Mohammed. They are reports from other people claiming to quote what the prophet Mohammed said verbatim. They can be on any matter or idea of law or theology. The term comes from the Arabic meaning, "report", "account" or "narrative".

Hadith is hearsay and would not hold up as evidence in court but they are second only to the Quran in developing Islamic jurisprudence. They are regarded as important tools for understanding the Quran and commentaries (tafsir) on it. Many important elements of traditional Islam such as the five salat prayers are mentioned in hadith but not the Quran. A salat is a very ritualized prayer used in Islam.

Muslims regard various hadith with different levels of importance, although all variants emphasize the Sunnah (the record of teachings, deeds and sayings of Mohammed). They can be second hand reports, such as a reliable person who claims the prophet said something on a particular occasion about a particular matter. Most of the early sources for the prophet's life, as also for the period of his immediate successors, consist of hadith in some arrangement or other. The closest modern corollary would be the Doctrine and Covenant of the Mormon Church, where the book of Mormon is considered scripture and the teachings contained within the D & C are held up as teachings used for clarification.

Because the hadith are oral reports that have been written down, they could have been easily fabricated or misunderstood. They were usually short phrases and as such did not contain the context in which the statement was made. The purpose of such reports was to validate Islamic law and doctrine. Some reports seem to contradict others and so they testify to intense conflicts over what was or was not the true teachings of Islam in the period up to the 9th century, when the material was collected and codified

The hadith literature is based on spoken reports that were in circulation in society after the death of Mohammed. Unlike the Quran itself, which was compiled under the official direction of the early Islamic State in Medina, a central authority did not compile the hadith reports. Hadiths were evaluated and gathered into large collections during the 8th and 9th centuries, generations after the death of Mohammed, after the end of the era of the "rightful" Rashidun Caliphate, over 1000 km or 621.3 miles from where Mohammed lived.

Each hadith is based on two parts, a chain of narrators reporting the hadith and the text itself. By "chain of narrators" it is meant that is it reported that each person who passed along the story is recorded. Each of these individuals must be found honest and the chain must be confirmed. Each hadith is classified by Muslim clerics and jurists into three categories: authentic, good, or weak. The problem is that the clerics do not always agree. If the hadith agrees with their personal view they are more likely to accept it as authentic. If a statement does not align with the teaching or belief of a group it would be easy to classify that hadith as "weak". This means that certain groups may tend to rely on certain collections of hadith.

The hadith could be used to bolster a faulty interpretation of the Quran since clerics were in the habit of taking lines of the Quran out of context and reinterpreting them in isolation or in light of some event in the prophet's life the verse had nothing to do with. Text without context is not only error but can be so tortured by lack of logic and context it can be made to say anything.

By keeping the Quran and Mohammed's teachings in context the rise of Islam can be related to developments in the world of late antiquity and understood in the correct light.

Logical interpretations of the Quran and the hadith should be combined with data collected via research and archeology to form a more informed picture of Islam. No interpretation of the Quran can be accurate unless historical interpretation proceeds and that will take the correct context and perspectives. Oddly, this is something most clerics seemed disturbingly unconcerned about.

So, we are left with lack of verifiable information regarding the life and times of Mohammed.

David Wood of North American Missions Board sums up the life of Mohammed like this:
"The Hadith are collections of sayings and deeds of Mohammed, usually arranged topically. The goal of the writers was to describe what Muslims should do in a given situation, based on the example set by their prophet. The Sira literature was quite different. Sira writers often attempted to write complete accounts of the life of Mohammed, and these writings are therefore quite similar to modern biographies. The two genres of historical writing employed slightly different methodologies, and Muslims today favor Hadith over Sira.

The sira literature includes a variety of heterogeneous materials, containing mainly stories of military expeditions undertaken by Mohammed and his companions. These stories are intended as historical accounts and used for veneration. The sira also includes a number of written documents, such as political treaties (e.g., Treaty of Hudaybiyyah or Constitution of Medina), military enlistments, assignments of officials, letters to foreign rulers, and so forth. It also records some of the speeches and sermons made by Mohammed, like his speech at the Farewell Pilgrimage. Some of the sira accounts include verses of poetry commemorating certain events and battles. Some of which are considered to be of a lesser quality and lacking authenticity, but the most serious of those are the ones by Hassan ibn Thabit.

The primary Hadith collections were written more than two centuries after Mohammed's death, and even the earliest extant Sira work (Ibn Ishaq's Sirat Rasul Allah) comes from more than a century after the life of Mohammed. Muslims themselves typically reject this source. We therefore have no detailed historical source written within a century of the prophet of Islam, and no source trusted by the majority of Muslims within two centuries. Such a time gap calls much of Mohammed's life into question, and some scholars hold that we can know virtually nothing about him.

Even pictures of Mohammed are virtually nonexistent. **Of course strict Muslims do not believe in having pictures of anyone, especially Mohammed, since it is said to promote idol worship.** *The Quran does not explicitly forbid images of Mohammed, but there are a few hadith which have explicitly prohibited Muslims from creating visual depictions of figures. It is agreed on all sides that there is no authentic visual tradition as to the appearance of Mohammed, although there are early legends of portraits of him, and written physical descriptions whose authenticity is often accepted. Many visual depictions only show Mohammed with his face veiled, or symbolically represent him as a flame; other images, notably from before about 1500, show his face. With the notable exception of modern-day Iran, depictions of Mohammed were rare, never numerous in any community or era throughout Islamic history, and appeared almost exclusively in the private medium of Persian and other miniature book illustration. Visual images of Mohammed in the non-Islamic West have always been infrequent. In the Middle Ages they were mostly hostile, and most often appear in illustrations of Dante's poetry."*

Adding to the list of documents and ideas shaping Islam, beside the Quran, Hadith, and Sira, is the idea of the fatwa. A fatwa is simply a judgment rendered regarding a subject by a cleric. In 2001, Egypt's Grand Mufti issued a fatwa stating that the show "Man sa yarbah al malyoon? "– Literally "Who will Win the Million?", modeled on the British show Who Wants to be a Millionaire?, was un-Islamic. The Sheikh of Cairo's Al-Azhar University later rejected the fatwa, finding that there was no objection to such shows since they spread general knowledge.

The Fatwa on Terrorism is a 600-page Islamic decree against terrorism and suicide bombings released in March 2010. This fatwa is a direct refutation of the ideology of Al-Qaeda and the Taliban. It is one of the most extensive rulings, an "absolute" condemnation of terrorism without "any excuses or pretexts" which goes further than ever and declares terrorism as kufr (blasphemy, impiety) under Islamic law. It was produced in Canada by an influential Muslim scholar Dr. Mohammed Tahir-ul-Qadri and was launched in London on March 2, 2010. Dr Qadri said during the launch "Terrorism is terrorism, violence is violence and it has no place in Islamic teaching and no justification can be provided for it, or any kind of excuses or ifs or buts." According to CNN experts, the fatwa was seen as a significant blow to terrorist recruiting. They were most definitely wrong. This is the nature of a Fatwa. It is one man or one group's view on a situation and carries no weight except to be a viewpoint posted by a particular cleric.

On July 2, 2013 at Lahore (Pakistan) 50 Muslim Scholars of the Sunni Ittehad Council (SIC) issued a collective fatwa against suicide bombings, the killing of innocent people, bomb attacks, and targeted killings declaring them as Haram or forbidden. The problem here is that each individual or group gets to decide who is innocent. In the view of many pious Muslims there are no innocent infidels (non-believers).

On March 11, 2015, Syed Soharwardy, the founder of the Islamic Supreme Council of Canada, and 37 other Muslim leaders of various Islamic sects from across Canada gathered in Calgary and issued a fatwa condemning followers of the Islamic State (ISIS) as non-Muslims. Soharwardy cited capturing opponents and beheading them, killing Muslims who disagree with ISIS's actions, destroying mosques, burning enemy soldiers alive and encouraging Muslim girls to join ISIS, among others, as acts by ISIS that violate Islamic law. Under this fatwa, anybody who even wishes to join the group will be "excommunicated from the Muslim community" and no longer considered Muslim. Fatwas do not matter to those who hold an opposite position and are convinced of their correctness.

Fatwas go from a plea for peace to an order to kill. One man's preacher is another man's Satan and fatwas reflect this. In an interview given on September 30, 2002, for the October 6 edition of 60 Minutes, American Southern Baptist pastor and televangelist Jerry Falwell said: "I think Mohammed was a terrorist. I read enough by both Muslims and non-Muslims, [to decide] that he was a violent man, a man of war." The following Friday, Mohsen Mojtahed Shabestari, an Iranian cleric, issued a fatwa calling for Falwell's death, saying Falwell was a "mercenary and must be killed." He added, "The death of that man is a religious duty, but his case should not be tied to the Christian community." I suppose Sheabestari proved Falwell's point about the violence of Mohammed and his followers.

Fatwas are meant to be issued by a religious/legal scholar, not by any political entity, but since Islam represents a political and religious state the separation of who speaks from a religious, political, or legal point of view is limited and often mixed. Generally, any given case may have many fatwas (legal opinions) written by the scholars of the region at the time. The fatwa backed by the State is the one with legal power if the state agrees to make it part of their body of law. Fatwas are useful only to the followers of the cleric that articulates them. The more important the cleric or the more people who follow him, the more weight the fatwa will have.

A Brief History of Mohammed

According to PBS.org "Mohammed: Legacy of a prophet" a general timeline of the life of Mohammed can be summed up as follows:

570   Mohammed's Birth and Infancy
Mohammed was born in the year 570 in the town of Mecca, a mountain town in the high desert plateau of western Arabia. His name derives from the Arabic verb hamada, meaning "to praise, to glorify." He was the first and only son of Abd Allah bin Al-Muttalib and Amina bint Wahb. Abd Allah died before Mohammed's birth and Mohammed was raised by his mother Amina, who in keeping with Meccan tradition entrusted her son at an early age to a wet nurse named Halima from the nomadic tribe of the Sa'd ibn Bakr. He grew up in the hill country, learning their pure Arabic.

575   Mohammed Becomes an Orphan
When Mohammed was five or six his mother took him to Yathrib, an oasis town a few hundred miles north of Mecca, to stay with relatives and visit his father's grave there. On the return journey, Amina took ill and died. She was buried in the village of Abwa on the Mecca-Medina Road. Halima, his nurse, returned to Mecca with the orphaned boy and placed him in the protection of his paternal grandfather, Abdul Al-Muttalib. In this man's care, Mohammed learned the rudiments of how to run a state. Mecca was Arabia's most important pilgrimage center and Abdul Al-Muttalib its most respected leader. He controlled important pilgrimage concessions and frequently presided over Mecca's Council of Elders.

578   Mohammed in Mecca in Care of an Uncle
Upon his grandfather's death in 578, Mohammed, aged about eight, passed into the care of a paternal uncle, Abu Talib. Mohammed grew up in the older man's home and remained under Abu Talib's protection for many years. Chroniclers have underscored Mohammed's disrupted childhood. So does the Quran: "Did God not find you an orphan and give you shelter and care? And He found you wandering, and gave you guidance. And he found you in need, and made you independent" (93:6-8).

580-594   *Mohammed's Teens*

As a young boy, Mohammed worked as a shepherd to help pay his keep (his uncle was of modest means). In his teens he sometimes traveled with Abu Talib, who was a merchant, accompanying caravans to trade centers. On at least one occasion, he is said to have traveled as far north as Syria. Older merchants recognized his character and nicknamed him El–Amin, the one you can trust.

594   *Mohammed is a Caravan Agent for Wealthy Tradeswoman, Khadija.*

In his early twenties, Mohammed entered the service of a wealthy Meccan merchant, a widow named Khadija bint Khawalayd. The two were distant cousins. Mohammed carried her goods to the north and returned with a profit.

595-609   *Mohammed's Marriage and Family Life*

Impressed by Mohammed's honesty and character, Khadija eventually proposed marriage. They were wed in about 595. He was twenty-five. She was nearly forty.

Mohammed continued to manage Khadija's business affairs, and their next years were pleasant and prosperous. Six children were born to them, two sons who both died in infancy, and four daughters. Mecca prospered too, becoming a well-off trading center in the hands of an elite group of clan leaders who were mostly successful traders.

610   *Mohammed Receives First Revelation*

Mecca's new materialism and its traditional idolatry disturbed Mohammed. He began making long retreats to a mountain cave outside town. There, he fasted and meditated. On one occasion, after a number of indistinct visionary experiences, Mohammed was visited by an overpowering presence and instructed to recite words of such beauty and force that he and others gradually attributed them to God. This experience shook Mohammed to the core. It was several years before he dared to talk about it outside his family.

613   *Mohammed Takes his Message Public*

After several similar experiences, Mohammed finally began to reveal the messages he was receiving to his tribe. These were gathered verse by verse and later would become the Quran, Islam's sacred scripture. In the next decade, Mohammed and his followers were first belittled and ridiculed, then persecuted and physically attacked for departing from traditional Mecca's tribal ways. Mohammed's message was resolutely monotheistic. For several years, the Quraysh, Mecca's dominant tribe, levied a ban on trade with Mohammed's people, subjecting them to near famine conditions. Toward the end of the decade, Mohammed's wife and uncle both died. Finally, the leaders of Mecca attempted to assassinate Mohammed.

622   *Mohammed and the Muslims Immigrate to Medina*

In 622, Mohammed and his few hundred followers left Mecca and traveled to Yathrib, the oasis town where his father was buried. The leaders there were suffering through a vicious civil war, and they had invited this man well known for his wisdom to act as their mediator. Yathrib soon became known as Medina, the City of the prophet. Mohammed remained here for the next six years, building the first Muslim community and gradually gathering more and more people to his side.

625-628   *The Military Period*

The Meccans did not take Mohammed's new success lightly. Early skirmishes led to three major battles in the next three years. Of these the Muslims won the first (the Battle of Badr, March, 624), lost the second (the Battle of Uhud, March, 625), and outlasted the third, (The Battle of the Trench and the Siege of Medina, April, 627). In March, 628, a treaty was signed between the two sides, which recognized the Muslims as a new force in Arabia and gave them freedom to move unmolested throughout Arabia. Meccan allies breached the treaty a year later.

630   *The Conquest of Mecca*

By now, the balance of power had shifted radically away from once-powerful Mecca, toward Mohammed and the Muslims. In January, 630, they marched on Mecca and were joined by tribe after tribe along the way. They entered Mecca without bloodshed and the Meccans, seeing the tide had turned, joined them.

630-632   *Mohammed's Final Years*
Mohammed returned to live in Medina. In the next three years, he consolidated most of the Arabian Peninsula under Islam. In March, 632, he returned to Mecca one last time to perform a pilgrimage, and tens of thousands of Muslims joined him.

After the pilgrimage, he returned to Medina. Three months later on June 8, 632 he died there, after a brief illness. He is buried in the mosque in Medina. Within a hundred years Mohammed's teaching and way of life had spread from the remote corners of Arabia as far east as Indo-China and as far west as Morocco, France and Spain.

The Meccan Period

Writing in the article, "Chronology of prophet Mohammed's Life" for the publication "Answering for Islam", Ehteshaam Gulam presents the following timeline for the periods of Mohammed's in Mecca and in Medina:

570 C.E. Mohammed is born in Mecca

595 C.E. Mohammed marries Khadija, who later becomes the first Muslim

610 C.E. Mohammed was in a cave on a religious retreat. Mohammed receives what he comes to believe is his first visitation from the angel Gabriel and revelation from Allah.

613 C.E. Mohammed begins preaching Islam publicly in Mecca

615 C.E. Friction with the Quraysh causes some Muslims to leave Arabia for Abyssinia

619 C.E. Khadija dies

620 C.E. The Night Journey prophet Mohammed is carried from Mecca to Jerusalem and then travels to the heavens and meets the previous prophets (Adam, Noah, Abraham, Moses, Jesus, etc).

622 C.E. The Hijra: Mohammed and the Muslims flee from Mecca to Medina

The Medinan Period

622 C.E. The Hijra: Mohammed arrives in Medina

624 C.E. The Nakhla raid. These raids were not solely designed to exact revenge from the people who had rejected the prophet who had arisen among them. They served a key economic purpose, keeping the Muslim movement solvent.

624 C.E. The Battle of Badr: the Muslims overcome great odds to defeat the pagan Meccans

624 C.E. Mohammed and the Muslims besiege the Jewish Qaynuqa tribe and exile them from Medina

625 C.E. The Battle of Uhud: the pagan Meccans defeat the Muslims

625 C.E. Siege and exile from Medina of the Jewish Nadir tribe

627 C.E. The Battle of the Trench: the Jewish Qurayzah tribe betrays Mohammed

627 C.E. Sa'd Ibn Mutab executes males of the Qurayzah tribe and enslaves the women and children.

628 C.E. Mohammed concludes the Treaty of Hudaybiyya with the pagan Meccans

628 C.E. Mohammed and the Muslims besiege the Khaybar oasis and exile the Jews from it.

630 C.E. Mohammed and the Muslims conquer Mecca

630 C.E. The Muslims prevail in the Battle of Hunayn and conquer Ta'if; Mohammed becomes the ruler of Arabia

631 C.E. The Arabian tribes remaining outside Islamic rule accept Islam

631 C.E. The expedition to Tabuk

632 C.E. Mohammed dies in Medina on June 8, 632 CE

We shall begin with Mohammed's call and revelation.
His experience is recounted in the writings of the eighth century Muslim, Ibn Ishaq, in his Sirat Rasul Allah:

When it was the night on which God honored him with his mission and showed mercy on His servants thereby, Gabriel brought him the command of God. "He came to me," said the apostle of God, "while I was asleep, with a coverlet of brocade whereon was some writing, and said, 'Read!' I said, 'What shall I read?' He pressed me with it so tightly that I thought it was death; then he let me go and said, 'Read!' I said, 'What shall I read?' He pressed me with it again so that I thought it was death; then he let me go and said 'Read!' I said, 'What shall I read?' He pressed me with it the third time so that I thought it was death and said 'Read!' I said, 'What then shall I read?' – and this I said only to deliver myself from him, lest he should do the same to me again. He said:

> *'Read in the name of thy Lord who created,*
> *Who created man of blood coagulated.*
> *Read! Thy Lord is the most beneficent,*
> *Who taught by the pen,*
> *Taught that which they knew not unto men.'*

So I read it, and he departed from me. And I awoke from my sleep, and it was as though these words were written on my heart."

Ibn Ishaq Sirat Rasul Allah (The Life of Mohammed), translated by A. Guillaume, Oxford University Press, 1980

At this point in his life is it possible that Mohammed had neither spiritual discernment nor an idea as to his purpose. The confusion is summed up by a quote from the Muslim scholar, Ibn Ishaq

"Mohammed was terrified by what happened to him. He believed that he had encountered a demon, and he became suicidal. His wife Khadija and her cousin Waraqah, however, convinced him that he was a prophet of God, and that he had met the angel Gabriel in the cave.

Mohammed spent the next twelve years preaching in Mecca, first only in private, then in public. During these early years, Mohammed preached a peaceful message. He called for religious tolerance, but he told people that they needed to turn to Allah. In general, the polytheistic Meccans hated him. The persecution eventually got so bad that Mohammed accepted an invitation to move to another city."

In 622, Mohammed and most of his followers moved nearly 300 miles north to Medina. The reasons for his move seem to be many. He was no longer welcome in Mecca. There were plans afoot to kill him. The polytheists were concerned about holding on to their religion and power. The town's folk were concerned that abandoning the old gods would upset Mecca's prosperity.

Mohammed was beginning to develop a reputation for being a holy man, so the people of Medina invited him to be a judge and arbitrator in their city, where there was growing tension between factions.

It's difficult to overestimate the importance of the move. It was in Medina that Mohammed began to define the Muslim community politically. The laws established here would become central to Islam.

Having been rejected by Mecca, Mohammed carried a grudge. We know that Mohammed took Mecca in what one could consider a war of revenge, but there were other factors at work, such as the persecution of the Muslims at the hands of the polytheists. Whatever the subtleties of reasoning for Mohammed's assault on the city of Mecca, this is considered to be his first Jihad

Most observant Muslims accept jihad as an integral part of Islam. It should be understood, however, that there are many kinds of jihad. Jihad may be internal or external. In Arabic language, the word jihad literally means striving and working hard for something. In Islamic terminology, it retains the literal meaning in two different dimensions, which are expressed by "major jihad" and "minor jihad".

In his article Peace and Jihad in Islam, published by Al-Islam, Sayyid Mohammed Rizvi writes:
"The major jihad is known as the spiritual struggle, a struggle between two powers within ourselves: the soul and the body. The conscience is in conflict with the bodily desires. This spiritual conflict is an ongoing jihad within each one of us. Islam expects its followers to give preference to the soul and the conscience over the body and its desires.
The fasting in the month of Ramadhan is an example of training personally for the major jihad.
The minor jihad is the armed struggle. However, that does not automatically mean unjustified use of violence. It is the external or minor Jihad that is the struggle of the sword, which has come to be known simply as jihad. "

Magnus Nilsson comments in his book, "Just War and Jihad: A Cross-cultural Study of Modern Western and Islamic Just War Traditions" that most modern day Muslims view jihad as their equivalent of the Bush Doctrine, where he gives the US the right to strike when attack seems unavoidable. In this position, paranoia would drive one to attack when there was no real aggression. Further, if one viewed a disagreement regarding religion or culture as an attack there would be no end to wars. This seems to be where we are today.

In Islam, war is justified and approved by God as a "holy war" if it is a response to oppression and aggression, or if it is to correct injustice. Of course, the problem here is that the injustice may be based on what is accepted or demanded under Shiria Law as opposed to what western laws or cultures deem just or correct.

The Quran supports the idea that war ought to be waged in self-defense and the moment some cleric declares that the west is the enemy of Islam or goes against Islamic values he has fulfilled the idea of defending Islam and in this light, however dim it might be, jihad is condoned.

The question arises, however: does the sira (biography) of the prophet Mohammed support such a view? Mohammed waged history's first jihad when he and his army stationed in Medina attacked the Quraysh of Mecca.

Did Mohammed wage a war against Mecca simply because the people there were infidels? Was he waging war out of revenge, or was he waging a war of self-defense? His motivations would be instrumental in formulating Islam's views of war and peace.

Mohammed was in Mecca when he was called and there he preached his message peacefully for over ten years, but his message was one that demanded change and the people did not want to change. He was seen as a troublemaker so the leaders persecuted him and his followers. The early Muslims suffered and some were killed. The persecutions of Mohammed and his followers reached such a level that Muslims were forced to flee.

Mohammed's uncle died and Mohammed was left with no tribal connections and thus no protection. This left him vulnerable to enemies within the city. But when he fled the city to Medina, 300 miles away, there was no reason to fear. He was no longer in harm's way. There was no reason to go back and kill anyone in Mecca. Here we must conclude that anger and revenge drove him to war, and not holy appointment.

Many on the Medina city board accepted Islam and promised to protect Mohammed. They secretly met Mohammed while he was still in Mecca, and took two solemn oaths to protect him, known as the First and Second Pledge at al-Aqaba. Under the cover of night, waves of Muslims began to flee Mecca to find refuge in Medina." Medinat al-Nabi (the prophet's city)

Mohammed was one of the last to leave Mecca. He traveled to Medina. This journey is called the Hijra, and is the Islamic equivalent of the Exodus. It was done in the year 622, which marks the beginning of the Islamic era. Thus AD 622 became for Muslims AH 1. Later, Mohammed would order his followers to make this "Hajj" as part of their worship.

Hajj is Arabic, meaning "pilgrimage". It is an annual Islamic pilgrimage to Mecca, and a mandatory religious duty for Muslims that must be carried out at least once in their lifetime by all adult Muslims who are physically and financially capable of undertaking the journey, and can support their family during the time it takes to make the journey.

The prophet arrived in Medina to take the position of a holy man and to be a judge or arbitrator to bring peace between the two major tribes of the city, which had been involved in a protracted civil war. The city elders had hoped Mohammed could find a way to settle the arguments between the two sides.

Merriam-Webster's Encyclopedia of World Religions, p.755 reports that Mohammed called for an end to tribal rivalries, preached brotherhood, and formed a united community (umma) out of groups. After establishing himself and taking advantage of the growing numbers of converts in Medina, Mohammed turned his attention to his former tormentors, the Quraysh of Mecca. The Quraysh were an Arab people and merchant tribe, of which Mohammed was a member and who from the 5th century, were distinguished by being religious custodians of the Kaaba (Kaabah) at Mecca before Mohammed's invasion. He first began attacking caravans from Mecca, robbing them and killing the riders. The people of Mecca sent around 1000 guards to protect their next caravan. The Muslims attacked with a much smaller force, and they won what came to be known as the Battle of Badr. Mohammed escalated and launched a war. The first military expedition against them was dispatched about seven to nine months after Mohammed's arrival in Medina in what is known as Hamza's Expedition to the Seashore. This is the beginning of the first Jihad.

For the next ten years until Mohammed's death in 632 AD, the Muslims never stopped fighting. Mohammed fought several more key battles against Mecca (the Battle of Uhud and the Battle of the Trench), finally taking the city in 630.

David Wood, in his article, "The Historical Mohammed: The Good, the Bad, and the Downright Ugly" writes:
Mohammed attacked other groups as well. In 629, Muslims attacked a Jewish settlement in the oasis of Khaybar in Northwestern Arabia. Shortly after the conquest of Mecca, Mohammed received Surah 9:29, which ordered Muslims to fight non-Muslims (including Christians and Jews) until they submit to Islam:

"Fight those who do not believe in Allah, nor in the latter day, nor do they prohibit what Allah and His Apostle have prohibited, nor follow the religion of truth, out of those who have been given the Book, until they pay the tax in acknowledgment of superiority and they are in a state of subjection."

Obeying this command to fight, Mohammed marched an army against the Byzantine Empire, though the Byzantines chose not to fight. Mohammed became sick and died shortly thereafter.

When one is following a religious leader one is emotionally invested in them and their lives. In such cases it is easy to see only the good characteristics and to completely ignore less desirable qualities.

Thus far we have seen Mohammed as a robber and as a warlord, waging battles for revenge and retaliation. When Mohammed allowed cities to be sacked and sex slaves to be taken he set up a situation where greed became one of the primary factors for men's rapid conversion to Islam. Mohammed used the spoils of war to entice converts to Islam.

An Islamic source quotes Mohammed defense of this tactic:
"Are you disturbed in mind because of the good things of this life by which I win over a people that they may become Muslims while I entrust you to your Islam?"
Sahih Muslim, Abdul Hamid Siddiqi, tr., Number 2313

Muslims try to compare the violence in the Quran to the violence in the Old Testament. However, verses in the Old Testament command a war or and act of violence against a particular people at a particular time for a particular reason. When the situation is resolved the violence ceases. In the Quran the violence is commanded and is not restrained by the historical situations, times, or context. The command is open-ended. To simply say, "kill all unbelievers" leaves no end to the bloodshed until the world is bathed in blood or converted to Islam. This is a statement unconstrained by time or circumstances. The commands become part of the eternal and unchanging word of Allah and must be obeyed forever. The Old Testament constraint of violence against a particular army or people at a certain time for a certain reason is why we do not see Jewish imperialism and killing word-wide, but Muslim violence does not cease. To strictly follow the Quran, it cannot cease. Islam must kill, destroy, and conquer to grow. This is the command.

Quran (17:16) - "And when We wish to destroy a town, We send Our commandment to the people of it who lead easy lives, but they transgress therein; thus the word proves true against it, so We destroy it with utter destruction." Osama bin Landen used this verse to justify attacking New York.

Quran (47:3-4) - "Those who disbelieve follow falsehood, while those who believe follow the truth from their Lord... So, when you meet (in fight Jihad in Allah's Cause), those who disbelieve smite at their necks till when you have killed and wounded many of them, then bind a bond firmly (on them, take them as captives)... If it had been Allah's Will, He Himself could certainly have punished them (without you). But (He lets you fight), in order to test you, some with others. But those who are killed in the Way of Allah, He will never let their deeds be lost."

Some say Islam is a religion of peace, but peaceful religions strive for peace both among their own followers and the with the rest of the world. Let us compare the above quotes with how the Torah tells Jews to treat strangers.
Leviticus 19:34 33 And if a stranger sojourn with thee in your land, ye shall not vex him. 34 But the stranger that dwelleth with you shall be unto you as one born among you, and thou shalt love him as thyself; for ye were strangers in the land of Egypt.

One may argue that the Jewish sect, now called Christianity, was the evolution of Judaism into the Axial Age. One may also argue that all of Judaism has evolved into the Axial Age if one observes that Judaism teaches equal treatment of all people when they are not at war and there is no more ritualized animal sacrifice, stoning, flogging, or other such punishment in Judaism today.

This is not to say that religions do not waver with acts, movements or splinter sects that are pre-Axial Age or post-Axial age, but a religion should be judged by how it generally embraces peace, grace, generosity, and love of mankind. Religions should not be judged on the national political movement that is predominately comprised of a faith. This is difficult, but one should not judge the people by the actions of their government. Nor, if the state and religion are separate, should we judge a religion by a nation. The Islamic State is different. The nation, government, and religion are one and must be judged as a single force.

235

If the world can be divided between people and faiths split between those that are pre-Axial Age and post-Axial Age it can be said without equivocation that Islam is a religion that represents all elements of the pre-Axial Age. It is ritualized, externalizes, and driven by a harsh set of rules and laws, all set in place to please a God who demands the killing of people and animals if one is to attain the carnally based heaven offered by Islam to its loyal followers and martyrs. This is the Islam of terrorism. It is said up to 20% of all Muslims hold to beliefs which lead to terrorism and killing non-believers. It will be up to the greater body of Islam to bring the faith firmly and completely into the Axial Age – an age of enlightenment – an age of peace.

Mohammed's Sexual Views

Mohammed had very liberal views regarding sex and marriage. Most Islamic sources report he married a total of eleven wives, but the maximum number of wives married at one time was nine. This makes the prophet an exception to his own rule of marrying a maximum of four wives. Among Mohammed's wives were a six-year-old child and a thirteen-year-old girl. In addition to his wives, Mohammed also had concubines and sex-slaves. Between slaves, concubines, and several divorces, numbers of wives have blurred through time. One slave girl was a Christian slave given to Mohammed by the governor of Egypt. Her name was Mariyam. After she gave birth to a son, some sources say Mohammed married her. Other sources disagree. Thus, the number of total wives vary between sources depending if one counts slaves and concubines he may have married, and if one counts divorces. Sources vary so widely on the number of wives he had that a list of women and their status is offered in Appendix "B".

Mohammed married his aunt, Zaynab bint Jahsh, who was one of his father's sisters. They married soon after she divorced Mohammed's adopted son, Zayd ibn Haritha.
Al-Tabari, Vol. 39, p. 180; cf Guillaume/Ishaq 3; Maududi (1967)

Marriage to cousins was common among Arabs at the time and remains so today. Culturally, marriage between first cousins is still regarded as the best choice. In the Middle East, alliances fall along lines of family/tribe, religion, and ethnicity. Marrying cousins keeps these lines strong and clear. Marrying cousins keeps inheritance of wealth, land and livestock concentrated within the family, adding to the value of the practice. Due to Mohammed's marriage to his cousin, Islam continues to encourage this type of inbreeding, which has led to many issues and has damaged the gene pool greatly.

In her New York Times May 1, 2003 article, Sarah Kershaw reported, "In some parts of Saudi Arabia, particularly in the south, the rate of marriage among blood relatives ranges from 55 to 70 percent, among the highest rates in the world, according to the Saudi government." The practice of inbreeding has produced a variety of physical and metal defects.

Nikolai Sennels, a Danish psychologist who has written about the problem of inbreeding in the Muslim communities, reports the percent of marriages between cousins is 67% in Saudi Arabia, 64% in Jordan, and Kuwait, 63% in Sudan, 60% in Iraq, and 54% in the United Arab Emirates and 54 % in Qatar. According to Sennels, research shows that children of consanguineous marriages lose 10-16 points off their IQ and social abilities develop much slower in inbred babies. The risk of having an IQ lower than 70, the official demarcation for being classified as "retarded," increases by an astonishing 400 percent among children of first cousin marriages. Spinal and neurological defects, including microcephaly occur. Due to inbreeding, microcephaly is so common in Pakistan they refer to those who suffer the condition as "rat people" due to the way their small heads make them look. (Consanguineous – blood relations)

According to a February 2016 report in Kristeligt Dagblad, a Danish newspaper published in Copenhagen, Denmark, the increased risk of insanity among children of marriages between cousins might explain why immigrant patients are stressing the psychiatric system and are strongly overrepresented among insane criminals. In June of 2007 the same paper reported, "In Sct. Hans Hospital, which has the biggest ward for clinically insane criminals in Denmark, more than 40 percent of the patients have an immigrant background."

If inbreeding among first cousins accounts for lower intelligence and increased criminal and psychiatric problems, it could explain the extreme acts of violence and disregard of logic and law we are now witnessing from the Islamic refugees. When these conditions were fueled and guided by fundamental Islam the result is the terrorism spewing from the Islamic nations and from ISIS.

In addition to encouraging marriage between cousins, Mohammed's choices also promoted pedophilia. Mohammed's third wife, Aishah, was only 6 when the arranged marriage took place. Aishah remained in her parent's house until she was nine, when the marriage was consummated. It is said Aishah was the favored wife of Mohammed and he died in her arms June 8, 632.

The religious scholar, Karen Armstrong writes:

"To the point that Aishah was only nine or ten years of age, it was common for arranged marriages to take place, even in absentia, in order to forge alliances between families. However, it was left up to the husband as to the time and at what age the marriage would be consummated. Sex with a pre-pubescent girl does fly in the face of our modern western senses. "

The scenario is summed up nicely in an article on the website "answering-islam.org", Mohammed, Aisha, Islam, and Child Brides by "Silas":

"A 49 year old man asks his best friend if he could have his permission to marry his 6 year old daughter. His friend agrees. The man then visits his best friend's house and speaks with the 6-year-old daughter. Her parents watch as the he proposes marriage to the child. He is serious; he wants to marry the little girl and is asking for her consent. The little child says nothing; she only stares at him in silence. She does not understand the concept of marriage or sex.

Mohammed proposed marriage to Aisha when she was 6. He assumed her silence constituted her consent. Some 2 to 3 years later, just after he had fled to Medina, he consummated his marriage with her. He was 52 and she was 9. This occurred prior to Aisha's first menses and by Islam's legal definition Aisha was still considered a child. Islam teaches that a child enters adulthood at the beginning of puberty. Sex before then leads to physical, and psychological, damage to the child."

Hadith of Bukhari, volume 5, #234

"As narrated by Aisha: The prophet engaged me when I was a girl of six. We went to Medina and stayed at the home of Harith Kharzraj. Then I got ill and my hair fell down (out). Later on my hair grew (again) and my mother, Um Ruman, came to me while I was playing in a swing with some of my girl friends. She called me, and I went to her, not knowing what she wanted to do to me. She caught me by the hand and made me stand at the door of the house. I was breathless then, and when my breathing became all right, she took some water and rubbed my face and head with it. Then she took me into the house. There in the house I saw some Ansari women who said, "Best wishes and Allah's blessing and good luck." Then she entrusted me to them and they prepared me (for the marriage). Unexpectedly Allah's messenger came to me in the forenoon and my mother handed me over to him, and at that time I was a girl of nine years of age."

Ibn Kathir born c. 1300, died 1373) was a highly influential Sunni scholar of the Shafil School. He was considered an expert in Quranic exegesis and jurisprudence, as well as a historian. In the Journal of Quranic Studies 16 (1): 3. 2014-02-01, Ibn Kathir writes regarding Quran 65:4:

"The `Iddah is the ritual periods based on cleanliness and the menstrual period." The ritual periods are set up so a man cannot divorce his wife until she has had her period and is clean and they have not had sex. This is to make sure she is not pregnant when they divorce. According to scholars there are three types of divorce. There is one that conforms to the Sunnah. Sunnah is the verbally transmitted record of the teachings, deeds and sayings, permissions, or disapprovals of Mohammed. There is another type of divorce called "innovated". The third type of divorce is for the very young or the very old wife, or the wife who refuses to have sex. The divorce that conforms to the Sunnah is one where the husband pronounces he is going to divorce his wife after she has finished her period and they have not had sexual intercourse. The innovated divorce occurs when one divorces his wife when she is having her menses, or after the menses ends, but he has sexual intercourse with her and then divorces her, even though he does not know if she became pregnant or not. There is a third type of divorce, which is neither a Sunnah nor an innovation divorce. This is done when a YOUNG WIFE HAS NOT BEGUN TO HAVE MENSES or the wife is beyond the age of having menses or one divorces his wife before the marriage was consummated.

Gaston Wiet tells us in his book "The Great Medieval Civilizations" that Al-Tabari (839–923 AD) was a prominent and influential Persian scholar, and historian. Today, Al-Tabari is best known for his expertise in Quranic commentary, law and history, as well as cultural and scientific development.

Al-Tabari said regarding the interpretation of the verse Quran 65:4, "And those of your women as have passed the age of monthly courses, for them the 'Iddah (prescribed period), if you have doubt (about their periods), is three months; and for those who have no courses (i.e. they are still immature) their 'Iddah (prescribed period) is three months likewise". The same applies to the 'idaah for girls who do not menstruate because they are too young if their husbands divorce them after consummating the marriage with them.

Abu-Ala' Maududi states:
"Therefore, making mention of the waiting-period for girls who have not yet menstruated, clearly proves that it is not only permissible to give away the girl at this age but it is permissible for the husband to consummate marriage with her. Now, obviously no Muslim has the right to forbid a thing which the Quran has held as permissible." (Maududi, volume 5, p. 620, note 13)

The only reason this type of marriage does not take place is the constraints of a society and its laws that forbid such imbalanced marriages from happening. The reason it is beginning to take place once again is that states such the Islamic State or ISIS have set up governments under Sharia Law, which permits this kind of act.

Sharia Law is a set of laws drawn up according to Mohammed's actions or words in the Quran and other writings, such as the hadith. Since Muslims believe Mohammed and the Quran are perfect, no Sharia Law can be altered. (More on Sharia law later.)

There seems to be a reactionary bend to Mohammed. When his first wife died, whom he seemed to love and with whom he maintained a happy marriage, he turned to polygamy and ended his days with nine wives, one of whom he had sex with when she was nine. After Mohammed's first wife died he seemed to lose his compassion and tolerance and declined into a more selfish lifestyle.

Likewise, when things did not go well for him and his new religion in Mecca and he was forced to flee for his life to Medina, his attitude of tolerance changed to that of a despot. He would later return to Mecca and take it over, killing those who had opposed him.

Although Mohammed endured persecution in Mecca, his attitude quickly changed when the number of his followers grew in Medina to the point where he could maintain control and fight those who opposed him. Soon he would tolerate no criticism whatsoever.

According to our earliest biographical source, a man named Abu Afak was more than a hundred years old when he wrote a poem criticizing people for converting to Islam. Mohammed demanded he be killed, and Abu Afak was murdered in his sleep. When a woman named Asma heard that Muslims had killed such an elderly man, she wrote a poem calling for people to take a stand against Islam. Ibn Ishaq relates what happened next:

"When the apostle heard what she had said he said, "Who will rid me of Marwan's daughter?" Umayr bin Adiy al-Khatmi who was with him heard him, and that very night he went to her house and killed her. In the morning he came to the apostle and told him what he had done and he said, "You have helped God and His apostle, O Umayr!" When he asked if he would have to bear any evil consequences the apostle said, "Two goats won't butt their heads about her," so Umayr went back to his people."
Sirat Rasul Allah (A. Guilaume's translation "The Life of Mohammed") pages 675, 676.

Mohammed's violence was directed towards groups as well. Mohammed once said to his followers, "I will expel the Jews and Christians from the Arabian Peninsula and will not leave any but Muslims." The Jews of Qurayza resisted Mohammed and attempted to form an alliance against him. When the alliance faltered, Mohammed acted quickly. His armies surrounded them and "besieged them for twenty-five nights until they were sore pressed and God cast terror into their hearts."
W. Muir in his Life of Mahomet, vol. III, pp. 276-279

When they surrendered, Mohammed confined them in Medina. Then Mohammed sent his men out to the market to dig trenches in the middle of the market. Then he sent for the captives to be brought to the market. There he placed them in the trenches and struck off their heads. Some sources place the number of deaths between 600 or 700. Other sources put the figure as high as 800 or 900.

Guillaume reports, "Every male who had reached puberty was killed on that day. Mohammed then divided the women, children, and property among his men (taking a fifth of the spoils for himself). "
Guillaume, p. 461-464., Peters, Mohammed and the Origins of Islam, p. 222-224., Stillman, p. 141f.

Mohammed was first and foremost a warlord, a military leader, and a conqueror. Many of his "revelations" came from god at opportune times conveying the correct messages to keep his troupes appeased during battle. As the Muslim armies raided towns and villages, they captured their women. These women were considered slaves and would be used, sold or traded. Since the Muslim army needed to be away from their wives for extended periods they wanted to use the women as sex slaves. Upon inquiring to Mohammed about the practice the prophet reported he had received a message from Allah to guide them. The revelation allowed the soldiers to rape the women as they pleased.

Wikipedia - en.wikipedia.org/wiki/Battle_of_Autas reports,
    "Allah's Messenger sent an army to Autas and encountered the enemy and fought with them. Having overcome them and taken them captives, the Companions of Allah's Messenger seemed to refrain from having intercourse with captive women because of their husbands being polytheists. Then Allah, Most High, sent down regarding that... Quran 4:24 Arberry Translation: and wedded women, save what your right hands own. So God prescribes for you. Lawful for you, beyond all that, is that you may seek, using your wealth, in wedlock and not in license. Such wives as you enjoy thereby, give them their wages portions; it is no fault in you in your agreeing together, after the due portion. God is All-knowing, All-wise.

Sayyid Maududi (d. 1979), a highly respected traditional commentator and scholar commented, "It lawful for Muslim holy warriors to marry women prisoners of war even when their husbands are still alive." He explains, "Forbidden to you are wedded wives of other people except those who have fallen in your hands [as prisoners of war] ."

Thus, it is lawful to have sex with multiple wives, slave girls taken in war, and children. Muslims are to emulate their prophet. Mohammed himself had sex with a prepubescent girl and this makes it not only legal but also something to be sought by Muslim men. Before his courtship of Aisha began Mohammed had a dream about her, which led him to believe that God wanted him to marry the young girl. Muslim sources report that Aisha still hadn't reached puberty. Aisha described her sexual experiences with the prophet. When she was six years old, he could not have intercourse with her due to her young age. As a consolation prize, he placed his penis between her thighs and massaged it softly. Aisha explained that "unlike other believers, the prophet had control over his penis."

Sam Shamoun, in the paper," An Examination of Mohammed's Marriage to a Prepubescent Girl And Its Moral Implications" wrote,
"After the permanent committee for the scientific research and fatwahs (religious decrees) reviewed the question presented to the grand Mufti Abu Abdullah Mohammed Al-Shemary, the question forwarded to the committee by the grand scholar of the committee with reference number 1809 issued on 3/8/1421 (Islamic calendar). The inquirer asked the following:
It has become wide spread these days, and especially during weddings, the habit of mufa'khathat of the children (mufa'khathat literally translated means "placing between the thighs" which means placing the male member between the thighs of a child). What is the opinion of scholars knowing full well that the prophet, the peace and prayer of Allah be upon him, also practiced the "thighing" of Aisha - the mother of believers - may Allah be please with her.
After the committee studied the issue, they gave the following reply:
It has not been the practice of the Muslims throughout the centuries to resort to this unlawful practice that has come to our countries from pornographic movies that the kufar (infidels) and enemies of Islam send. As for the prophet, peace and prayer of Allah be upon him, thighing his fiancée Aisha. She was six years of age and he could not have intercourse with her due to her small age. That is why [the prophet] peace and prayer of Allah be upon him placed his [male] member between her thighs and massaged it softly, as the apostle of Allah had control of his [male] member not like other believers.
Also see:
http://www.sout-al-haqe.com/pal/musical/mofakhaza.ram
http://www.islamic-fatwa.net/viewtopic.php?TopicID=8330

The problem here is not so much that an old man decided to have sex with a nine year old girl, or that a warlord gave his army permission to force themselves on women from cities they conquered and plundered.

These things have gone on throughout history. The problem is Mohammed is held up as the example to follow.

If one is a Muslim one attempts to emulate the behavior of Mohammed. If the man held up as God's prophet is cruel then the god he represents will be internalized as cruel and following the prophet of this god demands one become cruel and call it righteous.

It is said that Mohammed had an insatiable sexual appetite.

"The prophet used to visit all his wives in a round, during the day and night and they were eleven in number." I asked Anas, 'had the prophet the strength for it?' Anas replied, 'we used to say that the prophet was given the strength of thirty men." Bukhari (5:268)

Given this, is it easy to see why his heaven, the Islamic heaven, should have a definite sexual orientation. We are told the male believers of Islam will have 72 virgins awaiting their arrival in the after-life. The Quran does not specify the number as 72, it does say that those who fight in the way of Allah and are killed will be given a great reward. It goes on to stipulate that Muslims will be awarded with women with physical attributes of large eyes (Q 56:22) and big, firm, round "swelling breasts" that are not inclined to sagging (Q 78:33). The Quran refers to these virgins as houri, pure and well-matched companions of equal age. These bodily characteristics, including their virginity, gave rise to many hadiths (Hadiths are collections of the reports claiming to quote what the prophet Mohammed said verbatim on any matter. The term comes from the Arabic meaning "report", "account" or "narrative".) and other Islamic writings.

Hadith 2687 is where the number 72 is mentioned. "The smallest reward for the people of Heaven is an abode where there are eighty thousand servants and 72 houri, over which stands a dome decorated with pearls, aquamarine and ruby, as wide as the distance from al-Jabiyyah to San'a."

Quranic commentator Al-Suyuti, 1505 CE and Orthodox Muslim theologians such as al Ghazali , 1100 CE, and Al-Ash'ari, 930 CE, graphically describe the sexual and sensual pleasures provided to

Muslims in paradise. One likens it to a slave market where men may choose any woman and have sex with her then and there.

Al-Suyuti wrote, "Each time we sleep with a Houri we find her virgin. Besides, the penis of the Elected never softens. The erection is eternal; the sensation that you feel each time you make love is utterly delicious and out of this world and were you to experience it in this world you would faint. Each chosen one [i.e. Muslim] will marry seventy houris, besides the women he married on earth, and all will have appetizing vaginas."

Ibn Kathir, in his Qur'anic Commentary, the Tafsir ibn Kathir writes:
    "Women will have large, firm breasts that do not sag, large black eyes, appetizing vaginas, with resetting hymens (ever virgins) and men with erections that never go flaccid.... "

Abu Umama narrated: "The Messenger of God said,
    'Everyone that God admits into paradise will be married to 72 wives; two of them are houris and seventy of his inheritance of the [female] dwellers of hell. All of them will have libidinous sex organs and he will have an ever-erect penis.' " - Sunan Ibn Majah, Zuhd (Book of Abstinence) 39

On the whole, the Quran and the hadiths are filled with sexual fantasies that Muslim men are awarded when they reach Islamic heaven. Anas bin Malik, an Islamic scholar, claimed that "The prophet used to visit all his wives in a round, during the day and night and they were eleven in number... The prophet was given the strength of thirty (men)." Mohammed (hadith 24) apparently claimed that devout Muslims would be given the sexual strength of 100 persons upon their arrival in Heaven. (This is apparently more than what was attributed to the prophet himself).

One must ask what such carnality has to do with a spiritual heaven. The Islamic version of heaven, or Paradise, is nothing more than an extension of life here on earth brought to a place where all aspects of male Islamic life is perfected in such a way that those men of the 7th and 8th centuries would perceive it. This includes living under Sharia Law in a world where male appetite and domination is the cornerstone of the perfect society.

The sexual obsession by Muslim men as conveyed by Islamic writings, takes its cue from the founder of the religion. There is a world of difference, then, between the Mohammed of history and the Mohammed of faith.

Sexuality has become part of the Muslim war strategy. Muslim clerics are encouraging Muslim families in the UK, EU and US to have as many children as possible. "We will breed you out of existence," clerics warn. Some sources report an average birth rate among native EU, UK, and US families to be about 2.1 - 2.3 children per family. Muslims in the same countries are having 5 children per family on average. The activist, Pamela Geller reports :

"Afghan and Somali women in Britain have four times as many kids as UK born mums," by David Pilditch, Express, August 17, 2015: The UK is now home to more families containing four or more children than at any time since the early 1970s.

The average Afghan-born woman living in the UK has 4.25 children and the average Somali-born woman has 4.19 children.

The average for Pakistani women is 3.82. UK-born women have an average of 1.79 children, according to the data from European statistics agency Eurostat.

That compares with 2.19 for women living in the UK who were born in one of the 12 eastern European states, and 1.52 for women born in western European countries.

Meanwhile women born in Australia and New Zealand who live in the UK have an average of 1.38 children."

Pamelageller.com/2015/08

We shall see that these numbers vary between research groups. Governments are telling their people not to worry because the birthrates of Muslim families are dropping as they become westernized and discontinue their practices of polygamy and large families. We shall see. So far, this fits in with the warning that clerics have announced.

Pew Research, December 7, 2015 report states:

"There are two major factors behind the rapid projected growth of Islam, and both involve simple demographics. For one, Muslims have more children than members of other religious groups. Around the world, each Muslim woman has an average of 3.1 children, compared with 2.3 for all other groups combined.

Muslims are also the youngest (median age of 23 years old in 2010) of all major religious groups, seven years younger than the median age of non-Muslims. As a result, a larger share of Muslims already are, or will soon be, at the point in their lives when they begin having children. This, combined with high fertility rates, will fuel Muslim population growth.

While it does not change the global population, migration is increasing the Muslim population in some regions. Forty years after Sweden decided to welcome Islamic immigrants, cases of rape increased by 1,472%. Sweden is now number two on the list of rape countries, surpassed only by Lesotho in Southern Africa.

Why is the treatment of women so abhorrent among Muslim men? The religious and cultural views on women are quite negative and they are reinforced over generations.

The Quran says a husband has sex with his wife, as a plow goes into a field, and he can plow her as he wishes.
The Quran in Sura (Chapter) 2:223 your women are your fields, so go into your fields whichever way you like . . . . (MAS Abdel Haleem, The Qur'an, Oxford UP, 2004)

Hadith back up this position. 'If a man invites his wife to sleep with him and she refuses to come to him, then the angels send their curses on her till morning.' (Bukhari)

Husbands are a degree above their wives. The Quran in Sura 2:228 - Wives have the same rights as the husbands have on them in accordance with the generally known principles. Of course, men are a degree above them in status.

According to Mohammed, hell is full of women.
The Prophet said, 'I looked at Paradise and found poor people forming the majority of its inhabitants; and I looked at Hell and saw that the majority of its inhabitants were women.' (Bukhari)

Men are worth twice as much as a women. A male gets a double share of the inheritance over that of a female.
The Quran in Sura 4:11 - The share of the male shall be twice that of a female.

The word or testimony of a women is worth only half that of a man.
The Prophet said, 'Isn't the witness of a woman equal to half of that of a man?' The women said, 'Yes.' He said, 'This is because of the deficiency of a woman's mind.' (Bukhari)

Men may strike their wives if he thinks she is being disrespectful. Quran in 4:34 . . . If you fear highhandedness from your wives, remind them [of the teaching of God], then ignore them when you go to bed, then hit them. If they obey you, you have no right to act against them. God is most high and great.

Sharia Law

The church and state are one. There can be no separation. The church rules the state and all who live therein. Sharia Law is a set of laws based on the Quran and Islamic teachings, including the words and example of Mohammed. Mohammed's life is held up as "a beautiful pattern of conduct for anyone whose hope is in Allah" (Q33:21) and "an exalted standard of character" (Q68:4). Sharia Law is the body of Islamic law. The term means "way" or " path"; it is the legal framework within which the public and some private aspects of life are regulated for those living in a legal system based on Islam. Those laws based on the Quran cannot be altered, although there may be slight latitude given in interpreting the law at times. **Fundamental Muslims will always hold Sharia Law above a nation's civil law.**

Sharia deals with all aspects of day-to-day life, including politics, economics, banking, business law, contract law, sexuality, and social issues.

There is not a strictly codified uniform set of laws that can be called Sharia. It is more like a system of several laws, based on the Quran, Hadith and centuries of debate, interpretation and precedent.

Pure Islamic sharia law is not implemented in any country of the world except where violent fundamentalists are in control, such as in areas controlled by ISIS. Most Muslim countries have their own laws and have chosen laws from Islamic sharia as a foundation to their legal system.

Sharia law is the legal system of Islam. The Sharia (also spelled Shariah or Shari'a) law is derived from the actions, deeds, and words of Mohammed. This means the laws are derived from the Quran and the 'Sunnah'. The Sunnah is the verbally transmitted record of the teachings, deeds and sayings, silent permissions (or disapprovals) of Mohammed, as well as various reports about Mohammed's companions.

The Sharia law itself cannot be altered, but the interpretation of the Sharia law, called "fiqh," by imams is given some leeway.

As a legal system, the Sharia law covers a very wide range of topics. While other legal codes deal primarily with public behavior, Sharia law covers public behavior, private behavior and private beliefs.

The article from "simple.wikipedia.org/wiki/Sharia_law" gives us an overview of the laws and applications.

According to the Sharia law and after due process and investigation: Habitual theft past a specific threshold, and after repeated warnings, is punishable by amputation of a hand.

The punishment for adultery and fornication such that it becomes a public ordeal, according to the Holy Quran is lashing. Before the revelation of these verses, Mohammed followed the Judaic law in implementing the punishment of death by stoning. This was only given if the person admitted to it repeatedly, was not intoxicated and knew the repercussions. Even then, if during the punishment he repented, he was to be released. Although lately what we have been seeing is that once the first stone is thrown the bloodlust of the Islamic crowd deafens them to any cries of repentance by the accused parties and death by stoning occurs.

A woman is allowed to be accompanied by another woman in giving testimony in court for financial affairs.
A female heir inherits half of what a male heir inherits. The concept being that Islam puts the responsibility of earning and spending on the family on the male. Any wealth the female earns is strictly for her own use. The female also inherits from both her immediate family and through agency of her husband, her in-laws as well.

Sharia law is divided into two main sections: Acts of Worship and Human interaction.

The acts of worship, *or al-ibadat, called the 5 pillars of Islam:*
Affirmation (Shahadah): there is no god except Allah and Mohammed is his messenger. However, Allah is the same God of Isaac and Adam. Allah remains the same throughout time
Prayers (Salah): five times a day
Fasts (Sawm during Ramadan)
Charities (Zakat)

Pilgrimage to Mecca (Hajj)

Human interaction, *or al-mu'amalat, which includes:*
Financial transactions
Endowments
Laws of inheritance
Marriage, divorce, and child custody
Foods and drinks (including ritual slaughtering and hunting)
Penal punishments
Warfare and peace
Judicial matters (including witnesses and forms of evidence)

A Muslim can only marry a Muslim or Ahl al-Kitāb. He/She cannot marry an atheist, agnostic or polytheist.
A Muslim minor girl's father or guardian needs her consent when arranging a marriage for her.
A marriage is a contract that requires the man to pay, or promise to pay some of the wedding and provisions the wife needs. This is known as the dowry.
A Muslim man may be married to up to four women at a time, although the Quran has emphasized that this is a permission, and not a rule. The man must be able to house each wife and her children in a different house, he should not give preferential treatment to one wife over another. Marriage is a legal arrangement in Islam, not a sacrament in the Christian sense, and is secured with a contract.
"... marry women of your choice, two or three or four; but if you fear that you shall not be able to deal justly with them, then only one." (Quran 4:3)
Although a man may have a maximum of four wives, he is allowed to have sex slaves, the number of which is not specified.

Sharia recognizes three categories of crime:
Hudud: crimes against God with fixed punishment.
Qisas: crimes against Muslims where equal retaliation is allowed.
Tazir: crimes against Muslims or non-Muslims where a Muslim judge uses his discretion in sentencing.

There are 5 Hudud: theft, highway robbery, illicit sex, sexual slander (accusing someone of illicit sex but failing to produce four witnesses, and drinking alcohol

Sharia requires that there be four adult male Muslim witnesses to a hudud crime or a confession repeated four times, before someone can be punished for a Hudud crime.

Murder, bodily injury and property damage - intentional or unintentional - is considered a civil dispute under sharia law. The victim, victim's heir(s) or guardian is given the option to either forgive the murderer, demand equal retaliation or accept compensation in lieu of the murder, bodily injury or property damage. Under sharia law, the Diyya compensation received by the victim or victim's family is in cash.

The penalty for theft: Theft (stealing) is a hudud crime in sharia, with a fixed punishment. The punishment is cutting off the hand or feet of the thief.

The penalty for illicit sex: Sharia law states that if either an unmarried man or an unmarried woman has pre-marital sex, the punishment should be 100 lashes. There are some requirements that need to be met before this punishment can happen. For example, the punishment cannot happen unless the person confesses, or unless four eyewitnesses each saw, at the same time, the man and the woman in the action of illicit sex. Those who accuse someone of illicit sex but fail to produce four eyewitnesses are guilty of false accusation and their punishment is 80 lashes. Maliki School of sharia considers pregnancy in an unmarried woman as sufficient evidence that she committed the hudud crime of illicit sex and thus would subject the pregnant woman to 100 lashes under the whip. The Hadiths consider homosexuality as illicit sex.

The penalty for apostasy: The punishment for apostasy is thought to be death by several schools of Muslim thought, though the Quran has not advised such a punishment and in fact details that there is absolutely no penal punishment for apostasy. However, if someone does not convert or if a Muslim converts to another religion, or if a Muslim denounces or even criticizes Islam, most schools of thought advise killing the apostate.

An example apostate was Hashem Aghajari, who was sentenced to death for apostasy in Iran (in 2002) after giving a controversial speech on reforming Islam. His sentence was reduced to 5 years in prison, but only after international and domestic outcry.

There are two festivals that are considered Sunnah.
Eid ul-Fitr

Dr. Joseph Lumpkin

Eid ul-Adha
During these festivals, specific rituals are used:
Sadaqah (charity) before Eid ul-Fitr prayer.
The Prayer and the Sermon on Eid day.
Takbirs (glorifying God) after every prayer in the days of Tashriq (These are thought to be the days in which pilgrims stay at Mina once they return from Muzdalifah i.e. 10th, 11th, 12th, and 13th of Dhu al-Hijjah.)
Sacrifice of unflawed, four-legged grazing animal of appropriate age after the prayer of Eid ul-Adha in the days of Tashriq. The animal must not be wasted; its meat must be consumed.

Yes, Islam is not the only religion demanding the sacrifice of animals but is it one of the few. Muslims engaged in the Hajj (pilgrimage) are obligated to sacrifice a lamb or a goat or join others in sacrificing a cow or a camel during the celebration of the Eid al-Adha. Other Muslims not on the Hajj to Mecca are also encouraged to participate in this sacrifice to share in the sanctity of the occasion. It is understood as a symbolic re-enactment of Abraham's sacrifice of a ram in place of his son, a narrative present throughout Abrahamism. Meat from this occasion is divided into three parts:
For personal nourishment
For distribution among friends, family, and neighbors, and
as charity for the indigent

Other occasions where the lamb is sacrificed include the celebration of the birth of a child, reaching the final stages of building a house, the acquisition of a valuable commodity, and even the visit of a dear or honourable guest. For Muslims, the sacrifice of lamb was and is associated with celebrations, feasts, generosity, and the seeking of blessings. Most schools of fiqh hold the animal must be killed according to the prohibitions of halal sacrifice.

Dietary laws - Halal
Islamic law lists only some specific foods and drinks that are not allowed.
Pork, blood, and scavenged meat are not allowed. People are also not allowed to eat animals that were slaughtered in the name of someone other than God. Intoxicants (like alcoholic drinks) are not allowed under any circumstances. While Islamic law prohibits (does not allow) dead meat (meat slaughtered or prepared beyond a period of time after it dies. Animals must be killed in a certain way and prepared directly thereafter. This does not apply to fish and locusts.

254

Also, hadith literature prohibits beasts having sharp canine teeth, birds having claws, tamed donkeys, and any piece cut from a living animal.

Sacrifice: There are some specific rules regarding the killing of animals in Islam.
The animal must be killed in the most humane way: by swiftly cutting the throat.
The animal must not be diseased.
The animal must not have been exposed to feces, worms, and other impurities.
All blood must drain from the animal before being packaged.

Legal Under Sharia Law:

In his book, "Thirty Sharia Laws That Are Bad For All Societies", James M. Arlandson wrote:

The mosque and state are not separate. To this day, Islamic nations that are deeply rooted in sharia, like Iran and Saudi Arabia, do not adequately separate the two realms, giving a lot of power to courts and councils to ensure that legislation does not contradict the Quran (never mind whose interpretation). Most of the laws listed below come from this confusion. Back-up article: Mosque and State

A woman captive of jihad may be forced to have to sex with her captors (now owners). Quran 4:24 and especially the sacred traditions and classical law allow this. The sacred traditions say that while out on military campaigns under Mohammed's leadership, jihadists used to practice coitus interruptus with their female captives. Women soldiers fighting terrorists today must be forewarned of the danger.

Property can be destroyed or confiscated during jihad. Quran 59:2 and 59:5 discuss those rules. Sacred traditions and classical law expand on the Quranic verses. Modern Islamic law officially improves on the Quran: see Article Three of the 1990 Cairo Declaration of Human Rights, which is nonetheless based on sharia, but it outlaws wanton destruction of property. Would there be any conflict between old Islam and modern Islam in a war today? Back-up articles: Jihad and Qital and The Quran and the Sword

Jihad may be waged to collect spoils. Quran 8:1, 8:7, 8:41, and 48:20 show this clearly. Early Islam followed the old Arab custom of raiding caravans, but as its military grew, the raids were elevated to jihad. The spoils of war were coveted. Which Islam would prevail in a war today – the old one or the modern one?

A second-class submission tax, called the jizyah, must be imposed on Jews and Christians (and other religious minorities) living in Islamic countries. Quran 9:29 offers three options to Jews and Christians: (1) Fight and die; (2) convert to Islam; (3) or keep their religion, but pay a tribute or submission tax, the jizyah, while living under Islam. In Islamic history, vanquished Jews and Christians became known as dhimmis. This word appears in Quran 9:8 and 9:10, meaning a "treaty" or "oath," but it can also mean those who are "condemned" "reviled" or "reproved" (Quran 17:18, 17:22; 68:49). The word "submission" in Quran 9:29 can also be translated as "humiliation," "utterly humbled," "contemptible" or "vile." It can mean "small" as opposed to "great. Islamic nations today still seek to impose this second-class religion tax. Back-up articles: Jihad and Qital and The Quran and the Sword

Slavery is allowed. It is true that freeing slaves was done in original Islam (Quran 5:89 and 24:33), and the Quran says to be kind to slaves (Quran 4:36), but that is not the entire story. In addition to those verses, Quran 4:24, 23:1-7; 33:52 allow the institution. Mohammed owned slaves, even one who was black (so says a sacred tradition). He was militarily and politically powerful during his later life in Medina, but he never abolished slavery as an institution. Officially, Islamic nations have outlawed slavery (Article 11, which is still based on sharia). That proves Islam can reform on at least one matter. Can it reform on the other sharia laws? And we are told that "no other nation or religious group in the world treated slaves better than the Muslims did." The back-up article and next two items in this list contradict that claim. The legacy of slavery still runs deep in Islamic countries even today.

A male owner may have sex with his slave-women, even prepubescent slave-girls. See Quran 4:24 and 23:1-7; but it is classical law that permits sex with prepubescent slave girls and describes them as such. Some Muslim religious leaders and others still advocate this practice, taking the slaves as concubines (though sex with prepubescent slave-girls is another matter).

Slaves may be beaten. That's what sacred traditions and classical laws say. See Islamic Jihad: A Legacy of Forced Conversion, Imperialism, and Slavery

Apostasy laws, including imprisonment or execution, may be imposed on anyone who leaves Islam (an apostate). Normally this is a prescribed punishment, but it is also political, since it is about freedom of religion. Surprisingly the Quran does not cover punishing apostates down here on earth, though in the afterlife they will be punished. Can this modern Islam reform old Islam? Quran 4:88-89, 9:73-74, and 9:123, read in that sequence, might deal with earthly punishments. Mainly, however, the sacred traditions and classical law permit harsh treatment for anyone who leaves Islam. Islamic courts and laws still impose these punishments today, or religious scholars today argue for the law.

Blasphemy laws, including imprisonment or execution, may be imposed on critics of Islam or Mohammed. These verses should be read in historical sequence, for they show that as Islam's military power increased, the harsh treatment of mockers and critics also intensified, as follows: Quran 3:186, 33:57-61, 9:61-66, 9:73 and 9:123. Sacred traditions, classical laws, and historical Islam are unambiguous about the punishments, recording the people, often their names, who were assassinated for mocking Mohammed and the Quran. Islamic nations and pockets of Islam in non-Muslim countries still impose these punishments today.

Homosexuals may be imprisoned, flogged, or executed. Surprisingly, the Quran is not all that clear on this subject, but the traditions and classical laws are. Islamic nations to this day still impose those punishments, and religious leaders still argue for harsh punishments. Back-up article: Homosexuality

Adulterers may be stoned to death. The verse that says to stone adulterers to death went missing from the Quran, so says Umar, a companion of Mohammed and the second caliph (ruled 634-644). But he left no doubt that this penalty was done under Mohammed's direction, and the sacred traditions and classical laws confirm it. But a few rules of evidence must be followed, like confession of the adulterer or four eyewitnesses. In some interpretations of the law, if a woman is raped, but cannot produce four just and pious men who witnessed it, then she is slandering the alleged rapist (or gang rapists) – never mind that the four just and pious eyewitnesses did nothing to stop it, but stood there and watched it. Some modern Islamic nations still do this, and religious and legal scholars argue for it.

A woman inherits half what a man does. Quran 4:11 says it, and the hadith (traditions) and classical law confirm it. Modern Islamic nations still do this, and religious leaders still argue for it. Back-up article: Women's Status and Roles 23. A woman's testimony in a court of law counts half of a man's testimony, since she might "forget." Quran 2:282 says it in the context of business law. But the hadith (traditions) explains that women's minds are deficient; classical law expands this curtailment to other areas than business. Modern Islamic nations still do this, and religious scholars still argue for it.

A man may legally and irrevocably divorce his wife, outside of a court of law, by correctly pronouncing three times "you are divorced." Quran 2:229 says this, and the traditions and classical law explain and confirm it. A judge in a modern Islamic country will ensure that the husband did not speak from a fit of irrational rage (anger is okay) or intoxication, for example. Then the court will validate the divorce, not daring to overturn it, since the Quran says so. Sometimes this homemade and irrevocable divorce produces a lot of regret in the couple and manipulation from the husband in Islam today.

A wife may remarry her ex-husband if and only if she marries another man, has sex with him, and then this second man divorces her. Quran 2:230 says this, and the traditions and classical law confirm it. Supposedly, this rule is designed to prevent easy divorce (see the previous point), but it produces a lot of pain, in Muslims today.

Husbands may hit their wives. Quran 4:34 says it, and the traditions and classical law confirm it. There is a sequence of steps a husband follows before he can hit her, but not surprisingly this rule creates all sorts of abuse and confusion in Islamic society today.

A man may be polygamous with up to four wives. Quran 4:3 (and 33:50-52) allow this, but only if a man can take care of them. The traditions and classical law confirm it. Modern Muslims still push for this old marital arrangement even in the USA, and many Islamic nations still allow it. But some Muslims are fighting polygamy. The hadith (traditions) paints a picture of Mohammed's household that was full of strife between the wives.

A man may simply get rid of one of his "undesirable" wives. Quran 4:128 says this. The traditions say about the verse that the wife whom Mohammed wanted to get rid of was "huge" and "fat." She gave up her turn to his favorite girl-bride Aisha. He kept the corpulent wife. There is heartbreak in Islam today.

In December, 2014 Islamic reformists attempted to change the laws of Saudi Arabia on pre-pubescent marriages. The law stated that a mature man may marry a prepubescent girl. Quran 65:1-4, particularly verse 4, assumes, but does not command the practice. Classical law says a father may give away his prepubescent daughter, but she also has a few rights. Officially many Islamic nations have raised the legal marriage age, but pockets in the Islamic world still follow this old custom. The Grand Mufti of Saudi Arabia okayed marriage to ten-year-old girls.

Mary Chastain wrote about this in the December 2014 issue of the publication "Brietbart".
"Saudi Arabia's Grand Mufti Shaikh Abdul Aziz Al Shaikh announced there is "nothing wrong" with girls under the age of 15 getting married. This is a blow to human rights activists who hoped the strict Islamic country would at least set the minimum marriage age at 15.
"There is currently no intention to discuss the issue," he said.

In 2011, Saudi Arabia's Justice Ministry wanted to pass a law that set a minimum age to marry since many young girls are forced to marry much older men. Saudi Justice Minister Mohammed Al Issa said the issue came to light after "a surge in such weddings and growing criticism by local human rights groups."

Al Issa continued, "The Ministry is studying a draft law to regulate the marriage of teenage girls...the marriage of under-age girls in the country is not a phenomenon yet as some claim... those who say this are wrong." he said. "We are considering regulations in line with the Islamic Sharia to govern this kind of marriage."

The ministry submitted a study about the "negative psychological and social effects of underage marriages" to scholars and "requested a fatwa." However, the religious scholars never responded.

Today in Afghanistan the practice of pedophilia is rampant and has spread to the abuse of young boys. Men in power use boys as sex slaves. Owning these children is viewed as a status symbol.
Huffington Post, September 25, 2015 reported that the Pashtu (a large ethic group living in parts of Afghanistan and Pakistan) have a

saying that 'women are for (having) children and boys are for pleasure.' Social norms dictate that bacha bazi (boy play), is not un-Islamic or homosexual if the man does not love the boy. The sexual act is not reprehensible, and is far more ethical than defiling a woman. "

In his September 20, 2015 New York Times article, Joseph Goldstein reported: "Rampant sexual abuse of children has long been a problem in Afghanistan, particularly among armed commanders who dominate much of the rural landscape and can bully the population. The practice is called bacha bazi, literally "boy play," and American soldiers and Marines have been instructed not to intervene — in some cases, not even when their Afghan allies have abused boys on military bases, according to interviews and court records." One soldier complained, ""At night we can hear them screaming, but we're not allowed to do anything about it."

The Early Islamic Community

Mohammed's life as a preacher and leader of a community of believers has two major phases. Mecca set on a major trade road. Its citizens were mostly polytheists who believed there were gods guarding the city and making it successful. Most of the Arab world at the time practiced polytheism. Mohammed's message centered on monotheism. He proclaimed his message in a city in which the majority did not accept his teachings. In the eyes of the ruling people, Mohammed and his message would threaten the profit and success of Mecca and the region. It would have angered the gods protecting the city and causing it to prosper. Why change something that was working so well? The message presented in the "Meccan" period emphasizes the general themes of affirmation of monotheism and warnings of the Day of Judgment. Since the message was in conflict with the established financial and political structure of the city, the message represented a major challenge to the basic power structures of Mecca. The stress between the systems and the new religion demanded Islam become both a religious and political force and therefore, by default, a financial force as well. This would have demanded a redistribution of wealth and commerce in favor of Muslims and the conversion or relinquishing of power by the elite.

The second phase of Mohammed's career and the early life of the Muslim community began when Mohammed went to the city of Yathrib, which became known as Medina.

Although the fact is little publicized, more than one historian has affirmed that the Arab world's second holiest city, Medina, was first settled by Jewish tribes. The roots of Islamic anti-Semitism and the law of taxation of non-believers might be found in the initial plunder of Jewish settlements, and the imposition of a "poll tax" to fund Arab campaigns. Jews that did not convert were killed or taxed.

Bernard Lewis is a British-American historian specializing in oriental studies. He is also known as a public intellectual and political commentator, Professor Emeritus of Near Eastern Studies at Princeton University with expertise in the history of Islam and the interaction between Islam and the West. Mr. Lewis writes:

"Jizya or jizyah is a religiously required per capita yearly tax historically levied by Islamic states on certain non-Muslim subjects (dhimmis) permanently residing in Muslim lands under Islamic law. The Quran mandates Jizya. However, scholars largely agree that early Muslim rulers adapted existing systems of taxation and tribute that were established under previous rulers of the conquered lands.

"The city of Medina, some 280 miles north of Mecca, had originally been settled by Jewish tribes from the north, especially the Banu Nadir and Banu Quraiza. The comparative richness of the town attracted an infiltration of pagan Arabs who came at first as clients of the Jews and ultimately succeeded in dominating them. Medina, or, as it was known before Islam, Yathrib, had no form of stable government at all. The town was torn by the feuds of the rival Arab tribes of Aus and Khazraj, with the Jews maintaining an uneasy balance of power. The latter, engaged mainly in agriculture and handicrafts, were economically and culturally superior to the Arabs, and were consequently disliked.... as soon as the Arabs had attained unity through the agency of Mohammed they attacked and ultimately eliminated the Jews. Mohammed set up control in Medina and began growing his movement as one would grow a nation. In Medina Mohammed provided leadership in all matters of life."

According to Guillaume,

"At the dawn of Islam the Jews dominated the economic life of the Hijaz [Arabia]. They held all the best land. At Medina they must have formed at least half of the population. The prosperity of the Jews was due to their superior knowledge of agriculture and irrigation and their energy and industry. Jewish prosperity was a challenge to the Arabs, particularly the Quraysh at Mecca and ... [other Arab tribes] at Medina. The prophet Mohammed himself was a member of the Quraysh tribe, which coveted the Jews' bounty, and when the Muslims took up arms they treated the Jews with much greater severity than the Christians, who, until the end of the purely Arab Caliphate, were not badly treated.

Mohammed was changing his outlook with the rapidity of a man who had cast off the mantle of preacher and taken on the helmet of a warrior. He began his message in Mecca by preaching monotheism and a plea of conversion. He taught respect for Jews and Christians, whom he referred to as "Children of the Book." Yet, he and his followers treated the Jews in Medina with great cruelty.

It was in 622 Mohammed and his followers moved to Yathrib (Medina), and this emigration, or hijrah, is of such significance that Muslims use this date as the beginning of the Islamic calendar. The oasis became known as the City of the prophet, or simply al-Medina (the city).

In Muslim tradition the sociopolitical community that was created in Medina provides the model for what an Islamic state and society should be. The new community was open to anyone who made the basic affirmation of faith. Loyalty to the Islamic community was to supersede any other loyalty to clan, family or nation. The political structure of the new community evolved toward a sovereign monarchy or theocracy with a religious head. In this way Islam is frequently described as a social and political way of life rather than simply a religion."

Mohammed carried resentment for being thrown out of Mecca and he eventually exacted his revenge in blood. The Muslim army set out for Mecca on Wednesday, 29 November 629 (6 Ramadan, 8 hijra), joined by allied tribes. The Muslim army was swollen to 10,000 men. This was the largest Muslim force ever assembled to date. The army stayed at Marr-uz-Zahran, located ten miles northwest of Mecca. Mohammed ordered every man to light a fire to deceive the Meccans to overestimate the size of the already bloated army.

By the time of Mohammed's death in 632, Islam was established in Mecca, which would become very important to the Muslim world. The Kaaba, a cube shaped shrine in Mecca that had been the center of the polytheistic religious life and the draw of several types of pilgrimages was relabeled as Islamic. Mohammed announced that it was once an altar built by Abraham. Mecca became both the center of the Islamic pilgrimage and the place toward which Muslims faced when they performed their prayers.

Sunni, Shia, Salafis and Sufi

A religion based on behavior, deeds, and rituals, by its nature must become more and more exact in order to insure both its survival and its mission. If the target of this religion is heaven the bull's-eye will become smaller and smaller as rules are added and doctrine becomes more restrictive and specific. In time there will be a faction that splinters away because they will disagree with the main body on points of rule, control, or doctrine. They will see the main body as lacking in commitment or strictness. The main group may not be fundamental enough in the eyes of the emerging group to reach the narrowed goal of heaven. They will break away to gain heaven. Eventually they may even gain influence over the main group.

Suuni and Shia

The schism between the two main branches of Islam is somewhat reminiscent of the split between the Catholic and Orthodox branches of Christianity. Let us not forget it was the attempt to usurp power by the bishop of Rome, who at that time was simply one among many equals that was partially to blame for the great schism. Most schisms begin with a contest of power or control. Most religions containing a fundamental branch will, by its nature, come to a point of division since fundamentalist believe there can be no variation from what they hold as the truth. Anything outside, lacking, or beyond their core doctrine represents error and sin. Firm control over the faith and the faithful is the only way to insure compliance with the religion and the favor of god. So it was with the Sunni and Shia. In its most simple and basic description, the split between the Sunni and Shia was over who should control Islam after the passing of the prophet Mohammed. The point of contention was if control should come through bloodline or through political choice.

Islam had become a set of laws that ruled most aspects of life, including political authority, which was founded upon a monotheistic religion that incorporated some Jewish, Christian, and pagan doctrines. By the time of his death in 632, Mohammed had consolidated power in Arabia.

Less than a century after his death Muslims had built an empire that would reach from Central Asia to Spain.

The battles over the control, power and wealth of such an empire would be the downfall to a consolidated Islam. A battle over succession split the followers. Some argued that leadership should be passed to qualified individuals elected by the votes of the leading clerics. Others insisted that the only legitimate ruler must come through Mohammed's bloodline.

One faction turned to their leaders and cleric to elect a Caliph. The group of high-level leaders of Islam elected Abu Bakr, a companion of Mohammed. Others favored Ali ibn Abi Talib, Mohammed's cousin and son-in-law as the Caliph because he was a leader who shared a bloodline with Mohammed. The fierce opposition between the two choices eventually evolved into Islam's two main sects, the Shia and the Sunni.

Shias is a term that stems from shi'atu Ali, Arabic for "partisans of Ali". Shias believe that Ali and his descendants are part of a divine order, descending as a king or emperor should, through inheritance or blood. The party of Ali claimed that Mohammed had designated his son-in-law Ali ibn Abi Talib as his successor, and that the successor of Mohammed had to be a member of the prophet's household.

The Sunnis contended that the prophet of Islam had made no provision for a successor as political, military, and spiritual leader of the Muslim community, and therefore Muslims should choose the best man among them as their leader. Sunnis means "followers of the way" (sunna means way) of Mohammed. Sunnis are opposed to succession based on Mohammed's bloodline and believe succession should come through election.

Shias believe it was expected that the successor would have some of Mohammed's prophetic spirit, as well as infallibility in deciding disputed questions. It seemed to some that this ability could follow with the bloodline. Ali was finally chosen as the fourth caliph in 656. In 661 he was assassinated. Hassan, his eldest son and successor, was murdered in 670 on the orders of the Sunni caliph Muawiya. Then the

Sunni/Shi'ite split became definitive and permanent when Ali's younger son, Husayn, was killed in the Battle of Karbala in 680.

The Shi'ites (or Shias) were brutalized and their leaders murdered. This feeling of separation, loss and defeat became part of the Shi'ite theology and history. Thus, it affects their worship and behavior.

After the Sunnis beheaded Husayn, the Shi'ites continued a succession of Imams who were members of Mohammed's household. Each Imam was purported to have been poisoned by order of the Sunni caliph ruling at the time.

In a written report, The Council on Foreign Relations in their article "The Sunni Shia Divide" explains,

"Ali became caliph in 656 and ruled only five years before he was assassinated. The caliphate, which was based in the Arabian Peninsula, passed to the Umayyad dynasty in Damascus and later the Abbasids in Baghdad.

Shias rejected the authority of these rulers. In 680, soldiers of the second Umayyad caliph killed Ali's son, Husayn, and many of his companions in Karbala, located in modern-day Iraq. Fear of continuing reprisal resulted in the further persecution and marginalization of Shias.

Sunnis triumphed politically in the Muslim world and grow in number and thus in control. Shias continued to look to the Imams, who were clerics leading services and prayers in the mosques. These men were the blood descendants of Ali and Husayn and functioned as the legitimate political and religious leaders within the branch of Islam. Even within the Shia community, however, there arose differences over the proper line of succession.

Shia identity is rooted in victimhood over the killing of Husayn, the prophet Mohammed's grandson, in the seventh century, and a long history of marginalization by the Sunni majority. Islam's dominant sect, which roughly 85 percent of the world's 1.6 billion Muslims follow, viewed Shia Islam with suspicion, and extremist Sunnis have portrayed Shias as heretics and apostates.

The Shia sect continued to look to their Imams to guide them. Imams are the blood descendants of Ali and Husayn and the only men that can be their legitimate political and religious leaders."

The Council on Foreign Relations in their article "The Sunni Shia Divide" continues,

"Mainstream Shias believe there were twelve Imams. The majority of Shias, particularly those in Iran and the eastern Arab world, believe that the twelfth Imam entered a state of occultation, or hiddenness, in 939 and that he will return at the end of time. Since then, "Twelvers," or Ithna Ashari Shias, have vested religious authority in their senior clerical leaders, called ayatollahs (Arabic for "sign of God)".

The belief in the return of the twelfth Imam fits into an apocalyptic view, which fuels the terroristic tactics of some Muslims.
According to the traditions of Twelver Shi'ism, the official religion of the Islamic Republic of Iran, the twelfth of these Imams, a boy of five years old, disappeared under mysterious and disputed circumstances in the year 874. However, he remained alive and he communicated to the world through his four chosen agents. The last agent died in 941. At that point the Twelfth Imam went silent, entering the period of "Great Occultation" or a spiritual hiding.

The International Messianic Jewish Alliance wrote in the article, "They Await the Mahdi (ISLAMIC MESSIAH)",

"In his last message to the world in 941 the Twelfth Imam consoled his followers with prophecies regarding his reappearance. The prophecies are now being interpreted in a modern context. This modern view places Iran on center stage and brings fire and destruction to Israel and America. The two powers that the Iranian mullahs have long designated as the "Great Satan" and the "Little Satan" are America and Israel and they would be the first targets in an Iranian attempt to hasten the Twelfth Imam's coming."

Frontpage magazine November, 2013 article reports,

The Twelfth Imam, in his last message warned, "Hearts will become inaccessible to compassion. The earth will be filled with tyranny and violence, and the evil that Muslims were suffering was at its absolute apex.

In the Shi'ite tradition Mohammed prophesied (in the hadith) that the Twelfth Imam would be "the Resurrector" and would fill the world with peace and justice as today it is filled with violence and tyranny."

The Shi'ites teach that the Twelfth Imam would return at a time when the Muslims were oppressed as never before, and suffering worse than ever. The Imam, in the company of Jesus, would finally end the horrific persecution of the true believers, taking up arms against their enemies and conquering the world and establishing Islam throughout the earth.

Jesus is held as a prophet in Islam. Jesus will defer to Mohammed and in doing so prove that Muslims had it right all along and Christians would flock to convert."

Today modern, fundamental Muslims attempt to hasten the Twelfth Imam's return by fueling violence around the world. Their agenda is obvious. If they can make the entire world hate and persecute Islam and bring a global war against Muslims they will bring back the Twelfth Imam and with his help Islam would conquer the world.

The true believers of Islam will stop at nothing to bring about a world war against Islam. The world fears they may find a way by launching a nuclear strike against Israel to provoke retaliation that would subject the Muslims in Iran to war and even genocide. They believe this would bring back the Islamic messiah, the Twelfth Imam. Jesus would descend from heaven and order Christians to convert to Islam. Most of the world would convert. Muslims would then destroy those who oppose Islam. At that time they would establish their version of a world religion.

Sunni Shia - Modern Wars

Sects and denominations do not matter if there is no prejudice. In the U.S. one seldom cares if a person is an Orthodox, Catholic, or Protestant Christian because there is no discrimination between the denominations. That was not always the case and the lack of equal consideration fomented wars and fights. This is the tip of the problem when it comes to the Shia-Sunni divide.

Much of the ongoing conflict in the Middle East is fueled by the sectarian wars between the Shia and Sunni. These two sects are fighting proxy wars, where countries, which are either majority Shia or Sunni, are battling for control of large regions. It is not easy to identify these wars as sectarian because there are wars in which countries and not sects are fighting. But, below the surface these countries are simply the extensions of the sects that control them, and thus the wars conducted by the countries are proxy wars between Shia and Sunni.

An article in the Wall Street Journal, "Saudi Arabia vs. Iran: The Sunni-Shiite Proxy Wars" 4/7/2015 states in part,
"In today's Middle East the political and religious divisions are fueling the insurgency in proxy wars. One key driver of this instability is the fourteen hundred year-old sectarian split between Sunni and Shiite Muslim."

Several factors brought the old split back to the forefront. Iran's Islamic Revolution in 1979 deposed the Shah and established a theocratic rule over the country. This was the re-emergence of hard line Shia theology and the Sharia Law that came with it. Saudi Arabia promoted the fundamentalist Salafist strain of Sunni Islam to counter Iran's Shia ideology. Then, when Saddam Hussein was removed from power in Iraq in 2003 Sunni jihadism began and Iran began to influence Iraq. Today of the total Muslim population, 10-13% are Shia Muslims and 87-90% are Sunni Muslims. Most Shias (between 68% and 80%) live in just four countries: Iran, Pakistan, India and Iraq. Saudi Arabia is a driving force in the Sunni world and the largest exporter of terrorism driven by the Sunni sect. Iran is the largest exported of terrorism driven by the Shia sect. Much of the fighting in the Middle East is proxy wars for these two sects.

Now the sects are mixing and fighting within the countries themselves. This is the reason for the internal civil war of Syria.

Syria is a Sunni-majority country but it is ruled by members of a Shiite (Shia) sect. The fighting that began as anti-government has taken on sectarian overtones since the population is predominately one sect and the government and ruling class is of the other sect. That problem has spilled over to Iraq. Iraq's population is mostly Shia with a predominantly Shiite government, Sunni rebels increasingly trouble it. Iraq is caught in the middle between Iran, with its Shiite majority on one side and Saudi Arabia, which has a majority Sunni population.

Iran is exporting fighters to stir up trouble so it can take advantage. The major powers in Saudi Arabia and Iran have long pushed sectarian interests, resulting in civil and international conflicts.

Pew Research explains the conflict like this,
"Iran and Iraq are two of only a handful of countries that have more Shias than Sunnis. While it is widely assumed that Iraq has a Shia majority, there is little reliable data on the exact Sunni-Shia breakdown of the population there, particularly since refugees arriving in Iraq due to the conflict in Syria or leaving Iraq due to its own turmoil may have affected the composition of Iraq's population.

Neighboring Iran is home to the world's largest Shia population: Between 90% and 95% of Iranian Muslims (66-70 million people) were Shias in 2009, according to our estimate from that year.

Their shared demographic makeup may help explain Iran's support for Iraq's Shia-dominated government led by Prime Minister Nouri al-Maliki.

Iran also has supported Bashar al-Assad's government in Syria, where only 15-20% of the Muslim population was Shia as of 2009. But the Syrian leadership is dominated by Alawites (an offshoot of Shia Islam). Under Saddam Hussein's regime in Iraq, which was dominated by Sunnis, the country clashed with Iran."

There are countries where the Sunni and Shia get along and even marry. In these countries the distinctions, which are actually few, are overlooked. It is when people start focusing on the legalistic subtle details that differences are seen and dwelt on. Sunni and Shia are forms of Islam that can be legalistic and external. They tend to interpret the words and deeds of Mohammed literally and in doing so they condemn the religion to be crystallized and entrenched in the era of its creations, about 632 C.E. If there were a polar opposite of the Sunni and Shia, it would be Sufism. The Sunni and Shia are legalistic and religious, Sufism is mystical and spiritual.

Salafis

In one of the best articles on ISIS and Islam, Graeme Wood writes in The Atlantic Magazine 2015/03
What ISIS Really Wants

"The majority of Salafis believe that Muslims should remove themselves from politics. These quietist Salafis, as they are known, agree with the Islamic State that God's law is the only law, and they eschew practices like voting and the creation of political parties. But they interpret the Quran's hatred of discord and chaos as requiring them to fall into line with just about any leader, including some manifestly sinful ones. "The prophet said: as long as the ruler does not enter into clear kufr [disbelief], give him general obedience." The texts warn against causing social upheaval. Quietist Salafis are strictly forbidden from dividing Muslims from one another, for example, by mass excommunication.

Quietist Salafis believe that Muslims should direct their energies toward perfecting their personal life, including prayer, ritual, and hygiene. Much in the same way ultra-Orthodox Jews debate whether it's kosher to tear off squares of toilet paper on the Sabbath (does that count as "rending cloth"?), they spend an inordinate amount of time ensuring that their trousers are not too long, that their beards are trimmed in some areas and shaggy in others. Through this fastidious observance, they believe, God will favor them with strength and numbers, and perhaps a caliphate will arise. At that moment, Muslims will take vengeance and, yes, achieve glorious victory at Dabiq. But Pocius cites a slew of modern Salafi theologians who argue that a caliphate cannot come into being in a righteous way except through the unmistakable will of God.

The Islamic State, of course, would agree, and say that God has anointed Baghdadi. Pocius's retort amounts to a call to humility. He cites Abdullah Ibn Abbas, one of the prophet's companions, who sat down with dissenters and asked them how they had the gall, as a minority, to tell the majority that it was wrong. Dissent itself, to the point of bloodshed or splitting the umma, was forbidden. Even the manner of the establishment of Baghdadi's caliphate runs contrary to expectation, he said. "The khilafa is something that Allah is going to establish," he told me, "and it will involve a consensus of scholars from Mecca and Medina. That is not what happened. ISIS came out of nowhere."

The Islamic State mocks the Salafis by calling them "Salafis of menstruation," for their obscure judgments about when women are and aren't clean. ISIS calls this a low-priority and claims the Salafis waste

271

their time in minutia. Salafis are legalists and fundamentalist but not violent. They believe the conquests should be left to Allah. Salafis prepare themselves religiously while they wait for Allah to prepare the world for the end times.

Salafism offers an alternative to Baghdadi-style jihadism. If one seeks a conservative, uncompromising fundamental version of Islam without the jihad, Salafism may be the answer. Most Muslims would consider it an extreme form of Islam but the literal-minded would not find it ideologically hypocritical or blasphemous.

Graeme Wood continues with a warning to Barack Obama by saying it would be best for non-Muslims to refrain from weighing in on matters of Islamic theology, especially if they could be considered as an apostate Muslim themselves. Obama could be considered a Takfiri, which is when one Muslim accuses another of being an apostate, impure, or unbelief. When Obama accused ISIS (Islamic State) of not representing Islam and of not being Islamic at that point Obama, as the non-Muslim son of a Muslim, may himself be classified as an apostate. The takfir challenge from Obama elicited chuckles from jihadists. Wood reported that one member of ISIS tweeted, Obama is "Like a pig covered in feces giving hygiene advice to others".

Sufi

Sufism is less a sect of Islam than a mystical way of approaching the Islamic faith. It has been defined as "mystical Islam". Sufis believe and practice a way to seek divine love and knowledge through direct personal experience of God. Any religion or sect that seeks direct and personally communion with God is considered mystical.

Suf means wool. Sufi refers to the woolen garment of early Islamic ascetics. The terms evolved in Western languages in the early 19th century and derive from the Arabic term for a mystic.

Sufism has been a prominent movement within Islam throughout most of its history. It grew out of an early ascetic movement within Islam, which, like its Christian monastic counterpart, sought to counteract the worldliness, carnality, and literalism that came with the rapid expansion of the early Muslim community.

ReligionFacts.com in their article, "What is Sufism" reports,

"The earliest form of Sufism arose under the Umayyad Dynasty (661–749) less than a century after the founding of Islam. Mystics of this period meditated on the Doomsday passages in the Quran, thereby earning such nicknames as "those who always weep." Sufi interpretation of the Quran did not follow the rule of abrogation as the other two main branched did. Instead, they focused on the connection between God and humanity.

These early Sufis led an ascetic life of strict obedience to all Islamic scripture and were known for their night prayers. Many of them concentrated their efforts upon an absolute trust in God, which became a central concept of Sufism.

Another century or so later, a new emphasis on love arose in the faith and changed Sufism into a mysticism faith. This development is attributed to Rabi'ah al-'Adawiyah (800 CE), a woman from Basra who formulated the Sufi ideal of a pure love of God. This was a devotion that was beyond fear of hell or greed for paradise. It was a pure and unconditional love not based on the "bribe" of paradise of "threat" of hell. This type of pure love spills over into mankind and changes both practitioner and those who are astute enough to understand what they are witnessing.

Other important developments soon followed, including strict self-control, psychological insight, "interior knowledge," annihilation of the self, mystical insights about the nature of man and the prophet, as well as hymns and poetry. This period, from about 800-1100 AD, is referred to as classical Sufism or classical mysticism."

God's love for man and man's love for God is central to Sufism, and the subjects of most Islamic mystical poetry. The 13th century is considered the golden age of Sufism. The mystics wrote beautiful and soaring poetry. Figures such as Ibn al'Arabi of Spain, Ibn al-Farid of Egypt, Jalal ad-Din ar-Rumi of Persia, and Najmuddin Kubra of Central Asia emerged, changing the world with their poetry and prose of divine love and insight. Sufism permeated the Islam and began shaping the faith. The Sufi influence would not last as Islam would later give way to legalism and fundamentalism.

Sufis see God in everything and everything as part of God. Even though they testify that God is one and even though they believe in the Quran as the word of God fundamental Muslims sometimes accuse Sufis of monism or pantheism. The Sufis tend to believe nothing truly exists but God. They also believe nature and God are two aspects of the same reality. Because of these views, other branches of Islam might not consider Sufis orthodox.

Quba-e-siddique.com reports:
"The Path begins with repentance and submission to a guide or teacher. The teacher guides the disciple on a path that usually includes sexual abstinence, fasting and poverty. The ultimate goal of the Sufi path is to fight the true Holy War against the lower self, which is often represented as a black dog."

Mohammed taught that the greatest jihad or holy war is the one fought within, against our own baser nature.

religionfacts.com/sufism says,
"The Sufi will undergo changes in spiritual states. They are listed as:

Constraint and happy spiritual expansion,
Fear and hope
Longing and intimacy
Abiding in the moment
Interior knowledge, which is the gnosis of love.

This last state is a union of lover and beloved (man and God). In this final stage the ego is lost to the beloved and the person is transformed as the ego boundary is let down in order to allow the complete melding with the beloved. This stage is often accompanied by spiritual ecstasy.

Quba-e-siddique.com continues,
"After the annihilation of the self and accompanying ecstatic experience, the mystic enters a "second sobriety" in which he re-enters the world and continues the "journey of God."
Within the Sufi tradition are: Rituals: Prayers, Music and "Whirling." A rosary of 99 or 33 beads has been in use since as early as the 8th century for counting the thousands of repetitions of prayers and the names of God."

The well-known "Whirling Dervishes" are members of the Mevlevi order of Turkish Sufis, based on the teachings of the famous mystic Rumi (d.1273). The practice of spinning around is the group's distinctive form of sama (listening/meditation). The whirlers, called semazens, are practicing a form of meditation in which they seek to abandon the self and contemplate God, sometimes achieving an ecstatic state. The Mevlevi sect was banned in Turkey by Ataturk in 1925, but performances for tourists are still common throughout the country.

The Next Step In The Evolution of God and Man

In the beginning, the church was a fellowship of men and women centering on the living Christ. Then, the church moved to Greece where it became a philosophy. Then, it moved to Rome where it became an institution. Next, it moved to Europe, where it became a culture. And, finally, it moved to America where it became an enterprise.
Richard Halverson

Many religions have become superficial and narcissistic. Much of Christianity is now a diluted religion that has lost its roots of love and forgiveness. The church of the dark ages allowed no doubt or discussion, but condemned to hell all those who would challenge it. Modern Christianity is little better and has become so bogged down in doctrine and church laws that it is now legalistic and judgmental by nature and impudent in force.

Judaism has become so ritualized it has lost its connection to the idea of a living creator.

Islam has become the vessel of terrorism and hate around the world.

We are coming to a second Axial Age. We must. What it will entail, no one knows. While leaving the arena of the fatted, red-faced preacher yelling beratement, fear, and guilt to the congregation, we are rejecting the priestly protected pedophile. We now seek a higher path, an inner, personal path, and a mystical path. We will rid ourselves of our sedentary pride.

What is a mystic, and what is the meaning of "mystical"? To say glibly that religion will give way to the individual mystical experience serves no purpose if the term is not fully defined. Ah, but there's the rub. Such a word is impossible to define since it is utterly deep, personal, and spiritual. We have no terms for the experience. We may define it, and still not fully understand it. So, let's first define the terms as best we can, and then explore the writing of the mystics along with descriptions of their experiences so that we may gain insight into the future of human spirituality in the next Axial Age.

mystic |mistik|
noun
a person who seeks by contemplation and self-surrender to obtain unity

with or absorption into the Deity or the absolute, or who believes in the spiritual apprehension of truths that are beyond the intellect.

mystical |mistikəl|
adjective
1 of or relating to mystics or religious mysticism : *the mystical experience.*
• spiritually allegorical or symbolic; transcending human understanding : *the mystical body of Christ.*
• of or relating to ancient religious mysteries or other occult or esoteric rites : *the mystical practices of the Pythagoreans.*
• of hidden or esoteric meaning : *a geometric figure of mystical significance.*
2 inspiring a sense of spiritual mystery, awe, and fascination : *the mystical forces of nature.*
• concerned with the soul or the spirit, rather than with material things : *the beliefs of a more mystical age.*

What is a Mystic and what is the Mystical Experience?

There was once a path that was above organized religion and the stone-heavy, lifeless doctrine. The mystics, the desert fathers, and those who sought God without and beyond the rules forged it long ago. It is to this path I believe we will return. Thus, I wish to end this work with a discussion on mysticism. Although I hold to the path of the Christian mystic, I leave open the possibility, and pray it is true, that all contemplative paths lead to a single destination. Whether Buddhist, Jew, Muslim, or Christian, the inner and earnest search for God will lead us home.

It is possible the demise of contemplative worship in the West is a direct result of an ever-accelerating lifestyle of greed and selfishness. We now live in a world where there are more people living in greater personal isolation. We have turned away from intimate, face-to-face, conversations and replaced the eloquent, heart-felt letters of the past with sparse abbreviations of instant messaging. We text, Twitter, Facebook, and email snippets of thoughts, never becoming connected or close. Since it is more difficult to lie and cheat those we know, our society has begun to fall apart because our separation allows for ease of mutual destruction. Sadly, our lifestyle has influenced our worship, giving rise to drive-in churches and an ever-growing detachment from the deeper journey.

We seek entertainment, not connection. Our fast-food religion focuses on one or two exciting hours a week. There are no more voices crying in the wilderness, because the wilderness of the heart is left unexplored and there are none who dare venture into the dark regions of the soul where God awaits in the quiet, lonely darkness. Each church has substituted its own group of rules in place of the real journey and awakening. Like a committee following "Robert's Rules of Order," we try to live within the rules, but that does not allow us to meet the author. What shall we do?

I will speak here mostly of Christianity, since it is what I have practiced, yet the same formula could save any religion where form and ritual have eclipsed the spiritual search for God and where being right and righteous is more important than our fellow man.

The future of Christianity may lie solely in the mystical tradition, which demands a direct and personal relationship with God. Any hope of true salvation and personal growth in Christianity hinges on the depth of our relationship with God himself. The entire Christian faith is based on a direct and unique connection between the individual and God. In this aspect, Christianity is a mystical and dynamic faith. The Christian faith demands union and communion with the creator, wherein He teaches us, guides us, and loves us. Through gratitude, meditation, adoration, and prayer, we are joined with Him and transformed from within. Such love and transformation engendered by this relationship can reunite Christians with the power, grace, glory, and love meant for all who seek the living God.

With most people, and sadly, with most Christians, a crucial gap remains between God and man. We do not need more teaching of doctrine, law, or church tradition, or any social or moral message. We need a heart-to-heart dialogue with God. We need and long for a relationship with our creator in which He loves and teaches us as a father would a child. The modern church has forgotten the path to their father. It is still there, beneath the hedges of religion, rules, and pride. The hedges and briars of laws and church doctrine must be cleared away to find the path.

Jesus said:

Matthew 5:3   Blessed [are] the poor in spirit: for theirs is the kingdom of heaven.

Matthew 5:4   Blessed [are] they that mourn: for they shall be comforted.

Matthew 5:5   Blessed [are] the meek: for they shall inherit the earth.

Matthew 5:6   Blessed [are] they which do hunger and thirst after righteousness: for they shall be filled.

Matthew 5:7   Blessed [are] the merciful: for they shall obtain mercy.

Matthew 5:8   Blessed [are] the pure in heart: for they shall see God.

Matthew 5:9   Blessed [are] the peacemakers: for they shall be called the children of God.

Matthew 5:10   Blessed [are] they which are persecuted for righteousness' sake: for theirs is the kingdom of heaven.

Matthew 5:11   Blessed are ye, when [men] shall revile you, and persecute [you], and shall say all manner of evil against you falsely, for my sake.

Matthew 5:12   Rejoice, and be exceeding glad: for great [is] your reward in heaven: for so persecuted they the prophets which were before you.

How have we gone from meekness and love to this modern mess where everyday church members leave more wounded than when they arrived?

The formula of the worship of today is equal parts of emotional gratification, superficial study of scripture, and adherence to rules of denomination. We have neglected the one thing that stands as the banner of Christianity - a relationship with God through Christ our Lord. The Christian faith is the only religion in which God seeks out man. God seeks to engage man in a relationship that is personal, emotional, and unique.

Arguably, the Jewish faith encourages a relationship of this type. However, in Christ, we have a God who has shed his heavenly state in order to seek out man. He extends his hand to us so we may know that He understands us. God demonstrates this by living as we live, suffering as we suffer, and experiencing life as only man can. He does this in order that He, might have compassion (a word meaning to suffer together) on us and empathy (meaning to feel the same thing) with us, so that we may know that He knows us and can have a personal relationship with Him. For, if God is omniscient, He would have already known what it was like to be man, but we could not have conceived of His knowledge.

In Christ, we have the hero-God-king who relinquished everything including His life in order to seek, love, and save His people. There is nothing left emotionally undone in this formula God has given us. It is in the church of today that the formula becomes incorrect. Denominationalism has supplanted Scripture, and following a set of rules has become more important than love and forgiveness. It is essential to seek and know God if we are to be changed by His love into His image. Only in this marvelous transformation can we hope to come close to doing what He has asked: "Love God with your whole being. Love your fellow man as yourself." It is foolish to think that doctrine and Scripture could keep us on any path. If that were the case, Christ would have not needed to come or die. Theology serves to clarify ones' beliefs in order that they may be articulated, but declaring a belief is not that same as living it.

We may become theologians, but to no avail. The study of theology does not serve to edify man. It seems arrogant to endeavor to study He who is omnipotent and omniscient. Learning scripture and points of doctrine serves to enhance our knowledge, but not our heart. We may seek to gain insight into God's patterns and personality through study. This is admirable to a point; however, time may best be served by being in His presence. To know Him is always better than to study Him.

There are two states in a man's life – to love, and a call to be loved. We seek unconditional love because only through this God-like love we rest assured of being accepted with all sins and shortcomings that haunt us every waking hour and as well as in our nightmares. It seems right that we would seek to deliver this kind of love to those closest to us such as our children, spouse, and friends. This kind of love flows from the heart of God through us to others.

During the 1300's, a school of Christian mystics arose. From that school a book came to us as an explanation of the mystical life. "The Cloud of Unknowing," written by a young man entering and practicing the life of a monk within the mystical community. The book gives us insight and instructions in this meditative life.

Simply stated, if something can be sensed, tasted, felt, smelled, heard, or seen, it is not God. All that can be imagined or experienced is not the creator, but only a creation. To find the creator, one must eliminate everything else from the mind and heart. What an agonizing path! Yet, this path is not unlike what some monks in other faiths and in vastly distant parts of the world choose to travel.

Thomas Merton was a Catholic monk of the Trappists order. In the 1950s, Merton became fascinated with mysticism and other religions. He came into contact with the Japanese scholar on Zen, Daisetz T. Suzuki (1870–1966), who was greatly responsible for introducing Zen Buddhism to the West. They corresponded, and subsequently, some of their writings became the essay collection "Zen and the Birds of Appetite", a discussion of the similarities and differences between Zen Buddhism and Christianity. Gandhi was also influential upon Merton in saying that one can find the deeper roots of one's own religious tradition by becoming immersed in other religions-- and then returning "home" to see one's own heritage in a transformed way, with a transformed consciousness.

On October 15, 1968, with Merton aboard, a jetliner lifted off the ground in San Francisco bound for Tokyo and the Asia beyond: Joy. We left the ground--I with Christian mantras and a great sense of destiny, of being at last on my true way after years of waiting and wondering and fooling around. ... May I not come back without having settled the great affair. And found also the great compassion, mahakaruna... I am going home, to the home where I have never been in this body. " *(Asian Journal, pages 4-5).*

Merton would return to home, to Our Lady of Gethsemani monastery in Kentucky, very differently than when he headed east that day to a monastic conference in Bangkok, Thailand. Very different. Paradox, freedom, compassion, contemplation, emptiness and mysticism all played a role in Merton's Asian homecoming. He began advocating for inter-religious dialogue, especially between Buddhists and Christians. Merton's Catholicism had become more and more universal in its scope of possibilities for experiencing spiritual wisdom.

The Trappists were an order of monks focusing on living in a community of monks under the prescription "God Alone" and the motto "pray & work." Their way of life had changed little over the past 700 years. In this harsh environment, Merton developed a contemplative mind. This contemplative attitude and practice would later link him, at the root level, with Buddhists that he met.

The 1950s was a time of crisis for Merton. He awoke to the notion that monastic life was not an isolated enclave of holiness, separate from and superior to other ways of life. Individuals in most churches, most denominations, and certainly most orders believe that their belief and way of life are superior. It is likely because of the heavy personal investment it takes to commit to those things.

Merton became involved in worldly affairs of war and suffering. He began writing on the social issues of nuclear proliferation and the Viet Nam War. His religious superiors forbade him from further engagement in such things. However, Merton felt compelled to share his views. He felt his insights gained through Christian mysticism were of value, and he might have something positive to say about suffering in the world.

This was the time of Vatican II and the church began to open up to the idea that there may be something beyond the church walls and ways. A decree from the holy meeting came down to the priests and people:

"The Church therefore has this exhortation for her sons: prudently and lovingly, through dialogue and collaboration with the followers of other religions, and in witness of Christian faith and life, acknowledge, preserve, and

promote the spiritual and moral goods found among these men, as well as the values in their society and cultures (NA 2)."

Merton plumbed the depths of his own mystical experience and found an ancient teaching that he started to take very seriously in his study of Buddhism. Ambrose, a 4th century Christian bishop of Milan, had said that "all that is true, by whomever it has been said, is from the Holy Spirit," which can be related to the Buddhist Bankei's "the farther one enters into truth, the deeper it is."

In the preface to "Mystics and Zen Masters," Merton says that he has attempted not merely to look at these other traditions objectively from the outside, but in some measure at least, to try to share in the values and experience which they embody. In other words, he is not content to write about them without making them, as far as possible, "his own." Merton was able to "see" Buddhism and to be a Buddhist. His contemplative knowledge and experience of mysticism resonated with the Buddhist meditative experience.

Call to mind the instructions given to the mystic in the book, "The Cloud of Unknowing." If you clear from your mind everything that can be experienced or imagined, that which is left is God.

The great Zen Master, Dogen, said, "To study the Buddha Way is to study the self, to study the self is to forget the self, and to forget the self is to be enlightened by the ten thousand things." Thus, both types of meditation seek to clear the mind of everything and find what awaits us in the calm pool of our minds.

The mystics will tell you that this is not an easy path. As we clear the mind and reach toward God, again and again we get in our own way. In anguish, our soul cries out to God, but He does not answer. In despair, we sit alone and empty, in search of Him. We wish to die for Him. We wish to die to self. Our stubborn carnal hearts keep beating. We died because we cannot die. That is to say, we die inside through sin and sorrow because we refuse to die to self. We struggled to lay ourselves down and pick up His Cross, His glory, and His life in us. But the old man resists, fighting for each spiritual breath. This "not dying" is agony. We long for Him, waiting for Him with each breath we take, trying to get out of his way. Yet, no matter how we move ourselves, we are still in our own way.

The soul cries out, but God seems not to hear. Our hearts cry out for the beloved, but He cannot be found. We are poured out like water. Our hearts are like wax, melted and running away. We have waited for Him, prayed for Him, meditated on Him, beckoned Him, cried for Him, wept for Him, hurt for Him, and now we are in agony for Him. He is behind the Cloud. We cannot see Him nor can we feel Him. How can one who is everywhere be so far away? But He is. With prayer and desire, we beat against the Cloud, the wall that keeps us from God. We cannot get through the wall.

There is no night darker than this. Sorrow is a knife cutting the soul deeper and deeper, and so it becomes a bowl, capable of holding more joy when finally there is the joy of His coming. There is no night more sorrowful...but Joy cometh in the morning. We can do nothing but to await the Son. If we endure, this sorrow... this most deep and personal tribulation... will give way to patience and stillness.

LUK 21:19 In your patience possess ye your souls.

Desire will die and obedience will take its place.

ROM 6:16 Know ye not, that to whom ye yield yourselves servants to obey, his servants ye are to whom ye obey; whether of sin unto death, or of obedience unto righteousness?

Grace will be shed on us in obedience to God, and our hearts will receive his fullness.

ROM 5:2 By whom also we have access by faith into this grace wherein we stand, and rejoice in hope of the glory of God. 3 And not only so, but we glory in tribulations also: knowing that tribulation worketh patience; 4 And patience, experience; and experience, hope: 5 And hope maketh not ashamed; because the love of God is shed abroad in our hearts by the Holy Ghost which is given unto us. 6 For when we were yet without strength, in due time Christ died for the ungodly. 7 For scarcely for a righteous man will one die: yet peradventure for a good man some would even dare to die. 8 But God commendeth his love toward us, in that, while we were yet sinners, Christ died for us. 9 Much more then, being now justified by his blood, we shall be saved from wrath through Him.

...with no other light or guide than the one that burned in my heart.
The Dark Night by St John of the Cross

Where have you hidden, Beloved, and left me moaning? You fled like the stag after wounding me; I went out calling you but you were gone. *Spiritual Canticle by St John of the Cross.*

God, who is all perfection, wars against all imperfect habits of the soul, and, purifying the soul with the heat of his flame, he approves its habits from it, and prepares it, so that at last he may enter it and be united with it by his sweet, peaceful, and glorious love, as is the fire when it has entered the wood.
St. John of the Cross

What satisfies love best of all is that we be wholly stripped of all repose, whether in strangers, or in friends, or even in love herself. And this is a frightening life love wants, that we must do with the satisfaction of love in order to satisfy love. They who are thus drawn and accepted by love, and fettered by her, are the most indebted to love, and consequently they must continually stand subject to the great power over strong nature, to content her. And that life is miserable beyond all that the human heart can bear.
Hadewijch of Antwerp

Our task is to offer ourselves up to God like a clean smooth canvas and not bother ourselves about what the God may choose to paint on it, but, at every moment, feel only for stroke of his brush. It is the same piece of stone. Each blow from the chisel of the sculptor makes it feel -- if it could feel -- as if it were being destroyed. As blow after blow rings down on it, the stone knows nothing about how the sculptor is shaping it. All it feels is the chisel hacking away at it's, savaging it and mutilating it.
Jean Pierre Caussadede

When God is seen in darkness it does not bring a smile to the lips, nor devotion, or ardent love; neither does the body with the soul tremble or move as at other times; the soul sees nothing and everything; the body sleeps and speech is cut off.
Angela of Floigno

The eyes of my soul were opened, and I beheld the plenitude of God, wherein I did comprehend the whole world, both here and beyond the sea, and the abyss, and the ocean, and all things. In all these

285

things I beheld naught save the Divine power, in a matter assuredly indescribable; so that through excess of marveling the soul cried with a loud voice, saying, "this whole world is full of God!" ....
Angela of Floigno

Yet the creature does not become God, for the union takes place in God through Grace and our homeward turning love: and therefore the creature in its inward contemplation feels the distinction and the otherness between itself in God.
John Ruusbroec

Three parts of spiritual life, Worship, Study, and Prayer (communion) keep us in touch with God. Three strands making up the cord that ties us to God and keep us reaching upward to Him. They are Love, Praise, and Gratitude.

Worship is to seek and know the worth of God. What is He worth? What a strange question, you may say, but the answer underlies our actions. Is He worthy of praise? Is He worthy of our obedience? How about our study, prayers, love, gratitude... Are these areas in balance? One can love someone and not care to be with him. One can commune with someone and not love him. One can be grateful to a stranger. We can praise the actions of someone when we do not know their character. To get to know God, we have Worship, Study, and Prayer. To come into His presence, we have Love, Praise, and Gratitude. When all three of these attributes are brought to bear in one relationship there is fullness and joy.

For man, from the beginning of his creation, had been entrusted with the reins of his own volitions, with unrestricted movement towards his every desire; for the Deity is free and man had been formed after Him. *(The Image of God in Man According to Cyril of Alexandria)*

But, with a heart open and grateful to God we have joy and an enduring relationship.

PSA 100:2 Serve the LORD with gladness: come before his presence with singing. 3 Know ye that the LORD he is God: it is he that hath made us, and not we ourselves; we are his people, and the sheep of his pasture. 4 Enter into his gates with thanksgiving, and into his courts with praise: be thankful unto him, and bless his name. 5 For the LORD is good; his mercy is everlasting;

and his truth endureth to all generations. 101:1 I will sing of mercy and judgment: unto thee, O LORD, will I sing.

Out of gratitude and love springs charity. Charity flies forth from a heart filled with thankfulness and gratitude. All things are seen, as they are, a gift from God. We clearly see His love for us, and our hearts are joyous as we share God's gifts to us with others. Charity is the result of gratitude to God and God's love in us toward our fellow man.

COL 3:14 And above all these things put on charity, which is the bond of perfectness. 15 And let the peace of God rule in your hearts, to the which also ye are called in one body; and be ye thankful.

1 COR 13:13 And now abideth faith, hope, charity, these three; but the greatest of these is charity.

What is the secret of finding the treasure? There isn't one. The treasure is everywhere. It is offered to us at every moment and wherever we find ourselves. (In) All creatures, friends or enemies, it is ours abundantly, and it courses through every fiber of our body and soul until it reaches the very core of our being. If we open our mouths, they will be filled.
Jean Pierre Caussadede

Fickle and forgetful is man that he would trip over the truth, or through grace, fall headlong into it, and then rush off, forgetting all he had seen, learned, and felt in his deepest part. Not being reminded of the epiphany daily, man creeps into a mode of doubt and counts all of his communion and time with God as the dross of dreams and imaginings. In the dark nights of the soul, it is not knowledge that keeps us alive. It is faith, unshakable and tenacious. Faith trusts God is still there even if He cannot be seen. Faith knows God that is there, even if He cannot be felt. Faith sees the sun in the midst of night, and faith waits - for Joy cometh in the morning. Do you have knowledge of this faith? Is your heart fixed on God? Then the bridegroom will come and we will be one, transformed and conformed, we will be one.

PSA 57:7 My heart is fixed, O God, my heart is fixed: I will sing and give praise. 8 Awake up, my glory; awake, psaltery and harp: I myself will awake early. 9 I will praise thee, O Lord, among the people: I will sing unto thee among the nations. 10 For thy mercy is great unto the heavens, and thy truth unto the clouds. 11 Be thou exalted, O God, above the heavens: let thy glory be above all the earth.

But what passes in the union of the Spiritual Marriage is very different. The Lord appears in the centre of the soul, not through an imaginary, but through an intellectual vision ..., just as He appeared to the Apostles, without entering through the door, when He said to them: "Pax vobis" (peace be unto you) the soul, I mean the spirit of this soul, is made one with God, Who, being likewise a Spirit, has been pleased to reveal the love that He has for us by showing to certain persons the extent of that love, so that we may praise His greatness. For He has been pleased to unite Himself with His creature in such a way that they have become like two who cannot be separated from one another: even so He will not separate Himself from her.   *Teresa of Avila*

... it must not be thought that the faculties and senses and passions are always in this state of peace, though the soul itself is. In the other Mansions (i.e. those mansions which are exterior to the central one in which the soul now dwells) there are always times of conflict and trial and weariness, but they are not of such a kind as to rob the soul of its peace and stability -- at least, not as a rule. ...for it is difficult to understand how the soul can have trials and afflictions and yet be in peace... *Teresa of Avila*
... in this temple of God, in this Mansion of His, he and the soul alone have fruition of each other in the deepest silence. There is no reason now for the understanding to stir, or to seek out anything, for the Lord Who created the soul is now pleased to calm it and would have it look, as it were, through a little chink, at what is passing. Now and then it loses sight of it and is unable to see anything; but this is only for a very brief time   *Teresa of Avila*

And I am quite dazed myself when I observe that, on reaching this state, the soul has no more raptures (accompanied, that is to say, by the suspension of the senses), save very occasionally, and even then it has not the same transports and flights of the spirit. These raptures, too, happen only rarely, and hardly ever in public as they very often did before. Nor have they any connection, as they had before, with great occasions of devotion... *Teresa of Avila*

It is the nature of the Holy Spirit that I should be consumed in him, dissolved in him, and transformed wholly into love. ... God does not enter those who are freed from all otherness and all createdness: rather he already exits in an essential manner within them... *Meister Eckhart*

God is always near you and with you; leave Him not alone. ...I continued some years, applying my mind carefully the rest of the day, and even in the midst of my business, to the presence of God, whom I considered always with me, often in me. *Brother Lawrence*

... And the latter (union) comes to pass when the two wills -- namely that of the soul and that of God -- are conformed together in one, and there is naught in the one that is repugnant to the other. And thus, when the soul rids itself totally of that which is repugnant to the Divine will and conforms not with it, it is transformed in God through love. Saint John of the Cross
In thus allowing God to work in it, the soul ... is at once illumined and transformed in God, and God communicates to it His supernatural Being, in such wise that it appears to be God Himself, and has all that God Himself has. And this union comes to pass when God grants the soul this supernatural favour, that all the things of God and the soul are one in participant transformation; and the soul seems to be God rather than a soul, and is indeed God by participation; although it is true that its natural being, though thus transformed, is as distinct from the Being of God as it was before... *Saint John of the Cross*

I am not engaged to Christianity by decent forms, or saving ordinances; it is not usage, it is not what I do not understand, that binds me to it -- let these be the sandy foundations of falsehoods. What I revere and obey in it is its reality, its boundless charity, its deep interior life, the rest it gives to my mind, the echo it returns to my thoughts, the perfect accord it makes with my reason through all its representation of God and His Providence; and the persuasion and courage that come out thence to lead me upward and onward.
Ralph Waldo Emerson, sermon, Sept. 9, 1832

1TI 4:13 Till I come, give attendance to reading, to exhortation, to doctrine. 14 Neglect not the gift that is in thee, which was given thee by prophecy, with the laying on of the hands of the presbytery. 15 Meditate upon these things; give thyself wholly to them; that thy profiting may appear to all.

PSA 63:6 When I remember thee upon my bed, and meditate on thee in the night watches. 7 Because thou hast been my help, therefore in the shadow of thy wings will I rejoice. 8 My soul followeth hard after thee: thy right hand upholdeth me.

PSA 77:12 I will meditate also of all thy work, and talk of thy doings. 13 Thy way, O God, is in the sanctuary: who is so great a God as our God? 14 Thou art the God that doest wonders: thou hast declared thy strength among the people.

At first glance, there is no difference between the meditation techniques of the Zen Buddhist masters and those of the Christian mystics. Both demand the mind be still, quiet, and focused. Both demand we lose ourselves. Both demand patience and dedication. However, there is a great distinction between the two as to where the mind is placed. The teaching of the Eastern mystics directs the student to "go within," "empty themselves," and "center the mind." Concentrate on the center of the body or on the breath. First there is focus on sound or breath, then on the center where the breath arrives, and then even that disappears into nothingness until nothing is left, not even the self; not even nothingness. The students reach inside until in the depth all disappears into all and into nothingness.

For the Christian mystic, enlightenment is an ongoing and ever-changing, living relationship between God and man. As in any healthy relationship, we attempt to learn from and take the better part from the other into ourselves. Thus, God as both father and beloved, leads us, guides us, and teaches us. It is not only the mind, but the heart itself, that is focused on God. We do not seek to disappear, however, we seek union with Him, who is the creator of all, both Him and us together as lover and beloved. It is a great and total difference between seeking nothingness and seeking God's presence.

It is important to still the mind and stop the chaotic ramblings of thoughts so that we may be fully attentive to God. We may find it necessary to implement techniques, which will help us clear and fully focus our minds. This is where the two mystical communities of east and west break. The Christian mystics use the same centering techniques of breath and sound to still and center the mind, but the sound is a prayer or word that is meaningful to us in our relationship to God.

After the mind is brought under submission, there is a great difference in what happens next. The Eastern mystic focuses the mind inward or more specifically on nothing, while the Christian mystic begins to reach toward the heart of God. There is an immense yearning to be one with the spirit of God. It is a longing greater than life. Our heart is a room, a temple built for Him. We are waiting for the guest. It is the longing that does the work. We empty out our ideas of God and of ourselves. We want God to be who He is, not what we think He is. We want His fullness, not our limited idea of His fullness. No idea or imaginings can contain even the slightest portion of Him.

We reach for the Spirit without shape or form. We open wide the gates of our heart in anticipation of the arrival of the beloved. We keep the flame of our heart lit and burning, as one would light a candle to bid someone that we love to enter. We wait. We wait. We wait, and we reach. We reach until we find our limit. We reach until we find our hearts held down and captive under the cloud that separates us from God. It is then that we begin to beat against the cloud with all of the ferocity of a lover held inside a room, against their will, away from the beloved. We have reached as high as we can reach. Like a child who holds up his arms for his father, we wait for God to come, reach down, and pick us up. We wait to be gathered into His arms.

Christian Contemplative Prayer is the opening of mind, heart, and soul to God. It is beyond thoughts and words. It is bringing God into us, closer than thinking and feeling. The root of all prayer is interior silence. Only mundane and common prayer is of thoughts or feelings expressed in words. Contemplative Prayer is a prayer of silence, an experience of God's presence in us and we in Him. It is experiencing God which transcends the study of Him. Love is an experience.

SON 1:13 A bundle of myrrh is my well-beloved unto me; he shall lie all night betwixt my breasts. 14 My beloved is unto me as a cluster of campfire in the vineyards of Engedi. 15 Behold, thou art fair, my love; behold, thou art fair; thou hast doves' eyes. 16 Behold, thou art fair, my beloved, yea, pleasant: also our bed is green. 17 The beams of our house are cedar, and our rafters of fir. 2:1 I am the rose of Sharon, and the lily of the valleys. 2 As the lily among thorns, so is my love among the daughters. 3 As the apple tree among the trees of the wood, so is my beloved among the sons. I sat down under his shadow with great delight, and his fruit was sweet to my taste. 4 He brought me to the banqueting house, and his banner over me was love. 5 Stay me with flagons, comfort me with apples: for I am sick of love. 6 His left hand is under my head, and his right hand doth embrace me. 7 I charge you, O ye daughters of Jerusalem, by the roes, and by the hinds of the field, that ye stir not up, nor awake my love, till he please. 8 The voice of my beloved! behold, he cometh leaping upon the mountains, skipping upon the hills. 9 My beloved is like a roe or a young hart: behold, he standeth behind our wall, he looketh forth at the windows, shewing himself through the lattice. 10 My beloved spake, and said unto me, Rise up, my love, my fair one, and come away. SON 2:11 For, lo, the winter is past, the rain is over and gone; 12 The flowers appear on the earth; the time of the singing of birds is come, and the voice of the turtle is heard in our land; 13 The fig tree putteth forth her green figs, and the vines with the tender grape give a good smell. Arise, my love, my fair one, and come away. 14 O my dove, that art in the clefts of the rock, in the secret places of the stairs, let me see thy countenance, let me hear thy voice; for sweet is thy voice, and thy countenance is comely.

He is illusive. Our God, our lover, entices us to higher levels as we run after Him, seeking Him. We must keep Him in our hearts day and night. When we sleep, He is our breath and the beating of our hearts. When awake, we are ever watchful. With every fiber of our being, we anticipate our next encounter. We wait and our hearts long for Him. The longing draws us to Him.

SON 3:1 By night on my bed I sought him whom my soul loveth: I sought him, but I found him not. 2 I will rise now, and go about the city in the streets, and in the broad ways I will seek him whom my soul loveth: I sought him, but I found him not. 3 The watchmen that go about the city found me: to whom I said, Saw ye him whom my soul loveth? 4 It was but a little that I passed from them, but I found him whom my soul loveth: I held him, and would not let him go, until I had brought him into my mother's house, and into the chamber of her that conceived me.

We do not turn our minds off, nor do we seek to disappear into nothingness as the Eastern mystics do. We seek Christ, the beloved. We still our hearts and minds to listen for the rustle of His footsteps. We sit quietly, yearning for His approach, His breath upon our face, His fragrance as He enters the room, the mist we see covering His presence, the thin blue mist that surrounds Him. Our minds are turned outward to Him. The more quiet our hearts and minds, the sooner we will recognize Him whom we seek.

"The pursuit of God will embrace the labor of bringing our total personality into conformity to His. I do not here refer to the act of justification by faith in Christ. I speak of a voluntary exalting of God to His proper station over us and a willing surrender of our whole being to the place of worshipful submission, which the Creator-creature circumstance makes proper... Let no one imagine that he will lose anything of human dignity by this voluntary sell-out of his all to his God. He does not by this degrade himself as a man; rather he finds his right place of high honor as one made in the image of his Creator. His deep disgrace lay in his moral derangement, his unnatural usurpation of the place of God. His honor will be proved by restoring again that stolen throne. In exalting God over all, he finds his own highest honor upheld...We must of necessity be servant to someone, either to God or to sin. The sinner prides himself on his independence, completely overlooking the fact that he is the weak slave of the sins that rule his members. The man who surrenders to Christ exchanges a cruel slave driver for a kind and gentle Master whose yoke is easy and whose burden is light." *A. W. Tozer*

Let the remembrance of Jesus be present with your every breath. Then indeed you will appreciate the value stillness. *John Climacus*

As we begin our time of meditation and prayer, we must be careful. We must, first, still and focus the mind. This first stage, called centering, is somewhat like techniques used in Eastern mysticism. However, objects or words used in our Christian technique should be kept completely Christ centered in their representation. As we sit in meditation and prayer, many times, we find our minds in turmoil, with thoughts chasing themselves like a pack of monkeys. We must first have a way of clearing the mind of such thrashing. Before we can pray clearly, we must be able to think clearly. Before we can think clearly, we must stop the mind from running amok. Even in this preliminary stage of centering, it takes about twenty minutes to still the mind.

Excerpts from "Five Types of Thought" By Father Thomas Keating

"The most obvious thoughts are superficial ones the imagination grinds out because of its natural propensity for perpetual motion. It is important just to accept them and not pay any undue attention to them.... Sometimes they reach a point where they don't hear it at all..."

"The second kind of thought occurs when you get interested in something that is happening...This is the kind of thought that calls for some "reaction."... It is important not to be annoyed with yourself if you get involved with these interesting thoughts. Any annoyance that you give in to is another thought, and will take you farther away from the interior silence..."

"A third kind of thought arises as we sink into deep peace and interior silence. What seem to be brilliant theological insights and marvelous psychological breakthroughs, like tasty bait, are dangled in front of our mind's eye... If you acquiesce to a thought of this nature long enough to fix it in your memory you will be drawn out of the deep, refreshing waters of interior silence."

"As you settle into deep peace and freedom from particular thoughts, a desire to reflect on what is happening may arise. You may think, "At last I am getting some place!" or "This feeling is just great... If you let go, you go into deeper interior silence. If you reflect, you come out and have to start over.... As soon as you start to "reflect" on an experience, it is over...The presence of God is like the air we breathe. You can have all you want of it as long as you do not try to take possession of it and hang on to it."

"Any form of meditation or prayer that transcends thinking sets off the dynamic of interior purification....one may feel intense anger, sorrow or fear without any relation to the recent past. Once again, the best way to handle them is to return to the sacred word."

"Once you grasp the fact that thoughts are not only inevitable, but an integral part of the process of healing and growth initiated by God, you are able to take a positive view of them. Instead of looking at them as painful distractions..." *Five Types of Thought: By Father Thomas Keating*

It is not that we take a "positive approach to the unwanted and noisy thoughts, but we will acquire a passive approach to them. We will learn to dismiss them like twigs on the trail. We will keep walking without as much as noticing them.

"...the mind should retire into itself, and recall its powers from sensible things, in order to hold pure communion with God, and be clearly illumined by the flashing rays of the Spirit, with no admixture or disturbance of the divine light by anything earthly or clouded, until we come to the source of the effulgence which we enjoy here, and regret and desire are alike stayed, when our mirrors pass away in the light of truth. " *Gregory of Nazianzus*

Before we begin the first steps of meditation, we must find a comfortable and undisturbed place. Sit quietly. Close your eyes and relax. Find in your heart a sacred word. In your heart and soul, it must have a direct connection with Christ. Let the word be something special to you. Let it be grace, peace, love, hope, charity, or some word that connects you with Christ himself. Or, you may pick out some sacred object such as a cross or painting which you know will draw your heart to Him. Focus your mind and your heart upon this sacred word or object. Do not let it waiver and do not let it go.

It is common that after only a matter of moments your mind will start to wander. You'll find your focus lost, and your mind chasing itself and swirling like a storm. Your thoughts will become scattered and chaotic. Do not fret or worry, this is very common. It is the first obstacle to overcome in order to fully pray and meditate upon Him. God waits on the other side of chaos in our minds and hearts. This is the first step in the process of stripping away all of those things that stand in the way between our Lord and ourselves. The mind will protest and complain. It is like a stubborn mule which strains and complains against the bridle. But, we must bridle our minds. It will take infinite time and patience simply to learn to quiet and control our minds so that we can pray and meditate wholly on Him.

"Why does this little prayer of one syllable pierce the heavens? Surely, because it is offered with a full spirit, in the height and the depth, in the length and the breadth of the spirit of the one who prays. In the height: that is with the full might of the spirit; in the depth: for in this little syllable all the faculties of the spirit are contained; in the length: because if it could always be experienced as it is in that moment, it would cry as it does then; in the breadth: because it desires for all others all that it desires for itself...." *St. John of the Cross*

There are only two things in existence, the creator and created. As our minds become more still and quiet, we must continually push out all of the things that try to enter in. We must allow room only for God in our hearts and minds. Whether it is height, depth, blackness, emptiness, or nothingness itself, all things, save for God, must be pushed out of the mind and heart.

These two things exist -- God and creation are all there is in the universe. Everything that is not God, is creation. If we empty our minds and hearts of everything created, what is left will be God.

As we focus our minds' eye sharply on the attributes of the ineffable Godhead, we see it as existing beyond everything created. God transcends all intellect and all beings, and is wholly outside any imagined appearance, knowledge and wisdom. "dwelling in light unapproachable."

The poet Hafiz wrote
"The sun never says to the earth,
'You owe me.'

Look what happens with a love like that.
It lights up the whole sky."
"I searched for God and found only myself. I searched for myself and found only God".

"...it is the easiest exercise of all and most readily accomplished when a soul is helped by grace in this felt desire; otherwise, it would be extraordinarily difficult for you to make this exercise. Do not hang back then, but labour in it until you experience the desire. For when you first begin to undertake it, all that you find is a darkness, a sort of cloud of unknowing; you cannot tell what it is, except that you experience in your will a simple reaching out to God [a naked intent unto God]. This darkness and cloud is always between you and your God, no matter what you do, and it prevents you from seeing him clearly by the light of understanding in your reason, and from experiencing him in sweetness of love in your affection. So set yourself to rest in this darkness as long as you can, always crying out after him whom you love. For if you are to experience him or to see him at all, insofar as it is possible here, it must always be in this cloud and in this darkness." *Excerpts from The Cloud of Unknowing (James Walsh trans., New York : Paulist Press, 1981)*

God is unapproachable light. We cannot gaze on him. We see "*in a glass darkly and know in part" (1 Cor 13:12)*. Deity, God, the Godhead then, is wholly incorporeal, without dimensions or size, and not bounded by shape nor perturbed by them.

ROM 8:38 For I am persuaded, that neither death, nor life, nor angels, nor principalities, nor powers, nor things present, nor things to come, 39 Nor height, nor depth, nor any other creature, shall be able to separate us from the love of God, which is in Christ Jesus our Lord.

1 TI 6:16 Who only hath immortality, dwelling in the light which no man can approach unto; whom no man hath seen, nor can see: to whom be honour and power everlasting. Amen.

To become a saint of God, you must covet nothing in this world or the next and you must give yourself entirely to God and turn your face to Him. To desire this world is turning away from God for the sake of what is transitory. To covet the next world means turning away from God for the sake of what is everlasting.
Sufi Proverb

1 COR 13:12 For now we see through a glass, darkly; but then face to face: now I know in part; but then shall I know even as also I am known.

PHI 3:6 Concerning zeal, persecuting the church; touching the righteousness which is in the law, blameless.7 But what things were gain to me, those I counted loss for Christ. 8 Yea doubtless, and I count all things but loss for the excellence of the knowledge of Christ Jesus my Lord: for whom I have suffered the loss of all things, and do count them but dung, that I may win Christ, 9 And be found in him, not having mine own righteousness, which is of the law, but that which is through the faith of Christ, the righteousness which is of God by faith: 10 That I may know him, and the power of his resurrection, and the fellowship of his sufferings, being made conformable unto his death; 11 If by any means I might attain unto the resurrection of the dead.

True "religion" is to love and seek God, love and have compassion for others, and to express God's love to a dark and hurting world.

Never let the heart cease its cry. Never let it cease its reach for its creator. Day after day this process must be repeated. As we become accustomed to this toil of forgetting all things created, we must continually reach for God with our hearts and with every breath we take. Knocking, no, pounding with our heart's cry on the door that stands between God and us. This is called "praying without ceasing." Because there is a separation between God and us, it is a great mystery and paradox. Even though He is with us and in us, there stands a veil of "unknowing" whose only key is grace and only door is faith. God himself must lift the veil as He wills. In whatever faith we find ourselves, in whatever church, synagogue or Mosque, our search should follow the pure path of selflessness.

Truth has been planted in the center of your heart, entrusted to you by God for safekeeping. It becomes manifest with true repentance and with true effort. Its beauty shines on the surface when you remember God and do the dhikr [recitation of Divine Names]. At the first stage you recite the name of God with your tongue; then, when your heart becomes alive, you recite inwardly with the heart.
Sufi Proverb

1TH 5:16 Rejoice evermore. 17 Pray without ceasing. 18 In every thing give thanks: for this is the will of God in Christ Jesus concerning you. 19 Quench not the Spirit. 20 Despise not prophesying. 21 Prove all things; hold fast that which is good. 22 Abstain from all appearance of evil. 23 And the very God of peace sanctify you wholly; and I pray God your whole spirit and soul and body be preserved blameless unto the coming of our Lord Jesus Christ.

"In the inner wine cellar I drank of my beloved, and, when I went abroad through all this valley I no longer knew anything, and lost the herd which I was following." *St. John of the Cross*

"Now I occupy my soul and all my energy is in his service. I no longer tend the herd, nor have I any other work now that my every act is love." *St. John of the Cross*

"I want to deliberately and zealously encourage a mighty and ongoing longing for God. The lack of it has brought us to our present low estate. The stiff and wooden quality of our religious lives is a result of our lack of holy desire. Complacency is a deadly foe of all spiritual growth. Acute desire must be present or there will be no manifestation of Christ to His people. He waits to be wanted. Too bad that with many of us He waits so long, so very long, in vain."   *A.W. Tozer*

I hold you in my heart.
I rock and sing you to sleep.
You are everywhere in everyone,
The holy baby in all of us,
that plays there.

The beautiful one,
born when we love,
the glowing child.
You are the meaning that blooms in the heart.

Sufi Poem

MAT 13:18 Hear ye therefore the parable of the sower. 19 When any one heareth the word of the kingdom, and understandeth it not, then cometh the wicked one, and catcheth away that which was sown in his heart. This is he which received seed by the way side. 20 But he that received the seed into stony places, the same is he that heareth the word, and anon with joy receiveth it; 21 Yet hath he not root in himself, but endureth for a while: for when tribulation or persecution ariseth because of the word, by and by he is offended. 22 He also that received seed among the thorns is he that heareth the word; and the care of this world, and the deceitfulness of riches, choke the word, and he becometh unfruitful. 23 But he that received seed into the good ground is he that heareth the word, and understandeth it; which also beareth fruit, and bringeth forth, some an hundredfold, some sixty, some thirty.

Starting this journey may be easy; finishing is not. It takes tenacity and a unique stubbornness to complete what is started. The world has tribulations and enticements to sway us from our course. Our roots of desire for God must go deeper than our roots in the world.

Although the above passage is usually related to salvation, it shows the trials we will go through and has within it a warning. Many fail. Be prepared to endure and push on! Knowledge of God is not the same as acknowledging God. Accepting God in our lives is only the beginning of our journey. Many do not make it to the starting line.

They hear the word and do nothing with it. Then, there are some who receive the word of God and become saved by believing in Jesus Christ. Salvation fully equips us to meet the Lord in heaven, but now, while in this world, we must decide how high up the mountain we wish to climb. Most will start this mystical journey and grow tired of judging themselves. They will fatigue in seeking God. They will become distracted by the world. They will not endure the Dark Night of the Soul. They will hide their emptiness in the pursuits of this world. They will rest at the foot of the mountain. As for me, I wish to climb the mountain and touch the face of God. It is a costly journey. It will cost time, patience, and finally it will demand from us all we are. But, think of what we will have if we can give it all away.

Most who start this journey will repeat the same step over and over. They will begin, grow weary, fail, wander, come back, and begin again. They are caught in the midst between the emptiness they feel and the price they think they must pay to overcome. Like a seven-day fast, they abort after the first day; they will walk the same rutted road again and again. This does no good. It gets us no farther than the time before. Let us make a choice before we begin. After the journey is begun, it is either mysticism or recidivism.

Where is wisdom? Where is the path to God? How much has been discarded, covered, or destroyed by the church? Was it all in the name of power, greed, or control? Where is God in all of this?

There were hundreds, if not thousands of books that were examined and rejected from Christian canon. Many were rejected because they were not compatible with the doctrine of the emerging church power. Others seem to be spiritually sound, yet were dismissed because they invited too much personal freedom of faith. Too much personal freedom of faith would lead to an erosion of the much-coveted control sought by the Emperor and the church hierarchy.

Knowing that books may have been set aside for such political reasons raises a heretical question. Should we look outside the Bible in our search for God? In a word, yes.

Truth is found in a pinch of clay, as well as in the pages of some books. But only some have this truth. Others are simply stories devised for entertainment or for the expansion of nonsensical ideas no more true that the fables of the Titans. How then do we discern the difference? If we allow the spirit of God to judge what we hear or read, how can we go wrong?

We are holy vessels of a holy God. We are filled with His presence, and that presence communes with us moment by moment. Trust the Holy Spirit within you to guide you to truth. Use those things you know to be perfect and good as a signpost.

Look now at a few lines of one book that was rejected. Quotes below are from The Gospel of Thomas.

"Jesus said, If those who lead you say, "See, the Kingdom is in the sky," then the birds of the sky will precede you. If they say to you, "It is under the earth," then the fish of the sea will precede you. Rather, the Kingdom of God is inside of you, and it is outside of you.

Those who come to know themselves will find it; and when you come to know yourselves, you will understand that it is you who are the sons of the living Father. But if you will not know yourselves, you dwell in poverty and it is you who are that poverty.

Jesus said: Recognize what is in front of your face, and what has been hidden from you will be revealed to you. For there is nothing hidden which will not be revealed (become manifest), and nothing buried that will not be raised.

His Disciples asked Him, they said to him: How do you want us to fast, and how will we pray? And how will we be charitable (give alms), and what laws of diet will we maintain?
Jesus said: Do not lie, and do not practice what you hate, for everything is in the plain sight of Heaven. For there is nothing concealed that will not become manifest, and there is nothing covered that will not be exposed.

Jesus said: I have cast fire upon the world, and as you see, I guard it until it is ablaze.

Jesus said: I will give to you what eye has not seen, what ear has not heard, what hand has not touched, and what has not occurred to the mind of man.

His Disciples said: Show us the place where you are (your place), for it is necessary for us to seek it.

He said to them: Whoever has ears, let him hear! Within a man of light there is light, and he illumines the entire world. If he does not shine, he is darkness.

Jesus said: I stood in the midst of the world. In the flesh I appeared to them. I found them all drunk; I found none thirsty among them. My soul grieved for the sons of men, for they are blind in their hearts and do not see that they came into the world empty they are destined (determined) to leave the world empty. However, now they are drunk. When they have shaken off their wine, then they will repent (change their ways).

Jesus said: I-Am the Light who is over all things, I-Am the All. From me all came forth and to me all return (The All came from me and the All has come to me). Split wood, there am I. Lift up the stone and there you will find me.

His Disciples said to him: When will the Kingdom come? Jesus said: It will not come by expectation (because you watch or wait for it). They will not say: Look here! or: Look there! But the Kingdom of the Father is spread upon the earth, and people do not realize it.

Whether we read from the Torah, the New Testament, the eighty-one books of the Ethiopic Bible, the Quran, or the many books of wisdom such as the poems of the Sufi or the Gospel of Thomas, if we seek God we will find him in the words of an open and giving heart. This is religion true and pure, not found in form, ritual, or religion, but in hearts of compassion and love.

Our Idea of god has evolved from images of stone and wood whose anger cause disease and failure, and who are pleased by the sacrifice of children to ensure victory in war or a good harvest, to the idea of love and compassion toward others.

Yet, even though all major religions call on followers to seek God in spirit and truth, here we are in the twenty-first century still battling those who would kill others simply because they would call God by another name or practice their rituals in a different way.

So many religious people seem to be stuck in a mode and mindset that is pre-axial age. Indeed, this is now the fight that consumes the entire world. It is the battle between people of the pre and post-axial ages. Whether the "believer" is Jew, Christian, or Muslim, if anyone believes their finite religion, doctrines, or rituals can contain the infinite God they confess to worship they have not yet reached the fruit of the post axial awakening. If a person thinks that anyone worshipping differently or calling God by a different name must be punished or killed, they are still living a pre-axial existence. But hope remains. Maybe the religiously driven violence in the world today will force us to look at religion differently. Maybe we can spiritually evolve beyond outer forms of religion and learn to worship spiritually. It would be foolish to think we would not continue to evolve. Maybe, just maybe, one day we will unburden ourselves of religious forms, doctrine and labels and stand as a single people, all equal in the sight of God. After all, in war everyone believes God is on his or her side, the side of righteousness. It is not such a great leap to think that in time God would be with us all in peace and tolerance.

We await the second axial age. We await the next awakening.

Dr. Joseph Lumpkin

CPSIA information can be obtained
at www.ICGtesting.com
Printed in the USA
LVHW021532190222
711543LV00018B/1514